SCIENCE FICTION: Three definitions:

"Science fiction is a branch of fantasy identifiable by the fact that it eases the 'willing suspension of disbelief' on the part of its readers by utilizing an atmosphere of scientific credibility for its imaginative speculations in physical science, space, time, social science and philosophy."

— Sam Moskowitz

"Science fiction is what you find on the shelves in the library marked science fiction."

— George Hay

"Science fiction doesn't exist."

— Brian W. Aldiss

SCIENCE FICTION: WHAT *IS* IT ALL ABOUT

Illustration for *From the Earth to the Moon*
by Jules Verne.

128007

SCIENCE FICTION:
WHAT IT'S ALL ABOUT
Sam J. Lundwall

ace books
A Division of Charter Communications Inc.
1120 Avenue of the Americas
New York, N.Y. 10036

SCIENCE FICTION: WHAT IT'S ALL ABOUT

Copyright ©, 1971, by Sam J. Lundwall

This is a revised, enlarged, and specially translated edition of a work first published in Sweden under the title: Science Fiction—Från begynnelsen till våra dagar, and which is copyright ©, 1969, by Sam J. Lundwall, for Sveriges Radios förlag. Translated by the author.

An Ace Book. All Rights Reserved.

Cover art by Dean Ellis.

For Ingrid

Author's acknowledgments: For invaluable help and suggestions given to me during the work on this revised edition I am grateful to Alvar Appeltofft, Kenneth Bulmer, E. J. Carnell, Alan Dodd, Philip J. Harbottle, George Hay, Archie Mercer and L. Sjdanov. And, of course, to Donald A. Wollheim, who encouraged me to undertake the job of translating and revising the book.

— S.J.L.

Printed in U.S.A.

CONTENTS

INTRODUCTION

by Donald A. Wollheim

We science fiction readers whose native language happens to be English—that is to say we American, we Canadian, we British, and we Australian science fiction readers—tend to a curious sort of provincialism in our thinking regarding the boundaries of science fiction. We tend to think that all that is worth reading and all that is worth notice is naturally written in English. In our conventions and our awards and our discussions we slip into the habit of referring to our favorites as the world's best this and the world's best that. The annual American science fiction convention calls itself the World Science Fiction Convention, though every now and then it deigns to allow itself to meet overseas, but always with a strong cord attached so that it will return the next year to its "natural" heliocentric American habitat.

Of course we recognize with some moderate historical condescension that once there was a famous founding father named Jules Verne and that he was French. And we pay tribute to the fact that in the oldest issues of American science fiction magazines series appeared that had been translated from the German. Somehow, we also assume that abroad, in non-English speaking lands, there probably may be some local writers and even local magazines turning out stories and novels in the native tongues, but obviously going unnoticed and scarce worth translating.

To one sensitive enough to think about it and to

realize how provincial such a viewpoint surely must be, it comes therefore as something of a bewildering discovery upon going abroad to Western Europe or to Japan to find that these prejudices have real basis. Scan the published science fiction in Germany, or Holland, or Italy, Spain, Japan, France, Sweden, Denmark and —lo!—you will find that from eighty to ninety percent of it is indeed from English originals! Translations galore into every language, but always of the same American and British masters we honor in their original editions.

We come back to wondering how this came to be so. We come back perhaps also not a little pleased that this is so. What a pat to the ego to discover that "our" science fiction does indeed dominate the Western world and that the Hugos given as "World's Best" by some predominantly American readerhood may be quite justified in that designation.

(It goes without saying that all this does not apply to that mysterious world of literature masked by the unreadable Cyrillics of the Russians. There we hear rumors of a vast literature of science fiction having little in common with our own—of writers whose fame extends behind that side of the Iron Curtain but not on our side and where our Big Name writers are scarcely known over in that unexplored hemisphere.)

Surely, in the days of Hugo Gernsback's first magazines there were European writers of equal caliber with our own. Somehow, though, in the intervening decades, there has been a lapse. Somewhere the potential of European imaginative fantasy has been shunted aside.

What then is the true perspective of science fiction in literature? What is science fiction that it so seizes the minds of youth? What is science fiction today and what was it in the past? What does it mean to literature and society? In short—science fiction: what is it all about?

I myself tried to answer this in a book entitled *The Universe Makers: Science Fiction Today* published by

Harper & Row this year (1971). My views therein represent more the philosophical overview of the answers.

Perhaps a further enlightening perspective on this problem is to be found, not from someone at the center of this American-British dominated literature such as myself, but from a qualified observer on the perimeter —someone to whom English is a foreign language to be learned and mastered by hard study in order better to appreciate the ideas contained therein; ideas which may not be present in such quantity in the literature of a language limited by a much smaller audience. Such an observer has the advantage of both appreciating the virtues that exist and noting the oversights. He can see more closely the values of non-English-language writings, both past and present, and compare them with the giants we acclaim today. He can evaluate the impact of our writers in translation and he can point out the demerits of our perhaps overinflated self-importance in this field.

Such an observer is the author of this book, Sam J. Lundwall, a native of Sweden, student of science fiction and so sufficiently skilled in English as to have been able to translate this work itself into the English you see before you.

Sam J. Lundwall, still below thirty in age, started off, as most s-f writers do, as an active reader, as an active fan, and rapidly rose to the top of the small but very intensely competitive Swedish s-f fan world. Publisher of one of those fan magazines that briefly dominate those microcosms, *Science Fiction Nytt*, a journal of news and reviews, he became a leading authority on the subject of science fiction. Evidence of his status was confirmed by his first professional publication, a comprehensive *Bibliography of Science Fiction and Fantasy* in the Swedish language, published in 1964, and soon to reappear in a third and further enlarged edition. Reading English fluently, he became as versed in the writings of the United States and England as any of our native collectors and fans, and being talented, began to assert himself in the cultural sphere of his own country.

In the past several years, Lundwall has been connected with the government-operated Radio Sweden, and has written and produced television shows, directed plays, held down disc-jockey tasks in pop music, and has himself composed and sung folk music. He is widely known in his native land for his work in that field and has appeared on popular recordings in both 45 and long-playing records—and is soon to appear on casettes. Most recently, Lundwall has become the editor of a new line of paperback science fiction for the Stockholm publishers, Askild & Kärnekull, primarily translations but also to include original novels.

I first met Sam Lundwall when Radio Sweden sent him to England with a camera crew to interview science fiction personalities and to do a coverage of the annual British Science Fiction Convention, held that year at Oxford. I had the pleasure of working with him on that project and was myself interviewed, and I am told subsequently—ahem—starred in one such showing over the Swedish television network.

In any case, this apparently started the directors of Radio Sweden to thinking about science fiction and what it all meant and they commissioned Sam J. Lundwall to write a book about it. That book, whose title was *Science Fiction: från begynnelsen till våra dagar*, was published in 1969 and was an immediate success. We understand that it went into two or three printings —which is phenomenally good for Sweden. Essentially that book is the same as the one you have in your hand now.

It has been translated into English by its author, at my request, and in so doing Lundwall has slightly enlarged it, revised certain sections to be of greater interest to an English-reading audience, corrected some minor items, added others, and generally improved the work. Most of the original illustrations are included with this new translation and a few extra ones added.

INTRODUCTION

Although I think I know a lot about science fiction, I found it fascinating. Lundwall gives a depth to the field we do not find among other writers on the subject. He presents both a history of science fiction, a study of its roots and backgrounds, and a commentary. He covers it in all its aspects: books, magazines, comics, fans and fandom, juvenilia, series characters, and literary giants. He does this with accuracy and yet with wit. He does not stint in his admiration nor withhold his scorn when such attitudes seem to be called for. He can be bluntly harsh or admiringly applauding.

No one will agree with everything he says . . . I certainly do not . . . but reading him is educational, stimulating, and exciting. He brings to science fiction the perspective we dearly need—someone on the European perimeter, able to praise where praise is deserved, and able to prick overblown balloons when they need such deflation.

I commend this book to everyone who reads science fiction or who wants to know more about it. Sam J. Lundwall is eminently capable of telling the world what it's all about.

— DONALD A. WOLLHEIM

1. THE FANTASTIC NOVEL

There is a very short story, attributed to Fredric Brown, which better than any explanation gives an insight into the world of thought that is the substance of science fiction. It is exemplarily short, three sentences, and goes, approximately, as follows:

> After the last atomic war, Earth was dead; nothing grew, nothing lived. The last man sat alone in a room. There was a knock on the door . . .

I do not say that this is the archetype of all science fiction, or even that it is typical of the genre as such; but I can safely assert that if anything can be said to constitute the heart of the field, call it Sense-of-Wonder or whatever you wish, it must be found somewhere in those three sentences. For those readers who prefer more emphasis on the speculative scientific element in their science fiction, there is another and more venerable example, from Bishop John Wilkins' novel *A Discourse Concerning a New World and Another Planet* (1638):

> Yet I do seriously, and upon good Grounds, affirm it possible to make a Flying Chariot, in which a man may sit, and give such a motion unto it, as shall convey him through the Air. And this perhaps might be made large enough to carry divers Men at the same time, together with Food for their *Viaticum,* and Commodities for Traffique.
>
> So that nonwithstanding all these seeming impossibilities, 'tis likely enough, that there may be means invented of Journeying to the Moone. And how happy shall they be that are first successful in this attempt!

SCIENCE FICTION: WHAT IT'S ALL ABOUT

It might be thought that this is all pretty obvious and old hat, but how obvious it might seem this day, it was certainly not obvious in the year 1638. The first moon landing did not take place until July 20, 1969, which was somewhat later than the good Bishop had expected, but obviously there was both foresight and (some might say) some accuracy in the story. Personally, I do not think that John Wilkins did prophesy anything, least of all *Apollo XI*, but in 1638, this was Sense-of-Wonder in capital letters.

This might be called the We-told-you-so-didn't-we science fiction. The third example is of a somewhat later date, and if the earlier samples did not evoke the specific feeling of Sense-of-Wonder, perhaps this one will:

> The Gibbelins eat, as is well known, nothing less good than man. Their evil tower is joined to Terra Cognita, to the lands we know, by a bridge. Their hoard is beyond reason; avarice has no use for it; they have a separate cellar for emeralds and a separate cellar for sapphires; they have filled a hole with gold and dig it up when they need it. And the only use that is known for their ridiculous wealth is to attract to their larder a continual supply of food. In times of famine they have even been known to scatter rubies abroad, a little trail of them to some city of Man, and sure enough their larders would soon be full again.
>
> Their tower stands on the other side of that river known to Homer—*ho rhoos Okeanoio,* as he called it—which surrounds the world. And where the river is narrow and fordable the tower was built by the Gibbelins' gluttonous sires, for they like to see burglars rowing easily to their steps. Some nourishment that common soil has not the huge trees drained there with their colossal roots from both banks of the river.
>
> There the Gibbelins lived and discreditably fed. (1)

The principal characters of this story are by science fiction aficionados fondly referred to as BEM's, or Bug-Eyed Monsters; hostilely inclined creatures of some disagreeable kind, often green and decidedly slimy. The BEM's belong to the sf arsenal in the same degree as the old faithful ray guns and the space ships, and even though they nowadays only seldom twine their tentacles around the beautiful (and seminude) heroine's attractive figure, as the noble space-hero raises his trusty atomic blaster somewhere in the background, they still prosper in blissful abandon in the branch of sf that is known as Fantasy and Sword & Sorcery. It is the old fairy tale all over again, complete with the dragon and the milksop princess and the magic sword and the bags of tax-free gold. The above example is from Lord Dunsany's short story *The Hoard of the Gibbelins* (1912), which is a moral story with an unusually credible ending; the monsters devour the hero. The most well-known representative for this branch of science fiction is otherwise. J. R. R. Tolkien's mighty trilogy *The Fellowship of the Ring*, which contains all the time-honored ingredients, including BEM's, called Orcs. They are small, malignant and guaranteed atrocious.

Now the friend of order and discipline might ask how a literary genre with the pretentious name of science fiction can contain such disparate elements as space-flight and fire-breathing dragons. Where is the logic? And, above all, the definition of the genre?

The melancholy fact is that there does not exist any unitary definitions of the genre. Or rather, there exists about as many perfectly valid definitions as there are readers of what I here for simplicity's sake call science fiction. (For myself, I would prefer the term Speculative Fiction as being more descriptive.) The sf buffs present in this connection certain resemblances to a select club where the venerable old men in the reading room have sat and slept in their moldering easy-chairs since the early twenties, with *Amazing Stories* and *Astounding SF* over their white heads; this is the Old Guard, which reads their science fiction with the emphasis on *science,* expecting nothing in the way of purely literary merits and, consequently, getting nothing of that kind. Every deviation from the rule of scientific accuracy is a scathing sin against all decency.

SCIENCE FICTION: WHAT IT'S ALL ABOUT

The lovers of Space Opera are huddled behind enormous piles of *Startling Stories, Captain Future Magazine, Thrilling Wonder Stories* and the collected works of E. E. Smith, and follow with glowing eyes the latest super-scientific adventures of the glorious Space Patrol in the Crab Nebula, where green BEM's of the most atrocious sort are plotting vile schemes against Humanity. Atomic blasters blast, heroines cry, and the space ships leap in and out of hyperspace like frightened hens.

Right by, one can discern the Horror-lovers with their blood-curdling *Weird Tales* and H. P. Lovecraft. European members of this group might be more fond of E. T. A. Hoffmann. They are a small and persecuted minority, far from loved by the *Amazing* readers.

The Fantasy and Sword & Sorcery groups are crowded together in a small room behind the reading room, from which they look rancorously out toward the sleeping gentlemen, thoughtfully fingering at their gleaming broadswords. They are also a minority, but literarily acceptable since the recent upswinging interest in adult fantasy, and in strong need of *lebensraum*.

The group of social reformers sit by the bar, where they exchange views on the future overpopulation, the food crisis, environment pollution, the goal of Humanity etc., anxiously watched by the H. G. Wells phalanx which stands somewhere between the reading room and the bar and doesn't know exactly where they belong.

The "New Wave" advocates keep themselves company out in the cloak-room. This is a collection of bearded and long-haired persons who experiment with new literary forms; they are loud and bothersome and do not have deference for anything, not even for the founder of the club, old Uncle Hugo Gernsback, and they are regarded with deep distrust by all other members. Some of them are said to be supported financially by the Establishment. The members of the science fiction community are deeply worried.

And yet all those factions and branches are only different sides of the same coin, and the division into branches is the unhappy consequence of the labeling that the genre was subjected to around the turn of the century. The early writers of this particular literature, all the way from Lucian, Cyrano de Bergerac, Swift, H. G. Wells, etc., based their themes upon scientific facts known or suspected during their times, never suspecting that this particular branch of literature should be more "scientific" than any other. Their works were often woven around scientific achievements of a more or less speculative nature, granted, but so are many other works of literature than can't in any way be considered science fiction. The science was a background for the idea, something that the reader could suspend his disbelief with, not an end in itself à la *Popular Mechanics*. This label was glued to the genre around the turn of the century, when book and magazine distributors suddenly got books like *The War of the Worlds* and *Looking Backward* on their hands. The distribution system demanded a designation on these oddities; obviously, they were not love stories, and they were not Wild West or war stories, even if they contained elements of all these fields. Some enterprising gentleman leafed through these things that littered his surroundings, and discovered that they dealt with inventions of various kinds; time machines, space vehicles and other funny things. This must, then, be scientific adventures, and, consequently, it was labeled (among other, even more curious noms de plume) Scientific Romances. It had to have *some* name, didn't it?

Then came Hugo Gernsback, a Luxembourg-born naturalized American, who published a technical magazine called *Modern Electrics*. He had the commendable ambition to disseminate new theories and speculations in literary form, and in this respect he published some science fiction in his magazine, the most well-known being his own novel *Ralph 124C41+* which you probably haven't read. There is no need to feel badly about that, though, because the novel is completely unreadable. Gernsback was a good engineer and editor, but a dull writer, and *Ralph 124C41+* turned out as an unendurable bore of a novel, with great amounts of technical innovations—TV-telephones, weather control, synthetic food etc.—but the human angle of the story, par-

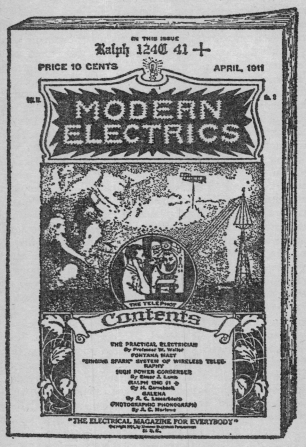

The first installment of *Ralph 124C41+*
appeared in this issue.

ticularly the compulsory love interest, was constantly on the level of the current masterpiece of drivel, the penny dreadful. Yet *Ralph 124C41+* formed the standards for science fiction for decades to come, and it was not until the forties that a lasting improvement set in. Some of the writers of sf have not changed yet. A sample from the first chapter of *Ralph*:

As the vibrations died down in the laboratory the big man rose from the glass chair and viewed the complicated apparatus on the table. It was complete to the last detail. He glanced at the calendar. It was September 1st in the year 2660. Tomorrow was to be a big and busy day for him, for it was to witness the final phase of the three-year experiment. He yawned and stretched himself to his full height, revealing a physique much larger than that of the average man of his times and approaching that of the huge Martians.

His physical superiority, however, was as nothing compared to his gigantic mind. He was *Ralph 124C41+*, one of the greatest living scientists and *one of the ten men on the whole planet earth permitted to use the plus sign after his name.* Stepping to the Telephot on the side of the wall he pressed a group of buttons and in a few minutes the faceplate of the Telephot became luminous, revealing the face of a clean-shaven man about thirty, a pleasant but serious face.

As soon as he recognized the face of Ralph in his own Telephot he smiled and said, "Hello, Ralph."

"Hello, Edward, I wanted to ask you if you could come over to the laboratory tomorrow morning. I have something unusually interesting to show you. Look."

He stepped to one side of his instrument so that his friend could see the apparatus on the table about ten feet from the Telephot faceplate.

Edward came closer to his own faceplate, in order that he might see further into the laboratory.

"Why, you've finished it!" he exclaimed. "And your famous—"

SCIENCE FICTION: WHAT IT'S ALL ABOUT

Ralph 124C41+ is still widely considered to be the first real, unalloyed science fiction novel; which of course is to stretch truth a long, long way. Actually, it is but one of the hundreds of Utopian novels that deluged the market around the turn of the century, propagandizing for some political or social idea or another.

The great classic in this field was Edward Bellamy's *Looking Backward 2000-1887*, which was a worldwide best-seller in 1880 and immediately was followed by a flood of plagiarisms. *Ralph 124C41+*, which was serialized in twelve parts starting April, 1911, was only one of these badly written, badly thought-out plagiarisms, lacking even the social pathos that, despite the inferior literary qualities, had made *Looking Backward* an important literary event, influencing millions of readers over the world. Bellamy's novel gave words to the hopes and dreams of an unprivileged and suffering lower class, seeking their Utopia in socialism, telling, in fact, more about the world of 1887 than about the highly improbable Utopia of the year 2000. It was, essentially, a pamphlet, not a novel in our sense. Gernsback's crude imitation was neither. There was science, but a science without meaning, coulisses without depth and without the slightest hint of contemporary significance. And whereas *Looking Backward* immediately catapulted into world fame, *Ralph* stayed in the science fiction field, which Gernsback made into a specialized literature.

This *science fiction* (called variously scientifiction or scientific fiction) went into full bloom in April, 1926, when Hugo Gernsback launched the sf magazine *Amazing Stories,* which still is being published, although the only thing the *Amazing* of today has in common with Gernsback's magazine is the title. *Amazing* contained scientific adventures, with the emphasis on the scientific side. An imposing array of experts in different sciences were attached to the magazine, and every story was allegedly subjected to examination as for its scientific accuracy. Considerably less interest was devoted to the literary merits; the plot could be unlikely and downright absurd, the characters stereotyped; nothing mattered as long as the imagination was kept within what was right and proper. The ray guns came (carefully checked by experts in physics and electronics), the fair heroine got into position, more slender and scantily dressed than ever before, and the BEM's of the Andromeda nebula started-up their gyroscope ships and prepared to participate in the common joy. The youthful readers of *Amazing* sighed with happiness, but there were others not quite that positive toward the phenomenon. The U.S. columnist Bernard De Voto wrote in 1939:

This besotted nonsense is from the group of magazines known as the science pulps, which deals with both the World and the Universe of Tomorrow and, as our items show, take no great pleasure in either . . . The science discussed is idiotic beyond any possibility of exaggeration, but the point is that in this kind of fiction the bending of light or Heisenberg's formula is equivalent to the sheriff of the horse opera fanning his gun, the heroine of the sex pulp taking off her dress. (2)

The "idiotic science" that De Voto lamented over was the numerous stories dealing with landings on the Moon, atomic bombs, satellites and other absurdities.

When one speaks about the origins of modern science fiction, one should keep this American development in mind. Gernsback separated speculative fiction from mainstream literature, put the emphasis on the scientific aspects and endowed it with a designation not too different from the one already in use. Science fiction appeared. The name was not new in any respect; the exact literary translation, *naturvetenskaplig roman*, was used in a Swedish science fiction magazine as early as 1916, and while Gernsback probably never had heard about this illustrious magazine, much less its designation of the genre, he could not have failed to be familiar with the widely used term *scientific romances*.

Orson Welles's reputed radio dramatization of H. G. Wells's *The War of the Worlds* on October 30, 1938, gave the genre a push forward; the specialized sf magazines grew like mushrooms, the first "World Science Fiction Convention" (strictly for the U.S.A.) was held in New York on July 2, 1939, and speculative literature, which hitherto had been a predominantly European phenomenon, suddenly became something typically American. Literary critics who have done surveys of the genre have often made fun of the sf buffs' eagerness to drag in Lucian and Milton and other literary giants in the field; and Gernsback's space ship-and-monster literature had surely not much in common with Milton. But Gernsback only isolated the technical aspect of the genre; that the whole field now is called science fiction can hardly be blamed on the readers—or the writers.

In order to make some semblance of order in the definitions, science fiction was divided into two general branches: on one hand sf as such, which principally deals with man and his relation to scientific and sociological innovations, probable physical occurrences like catastrophes etc., and on the other hand fantasy, where the scientific side is removed and the logic is constructed to suit the idea—e.g. Tolkien's *The Fellowship of the Ring* trilogy, which is rigorously logical within its own compass, even though elves, dwarfs, fire-breathing dragons, giants and malignant magicians hardly belong to the physical reality such as we see it.

A simplified definition would be that the author of a "straight" science fiction story proceeds from (or alleges to proceed from) known facts, developed in a credible way, whereas the author of a fantasy story starts with an idea and builds a world around it. The question of whether a certain story of imagination is a fantasy or a science fiction work would depend upon the device the author uses to explain his projected or unreal world. If he uses the gimmick or device of saying: "This is a logical or probable assumption based upon known science, which is going to develop from known science or from investigations of areas not yet quite explored but suspected," then one could call it science fiction. But if he asks the reader to suspend his disbelief simply because of the fun of it, in other words, just to say: "Here is a fairy tale I'm going to tell you," then it is fantasy. It could actually be the same story.

Many fantastic stories and novels these days are set upon another world inhabited by people, and if the author of a particular work was to start off by saying, "There is a world in space inhabited by people, and the natural laws of this world are somewhat different from ours, and they are magical," one could, generally speaking, say that this is fantasy. But if he says, "Here is this world,"—and it is the same story—leaving implications that this is the result of a colonization experiment from Earth of a thousand or two thousand or ten thousand years before, then it would suddenly become a science fiction story, because the reader has got a basis for suspending his disbelief. This could really happen, somewhere, somewhen. Fantasy is taking the author on his word, science fiction is taking him in on a logical assumption. He explains something in a logical way.

Fredric Brown gives in the introduction to his collection of short stories *Angels and Spaceships* (1954) a good example of the diffuse borders that separate science fiction from fantasy. He uses the story of King Midas. Kind Midas did the God Bacchus a favor, and got the customary wish as a reward. Midas wished that everything he touched would turn to gold. The wish was granted, but Midas soon found that the precious gift had certain drawbacks. He asked Bacchus to take the gift back, which was granted.

Now, this is certainly fantasy, and nobody expects this to happen in our orderly world. But, says Fredric Brown, let us now translate it to science fiction:

> Mr. Midas, who runs a Greek restaurant in the Bronx, happens to save the life of an extraterrestrial from a far planet who is living in New York anonymously as an observer for the Galactic Federation, to which Earth for obvious reasons is not yet ready to be admitted. Same offer of reward, same request. The extraterrestrial, who is master of sciences far beyond ours, makes a machine which alters the molecular vibrations of Mr. Midas' body so his touch will have a transmuting effect upon other objects. And so on. It's a science fiction story, or could be made into one. (3)

SCIENCE FICTION: WHAT IT'S ALL ABOUT

So much for the difference between science fiction and fantasy. It is really the old fairy tale once again, using the symbols of today—or, as the case may be, the never-never lands of myths—to give entertainment as well as comments to contemporary or suspected processes. Science fiction/fantasy is really not so much a literary genre as a point of view. We live in a scientific age, thus the emphasis on science. The renewed interest in mysticism and metaphysics, as exemplified in works by Hermann Hesse and the "New Wave" authors of science fiction is now challenging the scientific aspect, but though the forms might change, in the end it is all the same thing. Science fiction of today is neither particularly scientific, nor a specific literary genre, but designations are needed, so for simplicity's sake let's call it science fiction.

And why does one read this particular literature? There are lots of theories about what constitutes an avid reader of science fiction, from the extremely flattering (inside the sf fandom) to indulgence or condescension (from the inappreciative outsider). Exactly what this Something is, no one has succeeded in finding yet, even though the phenomenon has been given a name: Sense of Wonder. If you have Sense of Wonder, then you can appreciate science fiction. This obviously doesn't clarify matters much; however, I can say why I personally read it.

When I started to read science fiction seriously, about twenty years ago, it seemed to be offering a subversive thing, the prospect of change. Changes recur constantly in science fiction: changes in our environment, our future, our attitudes. No matter what you do, or how much you try to hold back the forces of amelioration, things are going to *change*. Now, the idea of change is deeply subversive to the Establishment, it must always be, and I think this is where H. G. Wells was subversive, this is why, in fact, he has never been really accepted into English literature. What he said was, in effect, that never mind whether it is going to be better or worse, it is going to be *different*.

This is, in my opinion, what makes the science fiction point of view different and makes it stand apart from mainstream literature, indeed the quality that makes it recognizable regardless of the literary form in which it is presented, be it that of the traditional fairy tale, the thriller, the religious allegory, the action story or what have you. Science fiction's strength has always been in its ideas, not in its forms, and the merits of the genre lie not in its paraphernalia of rockets, machines and distant worlds but in the message that nothing, absolutely nothing can be taken for granted, and that we always must be prepared for changes, both in our attitudes and in our environment. There has been a widespread notion that science fiction, according to its name, should predominantly deal with the technological hardware of future civilizations, and in Hugo Gernsback's time this was probably true—but *Ralph 124C41+* was written sixty years ago, and the science fiction field has not exactly stood still since then.

"It isn't really science fiction's business to describe what science is going to find," Frederik Pohl said in the introduction to his *Ninth Galaxy Reader* anthology (1965). "It is much more science fiction's business to try to say what the human race will make of it all. In fact, this is the thing —the one thing, maybe the only thing—that science fiction does better than any other tool available to hand. It gives us a look at consequences. And does it superbly."

At its best, science fiction fills this function, and does it well. The ray gun-and-monster branch's contribution to this end is usually small, but no one is pretending that all science fiction is great literature. Ninety percent of all science fiction is crud, the sf writer Theodore Sturgeon once said; but, on the other hand, ninety percent of *everything* is crud!

2. THE PREHISTORY

The pursuit of the origins of science fiction in the mists of the dim and distant past has always struck me as a little bit funny; it is following an established academic tradition whereby when someone asks you about something, you immediately have got to turn around and look behind you, to see where it started. For science fiction, which is mainly based on the future and what it might bring, this tendency seems to me somewhat odd. It is an attempt, I think, to make the subject respectable, providing an image for it, because you are not supposed to suddenly produce something new, it is very upsetting, you are not supposed to do that, you are supposed to prove that it came from somebody respectable with a long gray beard yesterday. In literature, age means respectability, no matter what the contents.

Science fiction is, actually, a very modern phenomenon, the result of the latest century's industrial, scientific and social revolution, and even though the ancient Greeks busied themselves both with Moon travels and robots, they did not live in the atmosphere of constant change that is so characteristic for our century, and which is the essential thing about (and the motivating force behind) all science fiction. Science fiction is, if perhaps not the only contemporary literature, undoubtedly the most typical literature of our time, the most sensitive indicator of social and intellectual tides. This is, of course, no new phenomenon. The *chansons de geste* of the Middle Ages faithfully reflected the rigid feudal society of its time, and later, when the power of the Church and the nobility was reduced due to social reforms and upheavals, the picaresque novel appeared as an expression of the skepticism that was born out of the new times. The fantastic novel, in the form we know it, appeared first during the Age of Enlightenment, with political satirists like Voltaire (*Micromegas*) and Ludvig Holberg (*Nicolai Klimii Iter Subterraneum*), at about the same time as authors like the Marquis de Sade explored the subconscious in works like *One Hundred Days in Sodom* and Matthew Gregory Lewis with *The Monk*. It is interesting to note the pyramidal success of Mary Wollstonecraft Shelley's novel *Frankenstein*, which, published in 1818, apparently gave voice to widespread misgivings toward the industrial revolution with its theme of forbidden knowledge coupled with Shelleyian romantic ideals. The Neo-romanticist (and, consequently, anti-scientific) ideals of the cultural elite of the time found its voice in multitudes of fantastic novels of this type, in the same way as the fears of the advancing technology later was voiced in works like Aldous Huxley's *Brave New World* and, more recently, John Brunner's *Stand on Zanzibar* and Harry Harrison's *Make Room! Make Room!* where the specter of overpopulation has taken the place of Frankenstein's monster as the experiment turning against its creator. This literature was—and is—typical of a world and a time in rapid change, with insecurity and great hopes and misgivings for the future. Science fiction of this type would obviously have been unthinkable in ancient Greece.

But of course there are old Greeks to be found, if one searches long enough. Some sf historians have searched until they have turned blue in the face, and have unearthed the most astounding discoveries, from the ancient Indian *Veda* books to the Apocalypse. In Sweden, some enthusiastic scholars seriously maintain that Dante Alighieri's religious allegory *Divina Commedia* was the first real science fiction work, with the radiant Beatrice the first astronaut. Bunyan's *Pilgrim's Progress* has also been nominated to science fiction's hall of fame, which, needless to say, strikes me as being somewhat odd.

Cyril Kornbluth said in *The Science Fiction Novel* (1964) that "Some of the amateur scholars of science fiction are veritable Hitlers for aggrandizing their field. If they perceive in, say, a sixteenth century satire some vaguely speculative element they see it as a trembling and persecuted minority, demand *Anschluss,* and proceed to annex the satire to science fiction."

This is, of course, a way to enlarge the field and enrich its image with some respectable names, if one professes to the one among the many definitions which asserts that it is the situation which makes sf—whether it is a scientific-sociological situation, or a fantastic fairyland with dragons, magicians etc.—and that the basis of the story is how man reacts in this situation. It can be a Utopian society, a visit to the Moon or Hades, a society where murder is socially acceptable, or one where eating is surrounded by as many taboos as sexuality is in our own society.

What reactions will such a situation start, and what will the consequences be? If one proceeds from this definition—and it is largely accepted in sf circles—one can find a lot of science fiction in ancient literature. The most commonly quoted example is Lucian of Samosata (born around 125 A.D.), who wrote a number of satirical dialogues based on fantastic ideas, e.g. *Icaromenippos, or a Journey through the Air* and *A True Story. Icaromenippos* describes a journey to the Moon with the aid of strapped-on wings, during which the protagonist not only gets the opportunity to visit the Selenites, but also Heaven, where he is invited to a feast among the Gods and witnesses how Zeus deals with the prayers that are sent up to him. (God, let my father die; God, make me rich and famous; God, please kill my wife, etc.) Menippos looks down at Earth from his elevated position and is far from encouraged by what he sees.

> I saw Ptolemaios sleep with his sister, Lyismachos' son plotting against his father's life, Antiochus Seleukos' son being in secret collusion with his stepmother Strantonike, Alexander in Thessalia being murdered by his wife, Antigones sharing bed with the wife of his son and Attalos' son give his father poison. Furthermore, I saw how Arsakes killed his wife and how the eunuch Arbakes drew his sword against Arsakes. The

rocket propulsion. He drops down in the Garden of Eden, meets the prophet Elias and gets thrown out after having insulted the worthy prelate. Later, on the Moon, he is jailed for maintaining that the Moon is a satellite to Earth; a dangerous view, since the prevalent opinion on the Moon is that it is the other way around. It is a witty and intelligent satire, but hardly science fiction in our sense of the word.

This also goes for the English priest Francis Godwin's novel *The Man in the Moone: or A Discourse of a Voyage Thither by Domingo Gonsales* (1638), in which the protagonist is left to die on the island St. Helena, but unexpectedly recuperates and tames a number of wild swans in order to have them carry him back to the mainland. It turns out, however, that it is time for the swans' annual emigration to the Moon, and the good Domingo Gonsales comes suddenly to a world where the inhabitants are nine yards tall and flies through the atmosphere of the Moon with the aid of artificial wings. The main point of this story is also the satire. Just as the previously mentioned novel by John Wilkins—being based upon the assumption that travels to the Moon might be possible, and developing this idea in a speculative way—obviously is science fiction, Francis Godwin's satire cannot by any stretch of imagination be considered one.

World literature is abundant with satires of this type, from François Rabelais's *Les Livres des faictz et dicts héroiques du noble Pantagruel* (1532-64), a humorous and satirical masterpiece, in which the giant Pantagruel travels through known and unknown countries, searching for the answers to all questions, finally finding them in the Oracle of the Golden Bottle, which simply tells him *Trink!* (Drink!), over Ludvig Holberg's *The Subterranean Journey of Niels Klim* (1741), a Swiftian excursion into the netherworlds, Voltaire's *Micromegas* (1752) in which a Sirian and a Saturnian visit Earth and get ample opportunities to be astounded by the human foolery, Samuel Butler's anti-Utopian *Erewhon: or, Over the Range* (1872), Jonathan Swift's *Gulliver's Travels* (1726), and on to the present-day's horror visions like *1984*, *Brave New World*, *Make Room! Make Room!* and *The Space Merchants*.

There is a bond uniting for example Lucian and the science fiction of today. The device of transferring contemporary anomalous states of things to an imaginary world on the Moon, forgotten valleys or the future, in order to subject them to a hard-hearted scrutiny in the disguise of overstatement, is still used in science fiction, but whereas the Moon-and-Forgotten-Valley satires dealt with contemporary problems, the science fiction author of today particularly works with subjects of a social, political or scientific nature that are likely to become topical in the near or foreseeable future. John Wilkins' *A Discourse Concerning a New World and a New Planet*, being speculative rather than satirical in nature, is very modern in this respect, as attested by his foreword where he says that:

It is my Desire, that by Occasion of this Disclosure, I may raise up some more Active Spirit to search after other hidden and unknown Truths. Since it must needs be of great Impediment unto the Growth of Sciences, for Men still to Plod on upon beaten Principles, as to be afraid of entertaining any thing that may seem to contradict them. An Unwillingness to take such things into Examination, is on of these Errours of Learning in these times observed by the judicious Verulam. Questionless there are many secret Truths, which the Ancients have passed over, that are yet left to make some of our Age Famous for their Discovery.

The Moon, being nearest to Earth and most easily accessible for observation, was the first and foremost goal for adventurous spirits seeking a place to show off their political or scientific theories. The first attempt that I know of traveling to more distant places is the German astronomer Eberhard Christian Kindermann's novel *Die geshwinde Reise auf dem Luft-schiff nach der obern Welt, welche jüngsthin fünf Personen angestellet* (1744), in which the author has made use of the Italian Jesuit Francesco Lama's theory of making a vehicle rise in the air with the aid of evacuated metal spheres which—Lama thought—would become lighter than the air and thus lift the vehicle. Neither Kindermann nor Lama seem to have given much thought to atmospheric pressure on the metal spheres, as attested by Guerick's evacuated globes of 1654, which could not be pulled apart by fourteen horses. Kindermann's travelers nevertheless managed to construct their space vehicle and steered, in a manner reminiscent of the hot-air balloons of the brothers Montgolfièr, toward Mars. Kindermann was, however, not the only scientist who was fooled by Francesco Lama's theory. It is known that Carl von Linné, the famous Swedish naturalist, thought the idea perfectly sound and argued for it in his book *Iter lapponicum* (Journey through Lapland, 1732).

The real breakthrough for science fiction came with the late industrialization, when the universe suddenly threw its gates wide open and nothing was impossible any longer. The holy machine was placed in the high seat, and with its help one could accomplish absolutely anything. This was the time of the unlimited belief in progress, and Queen Victoria sat with the sleeping lions at her feet and watched benevolently how the sky was darkened by smoke from railways and steelworks. In 1851, the first World's Fair was organized in London, arranged around the architectural masterpiece of the time, the Crystal Palace in Hyde Park, a magnificent construction in glass and steel, 115 feet high under the central dome. The whole Fair covered an area of 700,000 square feet, and during five and a half months more than 17,000 exhibitors displayed the grandest of human ingenuity and culture for six million visitors.

When the ninth World's Fair was arranged in Paris in 1889, the number of exhibitors exceeded 50,000, and the Fair was visited by more than twenty-six million people. This time the main attraction was the 1,000 feet high Eiffel Tower, the eighth wonder of the world, and a suitable symbol for the boundless self-confidence of industrialization. Two thousand years earlier, Archimedes had said, "Give me a fixed point to stand on, and I will move the Earth."

The Victorians had the fulcrum, and electric power would move the lever.

Jules Verne explored the interior of Earth in *Journey to the Center of the Earth* (1864), shot people to the Moon in a hollow cannonball in *From the Earth to the Moon* (1865), traveled around the world's oceans in the marvelous submarine *Nautilus*, complete with Wilton rugs and crystal chandeliers and the melancholy Captain, previously Maharajah, Nemo, in *20,0000 Leagues Under the Sea* (1869), repeated the performance in the air with *Robur the Conqueror* and *Master of the World* in which the current *übermensch*, the engineer Robur, flies around the world in the airship *Albatross*, a heavier-than-air vehicle that is a hundred feet long and looks like a sailing ship with seventy-four masts that carry helicopter rotors, and which could make James Bond green with envy anytime. In *The Mysterious Island*, a loose sequel to the more well-known *20,0000 Leagues Under the Sea*, a talented engineer was able to turn a dead island into a mechanical Victorian paradise, without any other equipment than his scientific knowledge plus a little bit of discreet assistance from the inevitable *deus ex machina*, the old graying Captain Nemo, who had retired from piracy and now devoted himself to charity from the bottom of a volcano.

The novel *The Begum's Fortune* was modeled as industrialization's apotheosis, with two super-cities, one humanistic (French) and one industrial (German). The holy machine had already begun to be dangerous, though, and sure enough it is the humanists in France-Ville that stand for the dream of the future, while the Stahlstadt of the German Doctor Schultze is described as hell on Earth. The evil doctor unfolds his philosophy for the captured hero:

My friend . . . Right-Good-Evil are purely relative, and quite conventional words. Nothing is positive but the grand laws of nature. The law of competition has the same force as that of gravitation. It is folly to resist, while to submit and follow in the way it points out is only wise and reasonable, and therefore I mean to destroy Doctor Sarrasin's city. Thanks to my cannon, my fifty thousand Germans will easily make an end of the hundred thousand dreamers over there, who now constitute a group condemned to perish. (4)

There was already a fly in the ointment. The future-dreamers had discovered that the machine's civilization was as bad as the preceding one. When Verne wrote *Propeller Island*, the floating city of the future, Milliard City, became a Utopist's paradise, a temple of Mammon and the holy science, with escalator-like pavements, magnificent marble palaces, concert halls where the greatest musicians of the time appeared. It was town-shaping on a gargantuan scale, as were the two cities in *The Begum's Fortune*, built by the immensely rich and offering undreamed-of luxury to a population of 10,000 inhabitants, of whom no one owned less than five million francs. The science is perfect—and yet this gigantic island is doomed to disaster, because its creators can't control the powers they themselves have set in motion.

In a later novel, *For the Flag* (1896), the traditional mad scientist, here called Thomas Roch, lets a new war's hell loose over the world. He uses guided missiles, with a payload comprised of something disquietingly like an atomic bomb, and with this anachronistic weapon in their hands, a group of pirates proceed to threaten all Atlantic shipping as well as America's Eastern Coast from their base in the Bermuda Islands, in a manner reminiscent of Ian Fleming's *Moonraker*. This does not imply that Jules Verne prophesied either the ICBM or James Bond, nor did he prophesy the modern submarine or *Apollo XI*. By reading up intelligently on the technical developments of his time, he was able to speculate on possible future developments, in the same way as later science fiction writers have done and still do. A somewhat more nearsighted form of this speculation is now done under the name of "future research" in private and military research centers. The science fiction writers—Verne and others—are not working with "future research." They are speculating in probabilities, and the mass destruction weapon was, of course, a possibility in Jules Verne's time.

SCIENCE FICTION: WHAT IT'S ALL ABOUT

The Victorians' confidence in the future stood unbroken in the shadow of the new steel wonders, the Utopists evoked the new world, where the machines would take over the workers' role and make mankind happy and prosperous over a single night. Certain writers, notably Jules Verne and H. G. Wells, had, notwithstanding, gotten a touch of the hangover. In 1888, H. G. Wells wrote the first outline of the novel *The Chronic Argonauts,* later retitled *The Time Machine,* in which he foresaw a future where the machine civilization had created two separate human races, the Morlocks and the Eloi. The Morlocks were descended from the factory workers of our time, who had been forced down into subterranean machine cities, where during millennia they had changed into repulsive, cannibal creatures who used the refined—and retarded—Eloi, the remainders of the ancient upper class, as food.

The idea was again brought forth by the German author Thea von Harbou in the novel *Metropolis* (1926), a masterpiece of drivel, which despite that, contains social implications that stood in glaring contrast to the type of Utopias that were popular at the time.

H. G. Wells, who at this time still deeply distrusted all Utopian schemes, had for a long time been preoccupied with the original *bête humain* and all its possible transformations. He believed, like many others, that most of our moral character is but results of habit and circumstances, and that man had undergone only "an infinitesimal alteration in his intrinsic nature since the age of unpolished stone." This belief was brought forth in a number of novels, notably *The Time Machine* and *The Island of Dr. Moreau.* The latter work, first published in 1896, was obviously influenced by Rudyard Kipling's Jungle Books, telling of Dr. Moreau's experiments in vivisection in order to create men out of animals. Scholars have pointed out the similarities between Kipling's "Law of the Jungle" and Wells's "The Sayers of the Law"; but, Ingvald Raknem says in his excellent study of H. G. Wells:

While Kipling's "Law of the Jungle" is a kind of idyllizing romance of jungle life, Wells's pictures of the Beast Folk are a veiled presentation of mankind trying to rise above the animal stage and worshipping their maker. Wells's chapter is indeed a demonstration of the process of development of man from the animal stage to that of a social and spiritual being, and a revelation of the superficiality of this transformation. (5)

These views were hardly in accordance with the beliefs of the progressive-minded generation of the nineties. One critic could only explain it "as a morbid aberration of scientific curiosity," it was the "perverse quest after anything . . . sensational," and "only an extreme instance of the horrible, the weird and the uncanny which characterize all his writings." Even those critics who attempted to see the positive sides of the novel misunderstood him completely:

The strong reactionary effect which is produced at the close of the story and the terrible fate which is meted out to the impiously daring vivisectionist are the saving points of the book. (6)

These reactions were again repeated in 1897, when H. G. Wells's next novel, *The War of the Worlds*, was published and met with anguished cries from the once again disappointed critics:

There are episodes that are so brutal, details so repulsive, that they cause insufferable distress to the feelings. The restraint of art is missing. We would entreat Mr. Wells to return to his earlier methods—to the saner, serener beauty of those first romances that cast their spell upon our imagination, and appealed to our finer sensibilities. (7)

This notwithstanding, Wells continued his excursions into the world of modern man. In the novel *The War in the Air* (1907) he described with horrifying fullness of detail all

ACE BOOK: 14253, 60¢

Jules Verne

THE "FITZROY" EDITION OF JULES VERNE. EDITED BY I. O. EVANS.

The Demon of Cawnpore

Cover of Ace Books edition.

the horrors of a modern war, horrors that only seven years later would turn out to be far worse than he ever could have visualized.

"I pointed out," Wells said later, "that the war in the air by making the war three-dimensional, would obliterate the war-front and with that the possibility of separating civilians from the belligerent, or to put an effective end to the war. This, I said, must not only sharpen but also change the common man's attitude to the ear. He cannot any longer regard it, as we did with the Boer War, as a lively spectacle, where his participation can be compared to that of a paying spectator at a cricket-match." (8)

In 1903, Wells had pointed out, in the short story *The Land Ironclads*, the revolution that would be the result of the tanks. The story directly leads the thought to the ruin of the Austrian cavalry during the first World War. It was the old world that rode out toward the machine guns, with gleaming epaulets, flags and sparkling flourishes of trumpets. The new world stood in gray uniforms behind the steel-blue, functional machines and swept away the cavalry as with an unconcerned giant's hand. The innocent romanticism of the turn of the century that was voiced in, for instance, novels like André Laurie's *Les Exiles de la Terre* (1889), in which the scientists visit the Moon by making a giant magnet and simply pulling down the satellite, was on its way out. In other novels people went on interplanetary sight-seeing trips, as in John Jacob Astor's *A Journey in Other Worlds* (1894) and George Griffith's *Honeymoon in Space* (1900) where the whole civilized paraphernalia was present, including lace curtains for the windows and frosty punch to the coffee as the bold travelers went around in the solar system, from the warlike Martians to the ethereal Venusians. These were the good old days, and when the beastly Martians or the stupid crew attacked, there was always an Eton-educated gentleman present to put a bullet or two between the villain's eyes.

World War I abruptly changed this. In 1920, the Czech writer Karel Čapek wrote the play *R.U.R.* (Rossum's Universal Robots), in which the robots took over the world, much in the same manner as the newts later did in Čapek's novel *War with the Newts* (1936). The play was an attack on the "scientific barbarism" which Čapek foresaw in the rise of nazism and fascism. The play was a success and was put on the stage all over the world; it was also filmed. The play is noted for being the source of the word "robot" in English and a number of other languages. The mechanical honeymoon was obviously over. The Victorians died with the *Titanic* and were buried in World War I.

"A jolt as the World War was needed," H. G. Wells later wrote, "to make the British people see that nothing stood still . . . All history is adaptation, and the only fundamental difference between our time and the past is the unprecedentedly changed scale and pace in which the necessity of adaptation has asserted itself." (9)

There was, once again, the message of the irrevocable change, now said with the experience of the World War's hell. After World War I, it became, of natural causes, fashionable to be a pacifist, and lean young men with Macassaroil in their hair walked around in the salons and argued that there never would be war again. H. G. Wells wrote the novel *The World Set Free* (1914) in which he prophesied new wars and the final weapon, the atomic bomb. After that, he sat back and waited. He didn't have to wait long.

3. UTOPIA

"Where do you want to partake of your dinner, madame? On the ground floor, in one of the big halls one, two or more storeys up? We have dining halls up to the eleventh floor. We also have private rooms, up to the fourteenth floor. Please make up your mind. The first elevator starts within one minute . . . My good ladies and gentlemen . . . Here we have the second elevator with octagonal parlours that hold fifty guests each. Here is the third elevator . . . Please step inside!"

It was one of the employees of the Central Hotel, an Escalator Major, who organized the ascendent to the dinner. The Central Hotel was situated in the old Humlegården, or rather in the place where this ancient park had been, and approximately on the spot where, five hundred years ago, a small building had been erected for the Royal Library, which was the name given to the government's rather insignificant collection of books during the days of the kingdom.

New guests arrived constantly, most of them by air-velocipedes, air-cabs and other flying vehicles. Only a small number, perhaps a couple of hundreds, let themselves be hoisted up from the ground floor. The others steered right into one of the upper floors, where the vehicles were received in a number of velocipede stables, checked and guarded . . .

When you entered one of the great dining-halls, you found that they were filled with bustling activity. Around the extensive buffets that lined the walls thronged the guests that didn't have the time to sit down for a real meal, but instead quickly swallowed some of the

41

universal-energy-extract pills that always were available and made it possible to eat in seconds the equivalent of two or three ordinary meals.

The guests that had more time on their hands sat at big or small tables, richly decorated by pieces of art made by the many newly discovered metals. At every table there were a certain number of buttons, similar to those that in ancient times were used for the so-called electric bell system, and on every button the name of a dish could be read. This was the menu of the time. You pressed a button, and immediately the desired dish appeared from the floor and was pushed over to the table. Waiters or waitresses were nowhere to be seen, but every time that a dish appeared on the table, an electric signal went to one of the cashiers by the entrance, where a machine immediately noted down the dish along with the number of the guest that had ordered it, and at the exit the guest must pay his bill before he walked out.

The Central Hotel was, like all other restaurants in Stockholm, amply supplied with eat- and drinkables from all parts of the world. One could have kangaroo-steak, tapir ham, peacock breast and other meat dishes from faraway places, everything fresh. The animal might have been killed the day before by one of the modern butchering- and hunting-machines and sent to the hotel by air freight . . .

"Look what we have won by putting science into the kitchen!" exclaimed Aromasia, as she brought her guests to a table in one of the big halls of the Central Hotel.

"But the poetry!" objected the poet. "Where is the poetry?"

"It seems you never can forget your railroad-poetry," Aromasia remarked smilingly, reading the food buttons.

"Alas! Where is now the poetry of the home!" continued the poet. "In the old days the husband gathered his family around their own table. Now the whole family goes to a restaurant and sits down in a public hall together with total strangers, and eats there. Can this be called family comfort? Do you know what in the old days was meant by domestic bliss?"

"Yes," interjected Aunt Vera, whom Aromasia also had invited to dinner, "with domestic bliss was meant that the housewife should do all the work and perhaps stand by the stove herself, if she wanted to make sure that the food wasn't ruined. She should be the servant of her husband and the whole family. All domestic care, all troubles rested on her. This was the domestic bliss of the old times."

This long extract from the Swedish writer Claes Lundin's delightful Utopian novel *Oxygen och Aromasia* (1879) is very typical of one aspect of the Utopian literature, namely the dream of the country of happiness as the place where all wishes have come true, where everything is orderly and beautifully thought-out, and where one, above all, lives in freedom from want. The beautiful, wonderful Schlaraffenland or Cockaigne or lubberland all rolled into one improbable thing, the country where dissenters are shot at sight and the laws are obeyed immediately or else. What makes Lundin's novel a strange bird in the peculiar world of the Utopias is its democratic inclination and its humor. Lundin is obviulsy not taking his Utopia entirely seriously. When the beautiful artist Aromasia plays the scent-organ, the "Odophore," for a group of devoutly groaning members of the local Society, both the scent-organ and the Utopia split wide open with a stench that abruptly terminates the heavenly concert. Lundin's description of the future evening papers *The Rapacious Wolf* and *Next Week's News* are not overly serious either.

Lundin described his Utopia with a pinch of humor, even if it contains all the time-honored ingredients of a true Utopian tale, including space ships (exactly like the *cavorite* sphere later described by H. G. Wells in *First Men on the Moon*), suspended animation, matter-transmitters and (almost) universal peace. Plus an anachronistic dissenter, a rather stupid poet. Weather control and TV telephones also appeared.

Title page for Claes Lundin's novel, 1878.

It should be noted that this novel was written five years before Hugo Gernsback, the "father of modern science fiction," even was born. Actually, *Oxygen och Aromasia* was at least sixty years before its time, being more modern than any science fiction written in the U.S.A. before 1930, both in imagination and quality of writing. Lundin even considered women as human beings, something that didn't dawn upon most sf writers until the middle of the twentieth century.

Other Utopias are considerably less foreseeing and—of course—not at all interested in the well-being of its poor citizens. As a rule, they show a contempt of men that would give them an honored place in the section for anti-Utopias. The inventors of these narratives from the burning hell have, with few exceptions, regarded themselves as Big Brother himself, who knows best and therefore is best suited to decide what is best for his fellow citizens. Unswerving obedience is the foremost principle of every well-arranged Utopia. I do not know how they have planned to dispose of the citizens that perchance should turn out to have different views on this; probably a firing squad was to be included somewhere.

The real horror in this sub-genre of science fiction is, of course, Plato, the old Nazi, who in his dialogue *The Republic* outlined a Utopia that leaves most others far behind. The first Commandment is naturally obedience before authorities, in this case equivalent to Plato and his friends. Moreover, every citizen's station in the society is fixed since birth, and under no circumstance is someone from the unworthy lower class permitted to ascend to higher positions. Race prejudice is systematized, and put into practical use, following a pattern that later on should be very familiar. After some typical comparisons to the breeding of dogs and the value of "pure" races, Plato turns to Man:

It follows from our former admissions, that the best men must cohabit with the best women in as many cases as possible and the worst with the worst in the fewest, and that the offspring of the one must be reared

45

and that of the other not, if the flock is to be as perfect as possible. And the way in which all this is brought to pass must be unknown to any but the rulers, if, again, the herd of guardians is to be as free as possible from dissension. We shall, then, have to ordain certain festivals and sacrifices, in which we shall bring together the brides and the bridegrooms, and our poets must compose hymns suitable to the marriages that then take place. But the number of marriages we will leave to the discretion of the rulers, that they may keep the number of the citizens as nearly as may be the same, taking into account wars and diseases and all such considerations, and that, as far as possible, our city may not grow too great or too small. Certain ingenious lots, then, I suppose, must be devised so that the inferior man at each conjugation may blame chance and not the rulers.

And on the young men, surely, who excel in war and other pursuits we must bestow honors and prizes, and, in particular, the opportunity of more frequent intercourse with the women, which will at the same time be a plausible pretext for having them beget as many of the children as possible. And the children thus born will be taken over by the officials appointed for this . . . The offspring of the good, I suppose, they will take to the pen or crèche, to certain nurses who live apart in a quarter of the city, but the offspring of the inferior, and any of those of the other sort who are born defective, they will properly dispose of in secret, so that no one will know what has become of them. (10)

It is interesting to compare texts and see how near the Nazis came to achieving the ideals of Plato. Jacques Delarue describes in his book *The History of the Gestapo* how the, possibly Plato-inspired, system of the Nazis worked:

. . . The S.S. man did not have the right to marry without the authorization of his superiors. His fiancée had to prove her Aryan descent back to 1800 if she wanted to marry a simple S.S. man or non-commissioned officer, and back to 1750 if she was to marry an officer. Only the *Hauptamt*, the head office, could validate the proofs provided and give the necessary authorization. Furthermore, the girl had to undergo a certain number of medical examinations and physical tests. She must be capable of ensuring issue to the race of Herrenvolk. After the marriage the bride had to attend one of the S.S. special schools, where she was indoctrinated with the political education and "ideology which springs from the idea of racial purity". . .

Himmler's system achieved its apotheosis with the creation of the Lebensborn—the fountain of life—a sort of human stud farm where young girls selected for their perfect Nordic traits could, free from all conjugal bonds, procreate with S.S. men also chosen according to the same criteria. The children born of these unions were fruits of a planned eugenics and belonged to the State, and their education was ensured in special schools. In theory they were destined to form the first generation of pure Nazis, fashioned in the ovum . . . (11)

It should be pointed out that the theory of "racial purity" worked out as badly for the Nazis as it should have for Plato and his philosopher friends. The pure-bred Aryans turned out to have an intellectual standard grossly below the average, and they did show a percentage of mental deficients four or five times higher than the normal. Or perhaps this is the sign of the Nazi/Plato thoroughbred; what do I know?

Other Utopias are somewhat more humanitarian than the Third Reich of Plato. St. Thomas More's *Utopia* (1516) (from the Greek *au topos*, nowhere) is light-years removed from *The Republic*. More has taken over the communistic society from Plato, but actually distributed a little bit of freedom to the people, keeping only ninety percent or so for the king. He is openly anti-militaristic, and even permits diverging religious faiths. The people of Utopia are merry, easy and without fear of the gods, and have a religion which favorably separates from the one of More's own time, foremost in that they maintain that:

> . . . a lesser pleasure might not stand in the way of a greater, and that no pleasure ought to be pursued that should draw a great deal of pain after it; for they think it the maddest thing in the world to pursue virtue, that is a sour and difficult thing; and not only renounce the pleasures of life, but willingly to undergo much pain and trouble, if a man has no prospect of a reward? (12)

As for religion, the nice advocate of Free Thought, King Utopus, gave every man of Utopia free liberty to believe in whatever religion suited him:

> . . . only he made a solemn and severe law against such as should so far degenerate from the dignity of human nature as to think that our souls died with our bodies, or that the world was governed by chance, without a wise overruling Providence . . . and they now look on those that think otherwise as scarce fit to be counted men, since they degrade so noble a being as the soul, and reckon it no better than a beast's; thus they are far from looking on such men as fit for human society, or to be citizens of a well-ordered commonwealth. (13)

This, in a nutshell, is the theory of Utopian life and code of conduct, not only for More's novel, but for all Utopian societies: Think what you wish, but think *right*.

More's *Utopia* is divided into two parts. The first is a vigorous attack on social evils of his time—despotism, intrigues, ruinous wars, an almost criminal taxation and a cruel legal system. The second part is the actual Utopian novel—a description of the imaginary communist society on the island of Utopia. The first part of the book is hard and uncompromising; the second is idyllic, and in fact the actual origin of the Utopian never-never land. The complete book is a work of scathing social criticism in which More's England contrasts glaringly to Utopia.

More was later beheaded by his king, Henry VIII, and somewhat later canonized, though not on account of this book.

A century after More, the Italian Dominican friar Tommaso Campanella wrote *The City of the Sun,* which to a great extent is an antithesis to Plato, but with Big Brother still present. Campanella's society is clearly socialistic, based on an authoritarianism that must seem less than desirable for a modern man. Children belong to the State, marriage as an institution is dissolved. All citizens are dressed in identical uniforms. The material prosperity is considerable, but here, as in all other Utopian societies, actual freedom seems to have been caught in a wedge under the writer's enthusiasm. He is obviously incapable of understanding that man might want something more than food, sleep and housing.

Utopian novels have many faults, the most obvious seem to be their single-mindedness and inability to regard man as a thinking, illogical creature with a will of his own. They are sort of sagas, really, or fairy tales, and even though all the classical Utopias—from Plato's dream of the Dorian ideal society over Augustino's Theocracy, Joachim di Fiore's "third society," Thomas More's *Utopia* and on to the ideal creations of Owens, Fouriers, Cabet, Saint-Simon and Huxley—were based on the factual conditions of their times, none has succeeded in making the speculation viable. Except in cases like More's *Utopia,* which clearly is an attack on the appalling social conditions of More's time, all Utopias are little but oversimplified escapist dreams.

In our time, the Utopian novel has found a worthy successor in works like those of Mickey Spillane, with their almost erotic dreams of fulfilled sadism. Not to mention the real Utopian literature of our time, the specialized Utopias of pornography, where everything is possible: the Pornotopia. This is not science fiction, though. What speculation there is, is purely on the monetary side—even though the Pornotopia obviously is fantastic enough.

The big fault with all Utopian literature is that it is illogical and muddily thought-out; it must always be. Chesterton once remarked that:

> The weakness of all Utopias is this, that they take the greatest difficulty of man and assume it to be overcome, and then give an elaborate account of the overcoming of the smaller ones. They first assume that no man will want more than his share, and then are very ingenious in explaining whether his share will be delivered by motor car or balloon.

The second objection—and this one might be even more serious—is that Utopias invariably are boring. Again, they must be so; this is in the nature of the Utopia. If everything is tops, what is there to live for? "I don't want comfort," cries Aldous Huxley's John Savage to the World Controller.

> "I want God, I want poetry, I want real danger, I want freedom, I want goodness, I want sin."
> "In fact," said Mustapha Mond, "you're claiming the right to be unhappy."

Mr. Savage does, heartily. And through Mr. Savage's reactions toward the apparent Utopia, a Utopia that has all the classical properties including unlimited food, drink and sex, *Brave New World* suddenly comes out as an anti-Utopian novel. The Utopian society described in the Fourth Book of *Gulliver's Travels* is viewed in the same way: (The Houyhnhms) may have all the reason, but the Yahoos have all the life. Voltaire's Candide voluntarily leaves Eldorado because it is boring. The anachronistic poet in Claes Lundin's *Oxygen och Aromasia* almost becomes mad in the all-too perfect world he is imprisoned in, and dies while trying to escape to the Moon with a newly invented space ship. The perfect Utopia bears in itself the seed of the anti-

Utopia. The perfect Utopia is like an army camp: you get fed, clothed and exercised, and nice people do your thinking for you. But who wants to live in an army camp for the rest of his life?

This violently totalitarian attitude is (with few exceptions) characteristic of all Utopias, whether they appear on unknown islands, in the Earth's interior or on the Moon, and could, as far as the implications go, as well be put into the section for horror visions, together with *1984* and *Brave New World*. Plato's *The Republic*, for example, could easily be changed into a true horror novel by making the narrator not one of the ruling elite, but one of those "inferior" citizens whose offspring was to be disposed of. The new Utopian writers are not quite that naïve, and do not persist in constructing their ideal states as concentration camps. In, for example, Ismar Thiusen's *Looking Forward* (1883), it was completely natural that the fair young ladies of the year 3,000 A.D. should be kept locked in, permitted to step outside only in the company of broad-shouldered old hags with daggers in their hands. Nowadays the young women might even go on three-week space tours together with the hero, without any other chaperons than their own accommodating consciences. If the old hag shows up, the hero probably would kick her out. This is, of course, a result of the more liberal outlook on sexuality and personal freedom of our days.

On the whole, the science fiction writers of today entertain a commendably suspicious attitude toward their ideal states, basing their speculations on the sound assumption that man will continue to be what he is, even though his environment will change. He will neither be saint nor slave, and the Utopia must be constructed according to this. In return, Utopia has grown considerably in size, and does hardly circumscribe itself to Earth or an insignificant part thereof. James Hilton's ethereal Shangri-La peacefully dreams away the years in splendid isolation behind impenetrable mountain ranges, but out in the starry void new empires appear—and disappear. The U.S. sf writer Isaac Asimov's well-known trilogy *Foundation* (1942-49) depicts a future that makes all other imagined societies bleak in comparison:

> . . . At the beginning of the thirteenth millennium, this (development) reached its climax. As the center of the Imperial Government for unbroken hundreds of generations and located, as it was, in the central regions of the Galaxy among the most densely populated and industrially advanced worlds of the system, it could scarcely help being the densest and richest clot of humanity the Race had ever seen.
>
> Its urbanization, progressing steadily, had finally reached the ultimate. All the land surface of Trantor, 75,000,000 square miles in extent, was a single city. The population, at its height, was well in excess of forty billions. This enormous population was devoted almost entirely to the administrative necessities of the Empire, and found themselves all too few for the complications of the task. . . . Daily, fleets of ships in the tens of thousands brought the produce of twenty agricultural worlds to the dinner tables of Trantor. . . . (14)

The central theme of all Utopian literature is Power. Power to change the environment, power to maintain the private or human individuality. The novels of Jules Verne belong, with few exceptions, to this branch, as well as most of the science fiction that was written during the time of the late industrialization. It was power to send man to the Moon, power to place man over the natural laws; with the help of human genius, power to create the ideal state on Earth. With a rough generalization, one can say that the Utopian novel dominated science fiction—with shining exceptions like H. G. Wells—until the nineteen thirties, when the Depression quickly put an end to the most naïve hopes for the future. It is interesting, though, to note that H. G. Wells, who started with anti-Utopias like *When the Sleeper Wakes* (1899) and *The Time Machine* (1895), in time became increasingly reactionary, until the scientific progress and evolutionary process whose end results are so gloomily predicted in the early stories, are held forth as the bases for desirable brave new worlds in, for example, *A Modern Utopia* (1905), *Men Like Gods* (1923) and *The Shape of Things to Come* (1933). *A Modern Utopia* describes the modern welfare state, governed by the usual Utopian rational elite, called *Samurai*, and the result is a world ruled by efficiency, proving, as many of Wells's subsequent works did, that he had no fondness for socialism in its classical sense, or even for democracy. This message is also brought forth in the other two mentioned novels, strange as it may seem when one knows that Wells once was an active member of the British Fabian Society, a socialistic movement. In these novels, Wells suddenly returns to the time-honored totalitarian state reminiscent of the government system proposed, among others, by Francis Bacon in *The New Atlantis* and by Plato in *The Republic;* a meritocracy with Science (or Philosophy) as an obedient servant standing behind the Masters. It is Utopia in all respects, chemically free of everything that possibly could make life worth living. The British critic David Lodge has observed regarding *A Modern Utopia* that:

> In a sense it was a generous attempt on Wells's part to imagine a social structure which would make available to everyone the kind of success and happiness he had personally achieved in the teeth of great disadvantages. Or, more cynically, you could call it the paradise of little fat men.

This also goes, in a lesser degree, for Aldous Huxley, creator of one of the most fierce and intelligent anti-Utopian novels, *Brave New World,* who as an old man wrote a straight Utopian novel, *Island* (1961) which is about as stimulating as any of the old stiff-legged and impossible Utopias.

The Utopian novel is escapist, as all dreams of the unattainable must be, and the science fiction writers of today are all too practical to go on escapist Utopian sprees. One of the very few exceptions I know of is the noted sf writer

SCIENCE FICTION: WHAT IT'S ALL ABOUT

Theodore Sturgeon's novel *Venus Plus X* (1960), which depicts a Utopia in the classic sense, complete with universal brotherhood, understanding, intelligence, love and no dissenters in sight. That the novel still manages to convey a message is entirely due to Sturgeon's obvious skills as a writer, plus the fact that this particular Utopia is built upon sexual and moral standards that in themselves make the novel interesting. Apart from that, this is Schlaraffenland all over again, and no beautiful machinery can make it credible. The societies created by other sf writers are far, far removed from this

A short story by Robert Sheckley, *Street of Dreams, Feet of Clay* (1969), joyously describes a seemingly perfect Utopia, a sentient city which is programmed to guard its inhabitants from all dangers, and to give them everything they can wish for. It behaves exactly as carpingly patronizing as an anxious mother, and the inhabitants can't wait to get out of it. Another short sf story describes a future where criminals are frozen into suspended animation and left for thawing in some distant Utopian future where people know how to handle them. The protagonist awakes in this future, is taken on a sight-seeing tour of the perfect Utopia, and soon becomes seized by claustrophobia. The continuance of Utopia is guaranteed by a simple surgical incision that is performed while the citizen is still a baby, and secures him a happy and peaceful life, free from unnecessary curiosity and rebelliousness. The protagonist has to choose between going through the operation and becoming a socially well-adjusted individual, or getting thrown out into the wilderness where the scattered remnants of various underdeveloped races live in horrible destitution. He chooses the savages.

In this story the good Utopians enjoyed themselves by spying on the appalling destitution of the savages through hidden TV cameras. In a recent story by Harlan Ellison, *The Prowler in the City at the Edge of the World,* the citizens of a future Utopia fetch Jack the Ripper and force him to prowl the sterile streets, killing and vandalizing, in order to satisfy the Utopians' demands for more and more

Illustration for Camille Flammarion's
1912 novel of the year ten million A.D.

perverted amusements. The citizens of More's esoteric Utopia were not unacquainted with the idea either. Of course they were strongly opposed to wars and such themselves, and in times of war the foremost task of the priests was to prevent (not preclude: that might put the soldiery out of jobs) unnecessary bloodshed. In the neighboring country Zapolet, however, live heartless, uncivilized brutes who are willing to fight Utopia's wars. The Utopians pay these killers to wage their wars for them, and complacently regard how they butcher each other. For their own part, the Utopians prefer assassinations, and assassins are both honored and well paid.

Imagined societies are still created in science fiction, but they are far from the escapist Utopias of yore. Robert A. Heinlein's and Isaac Asimov's highly complicated future societies are good examples of this. They are, on the whole, better than the societies of today, just as our world on the whole is better than that of a hundred years ago, but they are not perfect. No world will ever be perfect because man isn't, and no *deus ex machina* in the form of a brilliant new religious concept or some wonderful mechanical gadget will ever do the work for him.

When steam power was introduced, it was thought to pave the road to Utopia; well, it didn't, and neither did electricity, even though it certainly made life better. Later, atomic power, worldwide communications and space flight each in its own way contributed to the general welfare, but Utopia is still unattained. It will always be. Utopias make for interesting escapist reading at times, but they certainly have no place in reality.

The English professor John Ronald Reuel Tolkien's epic trilogy *The Fellowship of the Ring* (1954-55) probably comes as close to a Utopia as anything that has been written during the last fifty years, with its innocent Rousseauian escapism, but even here dangers always lurk in the shadows, threatening to tear the gossamer security into fragments at the first sign of weakness. Also, the story evolves in a mythical ancient past, well before man. When man is mentioned, it is as something threatening, something that will cause the destruction of the fairyland. Utopias, the science fiction writers seem to say, cannot exist. If they, notwithstanding, should exist, they could never work. And if they, against all common sense, should work, they would not be of any use anyway.

4. THE AIR-CONDITIONED NIGHTMARE

Many science fiction writers are incurable misanthropes. This might be the result of an uncommonly pessimistic inclination or a general perspicacity, but the fact is, that few modern sf writers have found reason to regard the future with any great hope. (I am now speaking of those works that deal with the future as a consequence of the present day, not those that depict a future situation according to its own terms. These will be discussed in a later chapter.) The future will turn out to be just like our own time, they observe—only worse. And then they summon forth a hell on Earth where the citizens are kept at bay by Thought Police and the big industrial trusts rule the people with a more or less obvious line of hard advertising, toward ever-increasing consumption and consequently rising opulence for the shareholders. The social dreams of the Victorians have been exchanged for scathing social criticism that, while most often based on cold, hard facts, sometimes topples on the borders of defeatism; the latter is commonly known as the "New Wave" syndrome of science fiction. The "fact" anti-Utopian novel, speculating in the results of processes already at work in our own time, might show a future à la Harry Harrison's *Make Room! Make Room!*, in which the year 1999 moves toward its end and New York is over-populated with thirty-five million desperate inhabitants, where hunger riots are the order of the day and where the minimum living space, as prescribed by law, is four square yards per person. Without water or outflow. The environment pollution has long ago passed the limit where it was merely catastrophic. Human lives are worthless. Over it all hovers the specter of the final war as a black, threatening shadow. And after the novel, the author adds a list of recommended reading which proves that it probably will turn out to be much worse. Or *The Jagged Orbit* (1969) by the brilliant British sf writer John Brunner, in which the twenty-first century is ruled by the huge, ruthless Gottschalk weaponry combine which sells weapons to anyone, anywhere, with predictable results; or *Teenocracy* (1969) by Robert Shirley, in which the teen-agers have taken over the U.S.A. for good, which means that if you ain't hip, you're out. The members of the Cabinet are chosen by a sort of Russian roulette, and the President is a tough rock star, name of The Fab. It makes one long for the uncomplicated golden days of *1984*.

As late as 1931, Aldous Huxley wrote *Brave New World*, originally as a conscious parody of H. G. Wells's *Men Like Gods*, as a horror vision of something that was possible but highly improbable: the artificial, promiscuous, drugged and enslaved humanity of the year 632 A.F. (After Ford). The most effective tool to keep the citizenry at bay was the same apathy drug, *Soma*, that Thomas More invented for the people of Utopia. Fifteen years later, the novel was furnished with a new foreword, in which Huxley sadly observed that the horror vision was not as distant as he in 1931 had thought. Huxley still thought that sanity existed, even though it was a rather rare phenomenon; he was convinced that it could be achieved and that he would like to see more of it. A critic retorted that Huxley was a sad symptom of the failure of an intellectual class in time of crisis. Huxley replied, and pointed out the real sinners:

The benefactors of humanity deserve due honor and commemoration. Let us build a Pantheon for professors. It should be located among the ruins of one of the gutted cities of Europe or Japan, and over the entrance to the ossuary I would inscribe, in letters six or seven feet high, the simple words: Sacred to the memory of the World's Educators. SI MONUMENTUM REQUIRIS CIRCUMSPICE.

Novels like George Orwell's *1984* (1949) and Karin Boye's

Kallocain (1940) are even more apparent in their fear of what man will do next. Both describe fascistic societies in a not too distant future, both are in a sense allegories on events that already had taken place when they were written. The authors are certain of their good cause, and do not squander on powder and shot. The terror is absolute, and the evil of the dictators is limitless. In 1984, O'Brien, the interrogator, says:

"Do you begin to see, then, what kind of world we are creating? It is the exact opposite of the stupid hedonistic Utopias that the old reformers imagined. A world of fear and treachery and torment, a world of trampling and being trampled upon, a world which will grow no less but *more* merciless as it refines itself. Progress in our world will be progress toward more pain. The old civilizations claimed that they were founded on love and justice. Ours is founded upon hatred. In our world there will be no emotions except fear, rage, triumph, and self-abasement. Everything else we shall destroy—everything." (15)

This was in 1949, when the author looked back at the second World War and began to fear for the probable evolution of the totalitarian state. Today, more than twenty years later, the dictatorate is usually more discreet—on the surface, that is—and the science fiction writers hardly expect the future dictators to use the same means as Big Brother of Orwell's novel. The future belongs to the multinational corporations, and against them nations and Big Brothers will cut poor figures. The earlier horror vision was founded on terror as a means for slavery. But a reign of terror means ineffectiveness, it reduces the Holy Production, and, even worse, the consumption. When the anti-Utopian writer of today looks into the probable future, he sees a consumption-oriented society which is not too far removed from ours, with a treacherous indoctrination that is far more effective than Big Brother's boots. Orwell is hopelessly out. No more than five years after the first publication of *1984*, the brilliant U.S. writer duo Frederik Pohl and Cyril M. Kornbluth brought out another sf novel, in which the new totalitarian state was shown in its fullest and most horrible detail:

"I don't have to tell you men that Point-of-Scale has its special problems," Harvey said, puffing on his thin cheeks. "I swear, the whole damned Government must be infiltrated with Consies! You know what they've done. They outlawed compulsive subsonics in our aural advertising—but we bounced back with a list of semantic cue words that tie in with every basic trauma and neurosis in American life today. They listened to the safety cranks and stopped us from projecting our messages on air-car windows—but we bounced back. Lab tells me," he nodded to our Director of Research across the table, "that soon we'll be testing a system that projects directly on the retina of the eye.

"And not only that, but we're going forward. As an example I want to mention the Coffiest pro—" He broke off. "Excuse me, Mr. Schocken," he whispered. "Has Security checked this room?"

Fowler Schocken nodded. "Absolutely clean. Nothing but the usual State Department and House of Representatives spy-mikes. And of course we're feeding a canned play-back into them."

Harvey relaxed again. "Well, about this Coffiest," he said. "We're sampling it in fifteen key cities. It's the usual offer—a thirteen-week supply of Coffiest, one thousand dollars in cash and a week-end vacation on the Ligurian Riviera to everybody who comes in. But—and here's what makes this campaign truly great, in my estimation—each sample of Coffiest contains three milligrams of a simple alkaloid. Nothing harmful. But definitely habit-forming. After ten weeks the customer is hooked for life. It would cost him at least five thousand dollars for a cure, so it's simpler for him to go right on drinking Coffiest—three cups with every meal and a pot beside his bed at night, just as it says on the jar." (16)

This nice picture from our advertisement-infected future comes from Pohl/Kornbluth's brilliant novel *Gravy Planet*, later retitled *The Space Merchants*, which tells about a not too distant future in which the big corporations have taken power and Money is king. The New York of *The Space Merchants* is diametrically opposite the London of *1984*, but in the end the slavery is all the same. Big Brother kicks his subjects into obedience; the new industrial tycoons drug them. "If you want a picture of the future," O'Brien says in *1984*, "imagine a boot stamping on a human face—forever." It hardly matters much to the victim if the boot bears the sign of a Swastika or a Coca Cola bottle. The difference is that in the latter case the victim can even be made to pay for the privilege of being trampled upon.

Pohl/Kornbluth have written a number of sf novels on this theme, among others *Gladiator-at-Law* (1955), which is an acid settlement with the multi-national corporations like Philips, General Electric, Kodak and so on. The distance of Orwell's boot-state is enormous. Here the world is ruled by a number of giant corporations which write their own laws, fight regular battles with competitive companies and unite only in the idea of the holy profit.

In Orwell's dictatorship the citizen can revolt, as Winston does, by escaping the system for a time, away from the spy eyes and the Thought Police. Or by turning out to be stronger than his tormentors, as Professor Burden in David Karp's *One* (1953), a more terrifying version of *1984* in which the protagonist is subjected to a thorough brainwashing within a government experiment concerning the best way to keep the citizenry in line. Professor Burden wins in a way: the government has to kill him. But in *Gladiator-at-Law* there is no Thought Police, no Ministry of Love. The industry doesn't need any executioners, it needs consumers. The British sf writer J. G. Ballard depicts in a short story, *The Subliminal Man*, an even more ingenious way to keep consumption up and people down; I have an uneasy feeling that the idea isn't entirely impossible.

A large neon sign over the entrance (to the super-market) listed the discount—a mere five percent—cal-culated on the volume of turnover. The highest dis-counts, sometimes up to twenty-five percent, were earned in the housing estates where junior white-collar workers lived. There, spending had a strong social in-centive, and the desire to be the highest spender in the neighborhood was given moral reinforcement by the system of listing all the names and their accumulating cash totals on a huge electric sign in the supermarket foyers. The higher the spender, the greater his con-tribution to the discounts enjoyed by others. The low-est spenders were regarded as social criminals, free-riding on the backs of others.

Luckily this system had yet to be adopted in Frank-lin's neighbourhood—not because the professional men and their wives were able to exercise more discretion, but because their higher incomes allowed them to con-tract into more expensive discount schemes operated by the big department stores in the city. (17)

The theme is, as I have said, widely used in anti-Utopian science fiction of today, and it seems as if the sf writers more and more now have turned from the earlier war and natural catastrophe themes to the results of our economic and environmental (mis)management and its impact on man. This way science fiction comes into the contemporary social and political debate, where it probably can do a lot of good through its unique qualifications for presumption-free evolu-tion and behavior analysis.

Personally, I believe there is a far more intelligent and presumption-free debate going on in the decried science fiction genre than in many of the so-called conscious and, for most people, incomprehensible, cultural magazines that are embraced with such great benevolence by the critics. That these critics never have come in contact with the genre, other than the Sunday paper's comic strip section, is not the sf writers' fault.

Science fiction has thus by its anti-Utopian branch returned to Lucian and his critical scrutiny of the follies of his time. The difference is partly that the objects for the satire of today are not present yet, though in most cases clearly recognizable as trends, and partly that the anti-Utopian writers of today are so clearly disillusioned. When an improvement comes in sight, it is immediately strangled by the conversationists, as for example in a short story by Mack Reynolds, *Subversive*. A new corporation called Freer Enterprises starts to sell gadgets for their real value. Soap is sold for three cents a bar, an electric razor for one dollar, a loaf of bread for one cent. Of course, Freer Enterprises are not allowed to go on like this. The Bureau of Economic Subversion (which in a final, clumsy and decidedly un-called-for backtracking turns out to be a front for the evil Communists) intervene and execute the conspirators of Freer Enterprises. Because where would the profits go if everything was priced according to its real value?

"Why, the consumers would be able to buy commodities at a fraction of the present cost!" says Mr. Flowers of Freer Enterprises.

Mr. Tracy, the evil Communist, "pounds the table with fierce emphasis."

"What would they buy with them?" he asks. *"They'd all be out of jobs!"*

The horrible thing is that Mr. Tracy is perfectly right and he will probably be even more so with time.

Robert A. Heinlein, one of science fiction's most brilliant and most keenly-debated writers, has outlined a similar problem in a short story, *Let There be Light*, which is part of his *Future History Series*, a grand collection of stories and novels that charts an ultra-reactionary future that might make Senator Goldwater giddy with joy. Here, a scientist who is somewhat ignorant in the ways of the world invents a combined light source and sun-powered energy source with an efficiency of ninety-eight percent that promises to wreak havoc with the power monopoly. Of course the inventor succeeds in the end, but before that Heinlein has given a pungent exposé of the powers that hold back amelioration.

Anti-Utopian science fiction is abundant with descriptions of future societies in which the now barely hidden sadism has been dragged out in the open and entered as an integral part of the everyday life. I have mentioned Frederik Pohl's and Cyril M. Kornbluth's *Gladiator-at-Law* in which the big industries settle their business by regular battles.

These tendencies have been brought further in novels like Robert Sheckley's *The Tenth Victim* (1966); here intending citizens are provided with licenses for murder and go out into life to kill other like-minded people who otherwise would have started wars and mixed up innocent bystanders in their private bloodthirstiness. The reasoning is seductive:

Though it gave the appearance of the utmost modernity, the Hunting Game was, in principle, not new at all. It was a qualitative reversion to an older, happier age when paid mercenaries did the fighting and noncombatants stayed on the sidelines and talked about the crops.

History is cyclical. An overdose of yin changes irrevocably into yang. The day of the professional (and frequently non-fighting) army passed, and the age of the mass army began. Farmers could no longer talk about their crops; they had to fight for them. Even if they had no crops to fight for, they still had to fight. Factory-hands found themselves involved in Byzantine intrigues in lands beyond the sea, and shoe clerks carried weapons into alien jungles and across frozen mountain-tops.

What did they do it for? In those days it all seemed very clear. Many reasons had been given, and every man adopted the rationale which suited his own particular emotionality. But what seemed obvious at the time became less so as the years passed. Professors of history argued, experts in economics demurred, psychologists begged to differ and anthropologists felt it necessary to point out.

The farmer, shoe clerk and factory-hand waited patiently for someone to tell them why they were really being killed. When no clear-cut answer was forthcoming, they became irritated, resentful and sometimes even wrathful. Occasionally they would turn their weapons upon their own rulers.

That, of course, could not be countenanced. The growing intransigency of the people, plus the technological possibility of killing everyone and everything, definitely overloaded the yang, thereby bringing forth the yin.

After five thousand or so years of recorded history, people were finally beginning to catch on. Even rulers, notoriously the slowest men to change, realized that something had to be done.

Wars were getting nobody nowhere; but there was still the problem of individual violence which untold years of religious coercion and police instruction had failed to curb.

The answer, for the moment, became the Legalized Hunt. (18)

Today we have the commonly accepted violence-pornography in the form of Wild West movies, usually of Italian make, which should be enough for anyone's bloodthirstiness. Contemporary folk heroes like Mike Hammer and James Bond also murder right and left, and display a remarkable contempt of men that obviously makes their millions of fans happy. This is, however, a violence by proxy that in the long run can't satisfy the real connoisseur.

One can, of course, go a bit farther out beyond the violence that TV and cinemas are distributing to devoutly drooling humanity, and give violence free rein with well-paid mercenaries, armed with science's latest and most sophisticated tools of murder. This would be real war, with beautiful close-ups of torn entrails and dying soldiers, realistic gas attacks with real mustard gas and machine guns and real dum-dum bullets. Then the whole thing would be distributed via TV all over the world to the peeping toms, and the worst killers would become national heroes like James Bond and Donald Duck (and the Green Berets) that every schoolboy would want to emulate. TV's coverage of the Vietnam war shows that we are not too far from this. The U.S. sf writer Mack Reynolds has outlined a probable development on these lines in the novel *Frigid Fracas* (1963), in which the somewhat degenerate Major Joseph Hauser with the aid of a clever PR man rises through the ranks to general and the declared hero of all children. The British film director Peter Watkins recently used a similar idea in the movie *The Gladiators* (1969), although he didn't give much interest to the cynical gamble for power that goes on behind the battlefield.

Man is obviously a killer by instinct, this most sf writers seem to be movingly unanimous about. But all sf writers do not regard this as something wholly *non possumus*. Robert A. Heinlein—formerly a professional military man, and since many years one of the sf genre's most brilliant writers, much-debated but always interesting—delineates in the novel *Starship Troopers* (1959) with obvious enthusiasm a future society in which the citizens have to go through military training with the hereto attached consequences, before they are permitted the minimum democratic right of voting. Military service is of course open to everyone, regardless of sex, race, mental and physical handicaps and so on, anything else would be undemocratic. It is the military indoctrination that is important—and the result is, predictably enough, a remarkably stable society with high morale, strong discipline, a one-party system and all the rest. Actually, this novel belongs rightly to the Utopian novels, as it describes an ideal society—ideal at least from Heinlein's point of view—and what few dissenters there are in the story all see the light before the story ends. Even the despised father of the hero, a rotten, cowardly pacifist, grabs a gun and earns his citizenship the hard way. The only thing that makes it less than a classical Utopian novel is that it contains so much violence and gore that no sane Utopian would stay there for five seconds. Utopians are a peaceful lot; Heinlein is not.

Now, this sounds like a thoroughly fascist state, and *Starship Troopers* has been subjected to a murderous criticism in sf circles, especially after it was awarded with science fiction's highly coveted Hugo Award in 1959. Myself, I would rather leave than love a country run along the lines of Heinlein's Utopia. But Heinlein has constructed his society with a logic that is rather seductive (you can accuse Heinlein for a lot of things, but never for faulty logic). In Heinlein's world the right to vote is thus a privilege that has to be earned with a specified, individual contribution of work. He proceeds, probably rightly, from the assumption that a person who is too lazy to earn this privilege also is too lazy to revolt against the established order of things. Thus, no "silent majority." If we look at our own society, the idea does not look so foolish. A great deal of the voters in the Western world do, as is well known, not vote so much on party platform as on the party candidate's appearance and morale, their own parents' political preferences and so on. A right to vote that had to be earned with hard labor in two or three years would probably be exercised with much more consideration. Heinlein's thesis seems, in short, to be that lazy people without knowledge of politics should not be permitted to participate in something as serious as politics. And who can dispute that?

What can be discussed is the fact that military service is the only chance to prove that you are not a lazy slob. And the horrible pacifists are already from the start excluded from any possibility of changing the rules. There are no conscientious objectors in Heinlein's world. Just voters (war veterans) and non-voters (draft-dodgers, effeminate snobs, pacifists and other animals of low standing). The belief in authority and the individual subjection that the military system impresses upon its disciples is—although commendable in a situation of war—hardly worth striving for in a democratic society.

Starship Troopers has, as I have said, been the cause of a very lively debate for and against the military establishment, in magazines, fan magazines (fanzines) and at least one sf novel, Harry Harrison's witty and intelligent *Bill, the Galactic Hero* (1966), a *Catch-22* on a magnificent cosmic scale. Whatever views one might take on the matter, one can't deny that *Starship Troopers* has done a lot of good in this respect, by stimulating an interesting debate. It is disturbing, and what shall good science fiction do, if not disturb?

As for the end-of-the-world type of science fiction that is most commonly associated with the genre, the sf writers have shown a remarkable wealth of imagination, all the way from the famous French astronomer and author Camille Flammarion's novel *La Fin du Monde* (1911), that dealt with the slow death of Earth ten million years hence, over more recent works like Ward Moore's *Greener Than You Think* (1947), wherein a new type of fertilizer mutates devil's grass which, ultimately, kills everything on Earth; Mordecai Roshwald's *Level 7* (1959) in which the final atomic war is triggered by mistake, leaving Earth a smoking wasteland, and the many end-of-the-world novels of J. G. Ballard where Earth alternately is flooded or dried up or more or less torn to bits by winds. It is interesting to note the upswing of this type of anti-Utopia during the high points of the Cold War, showing the extermination of mankind in a thousand imaginative ways but always conveying a deep distrust in man's ability to behave as a thinking animal.

This is, of course, the old Frankenstein trauma that is the basis of all anti-Utopian science fiction, the belief that sooner or later man's achievements will turn against their creator, be it the new society, man's inborn instincts or the hydrogen bomb. This apocalyptic tradition is not reserved exclusively for science fiction, but I think I am safe in asserting that nowhere else have these misgivings been voiced so repeatedly as in this particular genre.

I have already said that science fiction by its very nature must be a subversive thing, as it points out that there will always be changes, something that no establishment wishes to admit. The anti-Utopian novel is the most obvious ex-

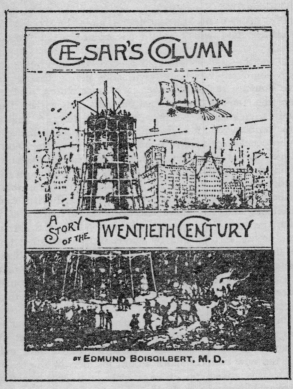

Cover of *Caesar's Column* by Ignatius Donnelly,
first published under a pen-name in 1890.

ample of this, as asserted in the treatment given anti-Utopian writers by totalitarian states not only in the past, but right now. The Russian writer Yevgeny Zamyatin is perhaps one of the most well-known examples, although not by any means the only one. Zamyatin (who died in exile in 1937) is one of the Russian authors—from Isaac Babel to Julij Daniel and Abram Tertz—who have been crushed or silenced because of their incisive social criticism. In 1924, his novel *We* was published in translation outside Russia. It was a forerunner to *1984* and *Brave New World*—in many respects actually more chilling than these more well-known works, dealing with a future super-communist society in which even the word "I" is forbidden as being a danger to the state. The novel earned Zamyatin complete censure and he was faced with renouncing his work or keeping silent. Zamyatin was lucky—he received permission to leave Russia. Other writers have not been as lucky. The fate of Abram Tertz and Julij Daniel is well-known—both of them had written science fiction criticizing the Communist state.

In 1969, the well-known Russian science fiction writers Arkadi and Boris Strugatsky, who are considered the best authors of Soviet science fiction and the only ones comparable to the best U.S. authors, were silenced by the Soviet authorities on account of four satirical sf stories dealing with bureaucracy and the right of a state to interfere with social development on other planets (read: countries). At the other end of the political spectrum, similar things have recently taken place in Spain, when the Political Police seized all the copies of an issue of the Spanish sf magazine *Nueva Dimension*.

This is, of course, not something that has happened only to science fiction. On the whole, the sf field has been spared the most mindless acts of the political censors. But with more and more writers turning to the science fiction story as a means to convey social criticism, it might be safe to assert that we will see more of this in the future.

It should be pointed out that criticism does not necessarily mean negativism. With so many of the well-known works of science fiction being anti-Utopian, the whole genre has gotten a somewhat undeserved reputation as being largely negativistic and defeatist in attitude, longing, in effect, back to the "good old days" that never existed anyway, and deadly afraid of what the future might bring. Actually, most sf writers seem to believe in progress, even though few are so naïve as to believe that the future will be all roses. Also, the anti-Utopian branch of science fiction occupies only a comparably small portion of the medium as a whole. Nevertheless, the anti-Utopian branch, with its roots in ancient satirical writings, has always proven to be the most popular outside of the circle of sf aficionados, and most easily recognized by the critics as "Literature."

"Straight" science fiction, being more optimistic in its outlook, and dealing more with the future as such, delineates future societies where conditions are vastly different from what they are here and now and constructs plot and human behavior as results of these assumptions—colonization of far worlds, new means of travel, new forms of (not necessarily evil) governments and so forth. Yet "straight" science fiction has never achieved the same impact on the literary scene. The reason for this might be that while the anti-Utopian novel is old as a literary phenomenon, the "straight" science fiction, depicting the future on its own terms, describing it as not necessarily better or worse but *different*, then taking this at its face value and trying to make the best of it, is new, and, therefore, somewhat suspicious.

Personally, I find the anti-Utopian science fiction extremely interesting—but it shows only one side of the matter. It is anti but never pro; it gives criticism, but never even attempts a solution. Just as the Utopian story is escapist, its antithesis is defeatist; it must always be so. There is an unfortunate tendency in all literature to view all changes with the deepest suspicion and to put the worst construction on everything new. It would be very strange indeed if this did not pervade science fiction to a degree as well. No doubt many people in the year 2025 will look back to the wonderful golden days of 1971 when everything was so much better, and regard the new star ships and what-have-you with grave misgivings, feeling the ground rock beneath their feet. This is as it should be, and the anti-Utopian novel has done a lot of good by pointing out faults in society's machinery—but one should not stare oneself blind on this side of the coin.

In 1660, the Italian Jesuit Francesco Lama was certain that God never would permit the construction of airships, because they could be used to throw things down at people. Airships *are* being used to throw things down at people, and in a much more horrible way than the good Lama ever envisaged, too, but they also are used to transport people in a perfectly peaceful way, and on the whole, it has been of much more good than evil, notwithstanding the old, often repeated cry that If-God-had-meant-us-to-fly/write /travel/live-he-would-have-given-us-wings/pens/wheels/hospitals. Well, he didn't; we did it ourselves.

Basically, the anti-Utopian novel is just a way of saying (as Cyril M. Kornbluth puts it in *The Science Fiction Novel*,) "I will show you what will happen if you don't listen to me and do as I say," as opposed to the Utopian message of "See here how beautiful and orderly everything will be if you make me dictator over the world." The difference is slight, and in the end they both come down to the same thing: an inability to face the present world. The anti-Utopian novel is interesting, and as a means of powerful social criticism, unsurpassed. It should be read with a pinch of salt, though. The future isn't all sour grapes.

5. THE MAGIC UNREALITY

When one comes to the type of science fiction that completely abandons the accepted idea of this universe for the benefit of another, more or less self-made one, so-called Fantasy, the question immediately arises as to which literature, properly speaking, does this branch of the genre belong, and why. Enthusiastic sf scholars have made remarkable plunges down into world literature and returned with the most astounding discoveries, from the Sumer epic of Gilgamesh to the old Norse Eddas, the Arabian Nights and so forth, not to mention the fairy tales of Hans Christian Andersen and the Brothers Grimm. With this definition, *The Sleeping Beauty* would make science fiction of prime quality, and Mother Goose would be a must in every true sf fan's library. Even the definition by situation that usually is applied to "straight" science fiction, gives peculiar results here. So, for example, we find religious allegories like John Bunyan's *Pilgrim's Progress* and Dante Alighieri's *Divina Commedia* among the works of science fiction, something that undoubtedly would have surprised the authors.

Fairy tales and religious allegories have existed since time immemorial, but the particular literature or point of view that we call Fantasy is, despite all eager efforts to prove the opposite, a comparably new occurrence, that appeared during the nineteenth century with works like Lewis Carroll's (Charles L. Dodgson) *Alice in Wonderland* (1865), *The Hunting of the Snark* (1876) and Frank L. Baum's *The Wonderful Wizard of Oz* (1900).

The difference between the traditional fairy tales and these works may seem slight—but there is a definite difference. We don't believe in demons, werewolves, fire-breath-

74

ing dragons and the rest (well—most of us don't), but once, and this wasn't too long ago, we certainly did. Everyone knew that these creatures existed; they were not imagination, they were fact. Sometimes they were seen. The fabled creatures of ancient and not too ancient times were a lot more familiar to those people than outer space is to the average man of today. Thor lived once, and the Earth was flat; and seven crystal spheres encircled the world of man. Of course we don't believe in this today, and any work of fiction assuming that these legends are true is purely fantasy. The difference lies in that the old sagas told about things that were considered facts, while modern fantasy—is fantasy.

Terry Carr says in his introduction to *New Worlds Of Fantasy/2* (1970) that ". . . fantasy springs from and operates on a basis of emotional symbolism, just as dreams do. Fantasy is, in fact, the literary equivalent of dreams." This is a good point, and tells a lot about the mechanisms of fantasy. Just as in dreams, anything can happen, anything at all. What logic and natural laws there are, can be changed at the slightest whim. And there are nightmares as well, as attested by the veritable armies of monsters, ghouls and malignant magicians who live in blissful abandon in this sub-genre of science fiction.

Most fantasy stories are based on an existing tradition of sagas and popular conceptions. This is exceptionally obvious in works like Charles Finney's *The Circus of Dr. Lao* (1935) and James Branch Cabell's stories from Poictesme—not to mention the Irish writer Lord Dunsany, heavily influenced by ancient folklore, who in his turn has influenced most modern fantasy writers. But it is striking in how high degree the authors have created their own universes, with highly specific natural laws, and how this has been done as a sort of intellectual game: creating worlds as frameworks to the narrative and molding them into shape with complete disregard for commonly accepted logic, much in the same way as the absurdists, Ionesco and Alfred Jarry and others, later did. It is also interesting to note that while many of these works of fantasy are commonly considered to be juvenile stories, e.g. *Alice in Wonderland,* they are actually highly sophisticated works that require an adult mind to comprehend them to their fullest extent. Still, they can be read and appreciated by anyone. As opposed, I might add, to some of the modern absurdist works.

Among the works of fantasy one can also find a number of stories bordering on far-out science fiction of the usual type, very intelligent and satirical works built within a framework of pure, undiluted fantasy; for example the French artist J. J. Grandville's sick, mystifying *Un Autre Monde* (1844), a hallucinatory vision in which steam-powered robots give mechanical concerts, where marionettes have formed kingdoms of their own and the botanical garden boasts a section for real, living heraldic animals. Grandville, a well-known illustrator of his time, was probably the world's first surrealist painter of the Dali school. He died in 1847 in a mental institution, his last works, done just a week before his death, being two strange, frightening surrealistic dream visions.

It is, of course, in the nature of fantasy literature that one can't draw up straight orientation lines for its development. The Italian writer C. Collodi's (Carlo Lorenzini) strange children's book *Pinoccio* (1880) with its touches both of Gothic horror and time-typical moral story, undoubtedly belongs to this genre, as well as the Finnish artist and writer Tove Jansson's *Moomin* books and the English philologist J. R. R. Tolkien's trilogy *The Fellowship of the Ring.* The English priest and Shakespeare scholar Edwin Abbott's mathematic fantasy *Flatland: A Romance of Many Dimensions* (1884), which is a square's (a geometric square, not a human one) description of its two-dimensional world, is likewise fantasy in the literal sense of the word.

The greater part of the fantasy literature that has been written during the last fifty years belongs, however, to the more easily handled groups of *science fantasy* (fantasy on an alleged scientific or logical basis, where the Newtonian cosmic system has been exchanged for one with a mystical or purely homemade basis) and *Sword & Sorcery* (swords and monsters of various kinds, usually with a strong influence of ancient Nordic folklore, including elves, giants, fire-breathing dragons, magicians and so forth).

The heritage from ancient mythology is considerable in the latter type of fantasy, and primarily the Gothic novel seems to have furnished a lot of its time-honored ingredients, from chivalrous feats to artificial creatures of all kinds —homunculi, golems, living dead and such, besides the usual ghoul ballet and its malignant conjurers. The Gothic novel, which appeared for the first time with Horace Walpole's *The Castle of Otranto* (1765) had obvious connections with the *chansons de geste* of the Middle Ages, the Arthurian legends and the legends of Charlemagne, of which especially Ludovico Ariosto's poetical work *Orlando Furioso* (1516, 1532) seems to have made lasting impressions. *Orlando Furioso* was a tale of chivalry with a motif from the alleged heroic deeds of Charles the Great, written in the style of the time. The plot is utterly dramatic, alternating between the pathetic and the grotesque, with lots of heroic deeds, swords, blood and thunder. Moreover, it contains some really imaginative episodes in the story of Asdolf's journey to the Moon and his highly improbable adventures there. This whole genre was murdered by Cervantes with *Don Quixote* (1605), and when its pitiable remnants again crawled inside the book covers, more than one hundred and fifty years later, it was thus in the guise of the Gothic tale.

The Castle of Otranto, and the literary genre that it gave birth to, can make the hair stand on end on the most obdurate person. It is a genre that almost exclusively occupies itself with dilapidated castles under the light of the werewolf moon, sepulchers with disagreeable contents, evil magicians, compacts with the Devil, noble heroines whose primary mission is to be abducted by all and sundry; noble heroes with peculiar names, kindhearted old men with noble features, old ladies with horrible secrets, and assorted monsters of the most horrible sort. The intrigues are usually complex onto the borders of insanity, and to complicate it all further, half of the characters are usually related to the other half, which gives birth to interesting incestuous situations à la some of the current teenage magazines.

This ghastly literature was, of course, a product of its time, in the same way as the current science fiction literature is the product of our specific situation. It belongs, partly, to the Romanticism of the eighteenth century, the longing back to times when everything was better (the old days were *always* better), as well as the Romanticist's well-known faiblesse for ruins and forgotten passages and such. But there was probably also a much more substantial connection with the real world. The Marquis de Sade makes an interesting observation in his *L'Idée sur les Romans* (1800) regarding the Gothic tale:

This genre . . . was the inevitable product of the revolutionary shocks with which the whole of Europe resounded. For those who were acquainted with all the ills that are brought upon men by the wicked, the romantic was becoming somewhat difficult to write, and merely monotonous to read: there was nobody left who had not experienced more misfortunes in four or five years than could be depicted in a century by literature's most famous novelists: it was necessary to call upon hell for aid in order to arouse interest, and to find in the land of fantasies what was common knowledge from historical observation of man in this iron age.

The "iron age" was the world in which people lived—if live it can be called—in indescribable conditions, condemned to a life of appalling suffering for the crime of being born; the world in which scholars spent years and healthy salaries arguing with learned friends about the placing of a comma in a poem and deciphering ancient stone tablets. The lower classes were starving, and in France, Marie Antoinette suggested that if the peasants didn't have bread, "let them eat cake." The Marquis de Sade chronicled the horrors of the time in a much more naked and effective way than any of his contemporaries, frequently repeating his conviction that, in modern civilization, virtue is persecuted—while crime not

THE
CASTLE of OTRANTO,
A
S T O R Y.

Translated by

WILLIAM MARSHAL, Gent.

From the Original ITALIAN of

ONUPHRIO MURALTO,

CANON of the Church of St. NICHOLAS
at OTRANTO.

L O N D O N:

Printed for THO. LOWNDS in Fleet-Street.
MDCCLXV.

Title page of the first edition.

only pays fabulous dividends, but, in the skillful hands of the man who is master of himself, goes unpunished.

Basically, the early Gothic tale was only the *romans de moeurs* in a new overcoat, still convinced that virtue will be rewarded in the end and vice justly punished, finding pleasure in "the beautiful horror which delights while it saddens," a sort of horror pornography, if you like. However much due to the influence that the Marquis had on his contemporaries, with works like *Justine ou les Malheurs de la Vertu*, *La Philosophie dans le Boudoir* and *Les 120 Journées de Sodome*, a change set in, in the Gothic tale. Vice did not always get punished. The Gothic tale became, not a picture of the contemporary world, but of its undercurrents of despair and hopelessness. The ghosts are within ourselves, as the tormentors of the Marquis' novels are projections of ourselves. In the imitation of the Marquis de Sade and, in a sense, of the Gothic tale as a whole, I can mention a modern work, Pauline Réage's painful and grandiose novel *Histoire d'O* (1954), which chronicles a woman's willful subjection to complete slavery of the most horrible kind. The Gothic tale had all this, although in a very inarticulate way, and this might be the chief reason why, outside of the sheer horror content, it is still readable. Its real terrors are real, but merely hinted at.

The Castle of Otranto, the first of the Gothic novels, had much in common with the *romans de moeurs* like *Manon Lescaut* and *Fanny Hill*—the pornographic interest was exchanged for the horror interest, but basically it was the same story, only much more crude. Instead of the bedroom we have the sepulchral chamber; instead of love, terror; instead of fornication, death (in womb-like subterranean passages). In later Gothic tales these two subjects, sexuality and death, were combined to form peculiar necrophilian situations. This is especially the case with Matthew Gregory Lewis's *The Monk*, which will be discussed later on. But in *The Castle of Otranto*, sex was exchanged wholesale for horror, and after a lot of gruesome spine-tingling occurrences, virtue was rewarded just as it should be.

THE MAGIC UNREALITY

The action is laid in the castle of Otranto, where the terrible sovereign Manfred reigns in the place of the rightful owner, who went out to participate in the Holy War and never returned. A terrible ancient prophecy haunts the background, and one day a giant helmet flops down in the courtyard, bashing in the empty head of Manfred's son Conrad, who quickly passes away, leaving Manfred with Conrad's bride-to-be, the beautiful Isabella. Manfred starts making unpleasant advances, just in the line of what one could expect of such a man, and before you know it, the circus is going full blast with bleeding statues, hollowly groaning ghosts, new giant articles of clothing that appear from nowhere when you least expect it, and other merry occurrences calculated to raise the spirit of any thrill-seeking reader. The atmosphere is gloomy, but all ends well despite everything. Manfred enters a monastery and the hero, a young and noble-looking lad who spends his days in the subterranean vaults of the castle, occupying himself with saving the life of all and sundry and finally turning out to be (surprise! surprise!) the long-lost heir to the castle, gets Isabella. The novel was originally published under the nom de plume of Onuphrio Muralto, "Canon of the Church of St. Nicholas at Otranto," and "translated from the original Italian by William Marshal, Gent." In the preface of the first edition, Mr. "William Marshal" speaks highly and without the slightest trace of unbecoming modesty of his own work:

The principal incidents are such as were believed in the darkest ages of Christianity; but the language and conduct have nothing that savours of barbarism. The style is purest Italian . . . The beauty of the diction, and the zeal of the author (moderated however by singular judgment) concur to make me think the date of composition was little antecedent to that of the impression . . . There is no bombast, no similes, flowers, digressions, or unnecessary descriptions. Every thing tends directly to the catastrophe. Never is the reader's attention relaxed . . . The characters are well drawn, and still better maintained. Terror, the author's principal engine, prevents the story from ever languishing; and it is so often contrasted by pity, that the mind is kept up in a constant vicissitude of interesting passions . . .

The unexpected success of the novel did, however, send Messrs. Muralto and Marshal back to whence they had come from, and Horace Walpole, himself an eccentric with many traits of the sovereign Manfred in his novel, stepped forth into the limelight to accept the applause.

An even better proof of the popularity of the novel was the flood of Gothic tales that immediately deluged the market; Ann Radcliff's *The Mysteries of Udolpho* (1794), William Beckford's *Vathek, An Arabian Tale* (1786), Charles Maturin's *Melmoth the Wanderer* (1820)—a variation of the legend of the Wandering Jew—and a veritable torrent of lesser but guaranteed blood-curdling works. The market for Gothic horror was substantial, and the offered goods satisfied all demands for perversions.

The culmination came with the young Englishman Matthew Gregory Lewis' novel *The Monk* (1796), which was a collection of atrocities of the worst possible kind, performed around the terrible mad monk Ambrosio, who is seized by wicked desires vis-à-vis his virtuous sister, and sells his soul to the Devil in order to satisfy his lusts. Ambrosio dogs the poor woman through moonlit castles and monasteries, sends demons after her, murders her friends and relatives and behaves in general in a way that hardly speaks of any particularly Christian temper. In between, he executes serenades at his desired's window, at which the instruments are handled by ghouls and demons with disagreeable looks, and the lyrics are of a kind that hardly could have improved the young woman's sleep, for example the song "Alonzo the Brave and the Fair Imogine" which later on was translated and subjected to some negligible changes and became known as the well-known and much loved Swedish "folk-song" *"Hjalmar och Hulda."* Lewis' original text is even worse than the macabre Swedish version. The fair Imogine has promised to wait for her beloved, the gallant knight Alonzo, while he slaughters the heathen in distant countries, but soon enough she forgets all about the promises she has made and prepares to marry someone else. And with good cause, one should think, as the gallant knight has died. The betrayed lover returns to Imogine's wedding as a decaying corpse, and "The worms they crept in, and the worms they crept out,/And sported his eyes and his temples about,/While the spectre addressed Imogine." The bridegroom dies on the spot, and the grim Alonzo carries the unfaithful Imogine down to the nether regions. The castle is hurriedly deserted, and from that day, no one sees the charming couple again. But—

At midnight four times in each year does her spright,
    When mortals in slumber are bound,
Arrayed in her bridal apparel of white,
Appear in the hall with the Skeleton-Knight,
    And shriek as he whirls her around.

While they drink out of skulls newly torn from the grave,
    Dancing round them the spectres are seen:
Their liquor is blood, and this horrible stave
They howl: "To the health of Alonzo the Brave
    And his consort, the False Imogine!"

After this softening, the monk Ambrosio rapes his poor sister in the monastery's sepulchral chamber, kills her and receives his punishment in good order. The novel was a scandal and Lewis had to rewrite parts of it. It is now available complete and unabridged in case someone should want something special and the Marquis de Sade, who seems to have influenced Lewis a great deal, isn't enough. (19)

The great classic of this genre, and the one that definitely brought the Gothic tale into the realms of science fiction came, however, in 1818. It was the result of the then twenty-one years old Mary Wollstonecraft Shelley's Swiss journey with the poet Shelley (Shelley was at this time still

married elsewhere, but his wife was pointedly not invited)
two years earlier. A typical portion of the text to evoke
the right feeling:

It was on a dreary night of November that I beheld
the accomplishment of my toils. With an anxiety that
almost amounted to agony, I collected the instruments
of life around me, that I might infuse the spark of
being into the lifeless thing that lay at my feet. It
was already one in the morning; the rain pattered dis-
mally against the panes, and my candle was nearly
burnt out, when, by the glimmer of the half-extin-
guished light, I saw the dull yellow eye of the creature open; it breathed hard, and a convulsive motion
agitated its limbs.

How can I describe my emotions at this catastrophe,
or how delineate the wretch whom with such infinite
pains and care I had endeavoured to form? His limbs
were in proportion, and I had selected his features as
beautiful. Beautiful! Great God! His yellow skin scarcely
covered the work of muscles and arteries beneath; his
hair was of a lustrous black, and flowing; his teeth of
a pearly whiteness; but these luxuriances only formed
a more horrid contrast with his watery eyes, that seems
almost of the same colour as the dun-white sockets in
which they were set, his shrivelled complexion and
straight black lips.

The object of this tender reflection is, of course, Frankenstein's monster, the greatest matinee idol of all time and
probably the most unappreciated BEM that ever has been
created in a mad scientist's gloomy laboratory. The monster
is a tender creature in Shelley's spirit, but his pathetic attempts to establish contact with human beings inevitably
ends in failures because of his horrific appearance. His gross
ignorance of fundamental human behavior also complicates
his existence. There is a tender scene in the novel, in which
the monster meets a small child by a woodland lake and
plays together with her. The play ends in catastrophe as the

monster notices the beautiful water lilies floating in the lake, and throws the girl into the water, believing that she also will float like a water lily. The members of the local village congregate in the bushes, armed with hayforks, flaming torches, etc., and the monster seeks asylum with an old hermit who luckily is blind and teaches him to behave like a real gentleman.

With time, the monster becomes really human, smokes a pipe, takes a drink before dinner, and starts to regard passing young ladies in a way that can't be misunderstood. He returns to Doctor Frankenstein, demanding that he create a female for him. Frankenstein firmly declines, and the monster retaliates by killing off Frankenstein's friends and relatives, whereupon Frankenstein and the monster pass the remainder of the novel stalking each other around the world. Frankenstein dies in the arms of a whaler in the Arctic Ocean, and the monster disappears in the eternal Arctic night to die as well.

At its best, *Frankenstein* is a moving tragedy with a contemporary significance. Harold Bloom writes in an afterword to an American pocket edition that:

> The greatest paradox and most astonishing achievement of Mary Shelley's novel is that the monster is *more human* than his creator. This nameless being, as much a modern Adam as his creator is a modern Prometheus, is more lovable than his creator and more hateful, more to be pitied and more to be feared, and above all able to give the attentive reader that shock of added consciousness in which aesthetic recognition compels a heightened realization of the self. (20)

However, the novel only seldom manages to climb over the level of the then current ten cent romance or "penny dreadful." *Frankenstein*'s strength lies in its implications, not its literary qualities. As it is, *Frankenstein* is not only a Gothic horror tale, but also the archetype of the anti-Utopian novel, as well as a unique introduction into the world of the Romantics: William Blake, Percy Bysshe Shelley, Lord Byron and so forth.

The theme of *Frankenstein* was not new, any more than other themes of Gothic literature. The artificial man, or homunculus, can be traced back to the legend of Daedalus, who built an artificial man for King Minos of Crete, and the homunculus can also be found in the Finnish epic *Kalevala*. In *Faust*, Goethe describes the creation of a homunculus by magical means, and his source was probably the old Jewish legend of the Golem, a homunculus molded in clay and infused with the spark of life by the rabbi Judah Loew Ben Bezalel in Prague, to defend the Jews against their tormentors. Golem turned against his creator, just as Frankenstein's monster later did, and was stopped only when the rabbi succeeded in taking away the paper inscribed with magical signs that gave life to the monster. This legend, one of the most recurrent in alchemistic dreams, was later used as the basis for a famous novel by Gustav Meyrink, *Der Golem* (1915).

Frankenstein was, at any rate, a thundering success, and was staged as a play all over Europe. The greatest success came later with the numerous films. The first came in 1910, produced by Edison Company ("Many repulsive situations have been eliminated," said the official press release), followed in 1915 by the Ocean Film Corporation of New York's *Life Without Soul* and then, in 1931, by James Whale's classic *Frankenstein* with Boris Karloff as the monster. Up to 1969, twenty Frankenstein movies had been released, most of them with very slight connections to the original novel. Werewolves, vampires and living dead were included as a matter of course, and in one film the poor monster even became a rock 'n roll star. Titles like *I Was a Teenage Frankenstein* (1957) and *Frankenstein versus the Space Monsters* (1965) speak for themselves. One of the latest editions to the Frankenstein myth, made by the reputable Hammer Films in England, bears the title *Frankenstein Must be Destroyed*. As far as the films are concerned, I am inclined to agree.

The second great movie star of the horror romance, is the

charming Count Dracula, an East European gentleman with sleek hair and burning eyes, not unlike Rudolph Valentino. The worthy count has been the subject of more movies than even his fellow-official Frankenstein's monster. His heyday came in the thirties, and his popularity seems to have rivaled that of a present-day pop star. Bela Lugosi, the good count's alter ego, said in 1935 that everyday he received as many letters as any romantic screen idol, ninety-seven percent of which came from women. (21)

The origin of Dracula and his blood-sucking brethren comes of course from ancient popular beliefs among the people of Asia and East Europe. The root of it lies probably in the ancient belief that the dead thirst after life-force, usually identified with blood. In Nordic popular belief, these creatures went by the name of *Pukes*, evil spirits, who nightly climbed down through the chimneys to nauseate the sleepers and suck the blood out of them. They also made a living as servants to the local witches, stealing milk and other useful necessities.

The first Gothic tale concerning itself with the exploits of the vampires was in the 1819 published story *The Vampire* by the Italian J. W. Polidori, who belonged to the group around Shelley and Byron and recorded it during the horror-story competition that gave birth to *Frankenstein*. The story was published in Lord Byron's name, to his exasperation, and proved to be an immediate success.

With the Irish writer Bram Stoker's *Dracula* (1897), the vampire appeared in the elegant top-hat-and-tails form that we now are accustomed to. The vampire is here a gloomy Transylvanian count who entices an innocent young man, the lawyer's assistant Jonathan Harker, to his terrible castle in order to prepare for his emigration to England and, at the same time, feed his vampirous sisters with the young man's blood. The novel is written in the form of a diary, and tells circumstantially of the count's attempts to kill the hero and how he later on appears in London, heralded by an army of rats, bats and other unpleasant animals. The ancient Slavic legend-making is scrupulously utilized, and Dracula follows all of the Gothic tale's rules of conduct all the way to his grandiose destruction on the desolate plains of Transylvania while the wolves howl in the background and the heroine swoons in the hero's hairy arms. It is an excellent novel, and a good representative of the Gothic tales.

The movie adaptations are legion, from Robert Vignola's *The Vampire* (1913), over F. W. Murnau's classic *Nosferatu* (1922) and Tod Browning's even more classic *Dracula* (1931) with Bela Lugosi as the count, to the present-day films like *Billy the Kid Meets Dracula* (1966) and Roman Polanski's delightful *Dance of Vampires* (1967) where the count at last is exposed as a homosexual, and which ends with everybody turning out as vampires. In the U.S.A. Dracula appears in various forms in immensely popular "come into my coffin" type TV shows, he is the big hero of the day, and according to an article by Raymond Lamont Brown, 6,500,000 women fans regularly watch ABC's Dracula-type TV show *Dark Shadows*. (22). It is so sick it is probably true.

The sf writer Richard Matheson has used the motif in the novel *I am Legend* (1954) which takes place in a future wherein everyone is a vampire. He even gives a scientific explanation of sorts to the phenomenon.

The werewolf, the last of the Big Three heroes of our time is, while a fairly ancient Central European mythological figure, rather new in the Gothic horror tale. The belief in werewolves or lycanthropes probably sprang from the suspicions of fooled game hunters that the wolf, or whatever it might have been, actually was a human being transformed into the animal. In France, during the sixteenth century, many werewolf-trials took place, during which people were charged with doing various atrocities while werewolves, and summarily burned at the stake.

The first novel dealing with the subject at any length was Guy Endore's *The Werewolf of Paris* (1933), the classic tale of the man changing into a wolf, prowling the streets of Paris at night, looking for something in which to sink his fangs. Endore drew heavily from the ancient werewolf tradition, even to the point of making the poor man, Bertrand Chaillet, a werewolf because he was born on Christmas Eve. Robert Louis Stevenson's *The Strange Case of Dr. Jekyll and Mr. Hyde* (1888) is of course an earlier example of the theme of man turning into monster. Jekyll/Hyde is actually just the werewolf theme, that of the *bête humain* dressed up with a slight scientific explanation. H. G. Wells used the theme with a twist in *The Island of Dr. Moreau;* he changed beasts into men. A more recent novel by Clifford D. Simak, *The Werewolf Principle* (1967), takes the theme a bit further: the protagonist of this novel is a triple werewolf, able to change himself into no less than three different animals—a wolf, a sort of alien intellect, and a man. He even finds himself a similarly equipped werewolf-girl at the end.

Otherwise, the werewolf is chiefly known through the horror movies—and, of course, through the ghastly horror comic magazines with which the market is abundant. The less said about these the better, though. I have a strong stomach, but these horror comics (made for children, mind you!) make it turn like a merry-go-round. The films are nicer.

The first one, *The Werewolf of London* (1934), told of the usual scientist, whose misguided research turned him into a howling wolf, whereupon he was firmly dispatched, although not until he had given his money's worth in torn throats, spilled guts, etc. The werewolf as a serial character came with *The Wolf Man* (1941) starring Lon Chaney, Jr. as the beastly hero. He managed to get shot in the end of the film, but nevertheless rose from the grave with moonlight reflecting on his glistening fangs, to howl himself through a number of increasingly silly horror films, starring against every monstrosity in sight, from Frankenstein's monster to Dracula and Abbott & Costello. Among the interesting additions to the modern werewolf myth, one might mention *I Was a Teenage Werewolf* (1957)—with Michael Landon of *Bonanza* fame as the howling and hairy hero—and *Werewolf in a Girl's Dormitory* (1961), with its theme song "The Ghoul in School."

The film *The Fly* (1958), in which the scientist almost

succeeds in changing himself into a common housefly, obviously belongs to this genre—although the clumsy scientist succeeds only partially. Only his head is transformed. Tsk, tsk.

To my knowledge, only two serious films have been based on the werewolf theme—both of them built on *Dr. Jekyll and Mr. Hyde.* They are Victor Fleming's *Dr. Jekyll and Mr. Hyde* (1941), with Spencer Tracy, Ingrid Bergman and Lana Turner—a strangely moving story; and Jean Renoir's *Le Testament du Docteur Cordelier* (1960), in which the scientist, Jean-Louis Barrault, actually becomes an elegant, interesting man while under the influence of the drug. Jerry Lewis's *The Nutty Professor* also plays along these lines, changing the awkward and shy scientist into a sleek-haired and thoroughly disgusting Elvis Presley-type hero at the downing of a retort of sickly-smelling liquid.

It is still horror, although not exactly of the classic type. Among the post-Gothic authors, Edgar Allan Poe (1809-1849) towers like a giant. His psychological insight and almost tender handling of his themes made him in a way the first serious Gothic writer, obsessed with pain and death, but using the obvious horror elements only as means to convey a deeper significance. The familiar picture of Poe is epitomized in two lines from a poem in his short story *Ligeia*; but it is far from the complete picture:

> And much of Madness and more of Sin
> And Horror the Soul of the Plot.

Poe was rather more complex than that. People who disliked Poe's writings, asserted that Poe wrote horror stories for their own sake; that he "had no heart." Chauncey Burr retorted in his *Memoir* (1850) that:

> Poe was undoubtedly the greatest *artist* among modern authors; and it is his consummate skill as an artist that has led to these mistakes about the properties of his own heart. That perfection of horror which abounds in his writings, has been unjustly attributed to some

moral defect in the man. But I perceive not why the competent critic should fall into this error. Of all authors, ancient or modern, Poe has given us the least of himself in his works. *He wrote as an artist.* He intuitively saw what Schiller has so well expressed, that it is an universal phenomenon of our nature that the mournful, the fearful, even the horrible, allures with irresistible enchantment. He probed this general psychological law, in its subtle windings through the mystic chambers of our being, as it was never probed before, until he stood in the very abyss of its center, the sole master of its effects.

Although Poe is renown for his Gothic horror stories, he also wrote a number of other works; his *The Murders in the Rue Morgue* (1841) is considered the first detective story, featuring as well Monsieur C. Auguste Dupin, whom Sir Arthur Conan Doyle later remolded somewhat as Sherlock Holmes. He also wrote a number of science fiction stories, and even a humorous story, *The Man That Was Used Up* (1840), in which a remarkably good-looking man turns out to be made up almost solely of protheses. It is interesting to note that Poe's most horrific story, *The Facts in the Case of M. Valdemar* (1845), a Gothic tale in all respects, generally was accepted as science *fact*, and during Poe's lifetime reprinted in England in the *Popular Record of Modern Science* as *The Last Conversation of a Somnabule* and later as a pamphlet entitled *Mesmerism, In Articulo Mortis*. A reception as curious as the theme of the story.

Among Poe's science fiction works, *The Unparalleled Adventure of One Hans Pfaall* (1836) and *The Narrative of Arthur Gordon Pym's Adventures* (1838) are the most noted. *Hans Pfaall* is a satirical variant of the old Moon journey; a balloon made of old newspapers lands in Rotterdam, and a dwarf climbs out of the gondola with the astounding news that he has just returned from the Moon. The story consists of the dwarf's narrative of his journey and the meeting with the people of the Moon. He concludes the story by promising to tell of his adventures on the Moon later on. It is apparent that his story probably is a joke on the good citizens of Rotterdam. The story might be a commentary on Richard Locke's reputed "discovery" of life on the Moon the preceding year, a revelation that was attributed to the English astronomer Sir John Herschel and was announced in the *New York Sun*; real yellow press journalism, without doubt.

Arthur Gordon Pym is a very ordinary sea story, until Pym comes to an island in Antarctica inhabited by peculiar black aborigines who get scared out of their wits at the sight of white objects. They slaughter everyone aboard the ship, excluding Pym and another man, who then proceed on to the Pole in a canoe, pursued by large white birds who terrify the aborigines. The novel ends with Pym and his friend being pulled down in a whirlpool at the Pole. The novel is unfinished, but it is probable that Pym was meant to drop down into some inner world of the usual type. Jules Verne later wrote a sequel, *The Ice Sphinx* (1897), which, however, did not include any inner world.

Poe wrote some other science fiction works, of which *Mellonta Tauta* especially, a picture of a future world in the style of present-day sf, is notable. His chief works were in the Gothic horror tradition, though, and it is stories like *The Fall of the House of Usher* (1839), *The Cask of Amontillado* (1846) and poems like *The Raven* (1845) that have given him his reputation as one of the greatest examiners of the dark undercurrents of man's mind, comparable even to the Marquis de Sade.

Despite the popular acclaim that met Poe's works, he lived in genteel poverty—and often not even that. When the book *Tales of the Grotesque and Arabesque* appeared, Poe's only payment consisted of a few complimentary copies of the volume.

The poem *The Raven* appeared in the New York *Evening Mirror* in January 1845, and Poe became, without question, a famous man. "The bird beat that bug all hollow," he remarked. During Poe's lifetime, the poem appeared in eleven periodicals as well as in book form. Still, Poe was even more troubled and impoverished than before. He became an occasional heavy drinker, and his wife Virginia's death in 1847 made his private sufferings all the worse. He died two years later, still impoverished, still suffering, still famous.

In ironic contrast to this, stands the value placed on Poe's letters after his death. A six-sentence letter to the Philadelphia publishers Lea & Blanchard, in which he suggested that ". . . you receive all profits (of a collection of stories) and allow me twenty copies for distribution to friends . . ." was less than a century after his death auctioned for $3,000, and recently a rare unpublished letter was auctioned for $5,200 to a New York manuscript dealer.

Poe's significance for the modern short story can hardly be overestimated. He has influenced Robert Louis Stevenson, Sir Arthur Conan Doyle and Baudelaire, among many others, and the modern science fiction genre owes a great and obvious debt to his works. It is known that *The Fall of the House of Usher*—unquestionably one of the masterpieces of short stories—influenced many artists to a great degree; among them was Debussy, who admitted to being "obsessed" by Poe and this story, and attempted to set the story in the form of a "symphony on psychologically developed themes."

These days, Poe is most well-known for the numerous films that he has been subjected to—chiefly by American International Pictures, whose vigorous director Roger Corman has been grinding out for years a steady flow of low-budget, low-quality adaptations from Poe's stories. These mostly have very slight connections with the original works —characterized by lots of fire and gore and sepulchers and burning castles and Vincent Price. They are interesting, in a sadistic way, but they don't have anything which makes Poe's work living and breathing and significant. They are painted backdrops with gory fronts and no content.

Poe laid the groundwork for the present-day fantasy— but the now prevalent type of fantasy came later on with two writers, both of whom utilized remarkable horror elements in their works. The writers were H. P. Lovecraft and William Hope Hodgson.

Hodgson's (1875-1918) novel *The House on the Borderland* (1908) is a narrative from a strange and repulsive world far beyond our reality. Two tourists find a lonely house situated at the edge of an unfathomable abyss during a walking-tour in a desolate part of Ireland. Before leaving the house, they find a diary kept by the last owner of the house, describing his experiences and the hideous underworld forces that focus on the place. It tells of the narrator's travels within the house, to other galaxies, to the center of the Universe and the fights with an inhuman "pig-people" who live in the abyss beneath the house. An aura of undefinable terror pervades the story, conjured not so much by the obvious terror elements as by the feeling of insecurity and alienness that is the keynote of this novel. Hodgson's novel is a typical example of the "new Gothic tale" that after the turn of the century began to appear, in which the time-honored vampires, living dead and so on slowly were being eased out for the benefit of far more fantastic creatures and plots. Hodgson's use of modern symbols in a traditional Gothic setting heralded the coming of the "science fantasy." This method is brought further in his novel *The Night Land* (1912), which depicts a world of total darkness millions of years hence, peopled with monstrous beasts and the remnants of humanity living in metal pyramids. With this novel, conjuring terror with the symbols of today, Hodgson actually became one of the first modern science fiction writers.

Howard Phillips Lovecraft (1890-1937) is a name practically synonymous with modern fantasy literature, not so much by his own works—his greatness as an author is disputed and from a literary viewpoint he is at best mediocre—as by the enormous influence he had on the writers who later on would shape science fiction literature: Ray Bradbury, Fritz Leiber, Henry Kuttner and others. Lovecraft was the most diligent contributor to the U.S. fantasy magazine *Weird Tales,* and he corresponded with almost all of the hopeful youngsters who later on would be writers;

he read their manuscripts, corrected them and gave advice. The stories of his kindness toward these aspiring writers are legion. Lin Carter says in the introduction to a collection of Lovecraft stories that:

> He was one of the most amazing letter writers of all times; at the peak of his voluminous correspondence, he was writing fifteen or twenty letters a day. Nor were they brief notes; as his disciple, friend, and sometimes collaborator August Derleth has written, "they sometimes covered thirty, fifty, or even seventy typewriter-sized pages, closely written." (23)

Lovecraft also wrote a number of stories and articles gratis for the fan magazines (fanzines) that were published in sf fandom, taking up a substantial part of his time and leaving less time for more profitable writings, which might have been one of the reasons for the poverty in which he lived at the end of his life.

Lovecraft's works are mostly pronounced horror stories, featuring demons of the worst kind: ghosts, ghouls, living dead and such things. The heritage from the Gothic tale is obvious, but Lovecraft is far more devilish and detailed than the Gothic writers ever were. Madness, unmentionable rituals and fear beyond all reason figure prominently in his stories, often coupled with acute claustrophobia; the horrid events usually take place in subterranean vaults and sepulchers, incredible ancient ruins and narrow passages deep under the modern cities, where indescribable creatures haunt the protagonist down and down until merciful madness darkens the poor man's mind forever. Black magic and rituals performed in ancient sepulchers are common occurrences in Lovecraft's stories, the dead walk again and ancient gods appear regularly.

Many of these stories are powerful, but they tend to be somewhat monotonous with time. His most enjoyable works are probably the dream-fantasies *The Dream-Quest of Unknown Kadath* (1925), *The Silver Key* (1926), and *Through the Gates of the Silver Key* (1932), all of them clearly influenced by the Irish writer Lord Dunsany. They are set in strangely beautiful never-never lands of imagination, far removed from the morbid fantasies of his other works.

In 1939, two sf fans, August Derleth and Donald Wandrei, started a publishing house, Arkham House, to publish works by H. P. Lovecraft and others. They also published eight issues of a fantasy magazine, *Arkham Sampler*, 1948-49, featuring among other works, *The Dream-Quest of Unknown Kadath*.

So much for the horror. I should perhaps point out that this branch of science fiction does not solely occupy itself with vampire castles and living dead. The greater part of the fantasy literature is noticeably temperate when it comes to the horror elements, and uses the fantastic situation in the same way as the more scientifically inclined branch of the genre, to construct a situation and follow it to its logical conclusion. I can mention Fredric Brown's *What Mad Universe* (1949), a parody on the clichés of science fiction, in which the protagonist drops down into a world dreamed up by a young and ardent science fiction fan. In Robert A. Heinlein's *Magic, Inc.* (1940) magic is a socially accepted occurrence, and is used in everyday business life.

A great part of the fantasy that is written today is, however, of the time-honored blood, sword and hero type and actually just the adventure story in its most straightforward form, featuring giants, magicians, beautiful princesses and the usual broad-shouldered hero with lots of muscles and no brow and eyes not an inch apart. It is the fairy tale all over again, with the monsters bigger and more horrible than before, and perhaps a wee bit more sadistic, but that is about the only difference. It is pure entertainment with a good measure of escapism thrown in, and it never purports to be anything else. You might call it a kind of Wild West in the never-never lands of unbridled fantasy. There are, of course, works of singularly literary qualities here as well as in the Wild West genre, as we shall see later on. This sub-branch of science fiction is called *Heroic Fantasy*, or *Sword & Sorcery*, both of them exceptionally fitting names.

L. Sprague de Camp, in his foreword to an anthology of heroic fantasy defines it as:

> . . . stories laid in an imaginary world, superficially somewhat like ours, but a world where magic works and machinery has not been invented. Sometimes this world is that in which the story-teller imagines ours was like in prehistoric times. Sometimes he fancies it will exist in the distant future, when the sun has dimmed, science and civilization have decayed, and magic has once again come into its own. Sometimes the scene is a world in another universe parallel to ours, where the laws of nature are different. (24)

In the foreword to another collection of fantasy stories (25), de Camp stresses the high entertainment value of this fiction, and ridicules the contemporary social novel ("should an heiress marry her chauffeur?") and the acknowledgment of sex as a driving force of man ("stories that reduce human beings to animated sets of genitalia with legs and other parts vaguely attached"). I agree with the high entertainment value of fantasy, but as for the rest, I don't. There is a lot to say about, for example, the undercurrents of sex in Heroic Fantasy. I will take this up in a later chapter.

This mixture of ancient Nordic sagas and Gothic tales that is called Heroic Fantasy or Sword & Sorcery appeared regularly chiefly in the U.S. magazine *Weird Tales*, without which the branch probably never would have become what it is today. It had existed in the form we now know it for some time, indeed since before the turn of the century, but *Weird Tales* encouraged writers like L. Sprague de Camp, Fritz Leiber, Clark Ashton Smith and Robert E. Howard who were to rise to predominance in the field. It proved immensely popular, but after World War II interest in the branch waned noticeably; obviously people had had enough of murder and violence. De Camp writes that:

> The cause, however, was the trend of the time, in

mainstream fiction and also in science fiction, towards stories with a strongly subjective, sentimental, psychological slant. In such tales, the anti-hero was often a wretched little twerp who could never do anything right. Instead of providing the reader with a heroic model with whom he could for the moment identify himself, giving himself a warm glow of vicarious heroism, the writer presented his reader with a protagonist so ineffectual and contemptible that the reader—the writer hoped—would enjoy the thought that at least he was better than *that*. (26)

After having delivered this unabashed praise to escapism, de Camp goes on to note the renewed interest in Heroic Fantasy ("The Hero shall ride again!") and in this respect he is undoubtedly right. Old classics are reissued by the score together with new stories of blood, thunder and well-sharpened swords. The spectrum goes all the way from the gentle novels of James Branch Cabell to the sadistic tales of Robert E. Howard and the almost Dickensian *Gormenghast* triology of Mervyn Peake. The source of this sudden interest in fantasy might be partly attributed to the success of J. R. R. Tolkien's *The Fellowship of the Ring* trilogy; however, looking at the state of the world—the real world —today, I can well believe there are some deeper reasons, too. There was a similar interest in heroes and mighty deeds in Hitler's Germany. Richard Wagner's *Der Ring der Nibelungen,* a heroic Sword & Sorcery fantasy of no mean qualities, was not the only work of its type popular at the time.

First among the writers of Heroic Fantasy stands Edward John Moreton Drax Plunkett, eighteenth baron of Dunsany (1878-1958), holder of one of the most ancient baronial titles in the British Isles and an aristocrat of the time-honored British big white bwana lion hunter type, the author of more than sixty books of drama, poems and fantasy (with a quill pen, his biographers note). His fantasy stories—built on elements heavily drawn from old Anglo-Saxon folklore and sprinkled with myths of his own making, characterized by a robust handling of the fantastic themes of monsters, heroes and elves as well as an almost tender, richly poetic language—influenced most of the following writers of the genre.

One might say that he practically invented the pastoral never-never land for fantasy. It had, of course, been there all along, in the fairy tale, but these tales had very seldom been written for anyone over the age of twelve. The Gothic tale only made use of the most ghastly elements of the old sagas. Dunsany used it wholesale, with his own details added, and did it for adult readers. He didn't use quite as many swords and spilled guts as his successors, though; that was for lesser geniuses to invent. Most of his books are now out of print, but two volumes of Dunsaniana have recently been issued under the editorship of Lin Carter.

Far away from Lord Dunsany's elves and magicians, and yet closely related to him in the use of ancient myths, although utilizing them with a greater awareness and more humor (and, many think, too much long-windedness) stands James Branch Cabell (1879-1958). His novels are usually set in a world bearing traits of classic mythology as well as the medieval world of Southern Europe. The country of Cabell's fantasy books is called Poictesme, a place bearing some modest relations with medieval Provence but actually a land of Cabell's own creation, formed under the influence of Cabell's extensive knowledge of medieval romance and ancient myths from all parts of the world.

The cycle of books that chronicles the adventures of kings, magicians and common people in this country is called collectively *Biography of the Life of Manuel,* Manuel being a swineherd who by various devious means rises to the position of Count of Poictesme. The story of his life is told in the second volume of the *Biography* (there are twenty of them, in all), *Figures of Earth,* while he appears as a much-revered statue in the third, *The Silver Stallion.* From having been a thorough rascal in his life, he is now considered as being something very close to a saint; and this is a way of turning things that can be found in all Cabell's fantasy works. Cabell is a romanticist with a difference, knowing that no object of admiration is quite worth the emotion it causes. Cabell is at the bottom disillusioned, and his humor, ranging from sarcasm to farce and burlesque only underlines 'this. *Jurgen* (1919), Cabell's most well-known novel, is a typical example of Cabell's subtle style. He regards his protagonist with the same kind indulgence with his many bad traits as he earlier showed toward Manuel in *Figures of Earth*. They don't behave like gentlemen, they are cowards and liars, you can never trust them, but such as they are, such is man and has always been.

Cabell looks at his figures, whether they are Achilles or Helena, the god Bacchus, mother Azra, the Devil or God, with the same irony; and Jurgen's hypocritical talks as he wanders from bed to bed in the strange lands of ancient sagas and myths becomes a quiet satire on all the ideals of religion and morality, of patriotism and romantic love. Nothing is really what it seems to be, he says, and when Jurgen gets the chance to fulfill his dreams in the shape of Queen Helena, the unattainable, he shies away because he is afraid of what he might come to know. *Jurgen* became the source of Cabell's fame as a writer, when the U.S.A.'s self-appointed moral guardian, John S. Sumner, boss of the Society for the Suppression of Vice, tried to suppress the book on charges of obscenity. Cabell was acquitted after a court battle that lasted for two years, and suddenly found himself a famous man. *Jurgen* has never been out of print since then. The guardians of morals are always the best advertisers for the very books they dislike. Which, of course, proves Cabell's thesis.

Actually, Cabell is far from immoral, and moreover rather difficult to get at. His works are abundant with references and metaphors that only a thoroughly classically educated reader can appreciate to their fullest extent, and his archaic, elegant prose makes him something of an anachronism in our day.

Cabell has been received with both utter enthusiasm and utter dislike. From having been one of the best-known American authors, he suddenly disappeared completely from fame in the early thirties, and it was not until very recently that he was rediscovered by any number of readers. The true aficionados have, of course, been here all along. The renewed interest in fantasy has brought Cabell back with fanfares, but only time will tell if he is back to stay or, as a critic has put it, "will be left alone to sardonic contemplation in the ivory tower built by his art."

Turning around completely, we come to Edgar Rice Burroughs, father of Tarzan, son of the apes, and a number of other hairy acquaintances—the absolute opposite of everything that Cabell stands for. Burroughs wrote a lot of Heroic Fantasy, actually making his debut with a novel called *Under the Moons of Mars* (1912), later retitled *A Princess of Mars*, the first of his renowned Martian novels, in which an able-bodied young man named John Carter transports his astral body to Mars, here called Barsoom, where horrible monsters spend their time chasing wonderfully beautiful princesses over the wastelands. It appears that this novel may have been influenced by a little-known novel by an English author, Edwin L. Arnold's *Lieut. Gulliver Jones* (1905; recently reissued by Ace Books as *Gulliver of Mars*). Richard A. Lupoff, an authority on Burroughs, says in a foreword to Arnold's novel that:

> . . . Gulliver Jones's Mars and John Carter's Barsoom bear such a resemblance as to stretch the long arm of coincidence far beyond the breaking point. Following Gully's unscientific advent on Mars (and John Carter's apparent astral projection to the red planet is hardly more feasible than Jones's flying carpet), he encounters a civilization remarkably like that of ERB's books, even down to the curious absence of old people and small children from Martian society.

Jones meets his Dejah Thoris—she is Princess Heru —and his Heliumites—the magnificently conceived Hither People. He duplicates Carter's rescue of Dejah as recounted in *A Princess of Mars*, and Carter's voyage down the Iss as described in Burroughs' *The Gods of Mars*. And his return to Earth near the end of Arnold's

book parallels Carter's return at the end of *Princess*.
(27)

Eleven more Martian books followed, most of them with
John Carter as the main figure, and contemporaneously with
these Martian stories and the equally fantastic *Tarzan*
novels (twenty-seven in all, a great deal of them of the
monster-and-lost-empire type) he ground out four novels of
Carson Napier's adventures among the creatures of Venus,
three Moon novels and nine novels dealing with Pellucidar,
the subterranean world, the latter with the hero David
Innes as the most common denominator. The Earth being
hollow and provided with a small central sun, in Pellucidar
everything is about as it is here, only more wild and more
monstrous. Here David Innes lived merrily with swords and
gorgeous princesses, now and then in company with the
great Tarzan, who flopped down into the subterranean world
when he didn't have anything else to do. The first Pellucidar novel, *At the Earth's Core*, came in 1922.

Burroughs' fantasy novels have proved immensely popular,
despite the fact that every one of them on close scrutiny
turns out to be rather old hat. This not only goes for the
Pellucidar books—the hollow Earth is one of the oldest
and most common clichés of science fiction. Jules Verne's
Journey to the Center of the Earth being only one among
many works utilizing this idea. Likewise, the Burroughs
adventure formula doesn't differ much from other action
novels.

The answer might lie in the quick, breathtaking pace of
the stories, and the skillful handling of the prose. Burroughs
was out to write entertainment, and this he did, splendidly.
It is far from great literature—you hardly know more about
the people in the stories when you finish them than when
you began—but there is suspense in them from beginning
to end, and in Heroic Fantasy, this is what counts. The
Rev. Henry Hardy Heins has in his preface to a book
about Burroughs' life and works found yet another reason
to the greatness of Burroughs' novels:

ERB knew the difference between right and wrong, and he spun his yarns so that there was never any doubt in his reader's mind either. His heroes and villains, together with the characteristics of each, were painted in unmistakable terms of black and white. And he was always scrupulous to keep his stories *clean*, even though they might also include violent battles and the spilling of countless buckets of blood. This is why it seems downright foolishness to me to hear of anyone alleging that Burroughs' works are unfit for children. Actually, taken in *toto*, they depict most clearly the relative merits of Good and Evil, along with an exaltation of the simple virtues such as honesty, kindness and family devotion—with the opposing vices often played up in order to intensify the contrast. (28)

To me, this seems to be a pretty good explanation as to why Burroughs never should have seen print at all and why (as actually once was done in Burroughs' home town, Tarzana) his books should be banned in every library ever frequented by people under the age of fifteen years. Perhaps the Rev. Heins thinks that "the spilling of countless buckets of blood" belongs to the "simple virtues" of life. I don't. I much prefer "dirty" (and natural) sex to the senseless killing so exultantly praised by this Burroughs advocate.

The "clean" virtues listed by the Rev. Heins above are, however, common for all Heroic Fantasy heroes: they kill like maniacs, but they are *clean* (which probably means that all of them still are virgins; how they should be able to have clean consciences after what they have done, escapes me). The facets of Good and Evil are also very easily discernible; everyone intellectual or not broad-shouldered enough is a baddie. Same goes for everyone with physical deformities. 'Tis a beautifully uncomplicated world, this one.

One of the very few cases of Heroic Fantasy heroes turning out to be somewhat less than spotlessly clean in word and deed, is in Fritz Leiber's stories of Fafhrd and the Gray Mouser, two dubious heroes working with poison and

Illustration by J. Allen St. John for
The Master Mind of Mars by E. R. Burroughs.

daggers when the need arises, drinking themselves drunk when the chance comes and harboring foul thoughts most of the time. They are by far the most interesting and individual heroes I have encountered in this particular type of fiction—but they are quite alone. It should be noted that Fafhrd has a sex life—something almost unique in this collection of oversized eunuchs.

Modern Heroic Fantasy takes place in a strange world of sword-toting heroes, terrifying monsters and women (usually princesses) almost too beautiful to be true. The scene of action may change, the monsters might vary in size and shape, but the fundamental idea is always the same. The heroes usually sport magic swords, with which they without any great compunction murder people right and left. Their attitude toward the heroines is also far from gallant. If they are of the rare type equipped with a sex drive, they usually rape her on the corpse of the murdered antagonist, whereupon they kill her as well and scamper off toward new gory heroic deeds. The rest of their time these heroes divide between damp caves where miscellaneous shady magicians wander about conjuring beasts, and the sackings of one defenseless city or another. There is a lot of gore in these stories, and action enough for ten ordinary novels in every one of them.

Usually, the Heroic Fantasy, or Sword & Sorcery, is so absurd that no one ever can take it seriously, which admittedly weakens some of the objections against it as to its overemphasis on violence. True, fantasy takes a lot of "suspension of disbelief" to appreciate it as entertainment, but it is really no more improbable than the typical story of the broad-shouldered private eye who fights fifteen Russian agents single-handedly and shoots beautiful blondes in the belly. It's just the setting that is different. Basically, I believe that Heroic Fantasy shares with the Wild West and the tough detective story the trait of being essentially Utopian: that is, to again quote de Camp, "providing the reader with a heroic model with whom he for a moment (can) identify himself, giving himself a warm glow of vicarious heroism." As far as entertainment goes, I can't see anything wrong with this. Though I still dislike the over-emphasis on violence.

The masters of this particular form of entertainment are generally considered to be the American writers Robert E. Howard, Clark Ashton Smith, Fritz Leiber, and the British Michael Moorcock. Robert E. Howard (1906-1936) is the crowned king of the branch, practically canonized by his many fans and followers. Howard, a man with an unhappy mother complex who committed suicide when his mother died, created in his stories a never-never land called *Hyboria*, in which his gigantic and unbelievable sadistic hero Conan carried on like a devil, killing women, children and old bootmakers with the same merry spirit. Conan was a great ladies' man as well, and all the wonderfully beautiful queens were crazy about him. The stories of Conan and his bloody sword appeared chiefly in the magazine *Weird Tales* during the thirties. They have also been published as books (six of them, plus an additional one, *Return of Conan* by Björn Nyberg and L. Sprague de Camp). Howard also created a number of other equally fearless heroes, Almuric and Bran Mak Morn being some of the most Conan-esque. Conan has proven immensely popular in fantasy circles, a "Hyborian Legion" was formed in 1955, and fan-zines are to this day published, devoting themselves to the exploits of The Hero. Conan's originality is not so great as to necessitate any deep analysis; it is basically the time-honored adventure formula all over again, but for anyone looking for good, clean murder, slaughter and sadism, this is a must. This formula for Heroic Fantasy has been admirably exemplified by Michael Moorcock, who should know, as:

A) Hero must get or do something,

B) Villain disapproves,

C) Hero sets out to get what he wants anyway,

D) Villain thwarts him one or more times (according to length of story), and finally

E) Hero, in face of all odds, does what the reader expects of him. (29)

THE MAGIC UNREALITY

This goes for all Heroic Fantasy, but Howard's heroes are even less subtle than the others of the branch. They go from start to finish like steamrollers, pausing only to wipe the blood from their swords, and if the exploits are downright impossible, that's part of their undeniable charm. According to E. Hoffman Price in *A Memory of R. E. Howard,* Howard made his heroes so simple so that when "you get them in a jam . . . no one expects you to rack your brains inventing clever ways for them to extricate themselves. They are too stupid to do anything but cut, shoot, or slug themselves into the clear." (30)

Fritz Leiber is in many ways a strange bird in the world of Heroic Fantasy. His heroes, notably Fafhrd and the Gray Mouser, are not only cutpurses and rogues, they only kill when they have to (a most uncommon trait in this fiction) and they even have sex urges (Conan once sported one, too, in *Return of Conan,* but it was censored by the publisher). Leiber's heroes also have a humorous trait that makes me rather favorably inclined toward them. Leiber doesn't seem to take his heroes quite as seriously as his fellow Heroic Fantasy writers. It should be noted that Fritz Leiber has shown himself well acquainted with the art and uses of ancient magic, as shown not only in his Heroic Fantasy stories but also in a number of other works. Most notable is his novel *Conjure Wife* (1953), one of the most frightening and thoroughly convincing horror stories of this century, dealing with witchcraft in the peaceful setting of a university town. This is fantasy, although hardly of the heroic type—which also to a degree goes for his *Gather, Darkness!* (1943), the story of a battle between pseudo-religion and pseudo-magic. In *Gather, Darkness!* Leiber actually proved that the gulf between "straight" science fiction and Sword & Sorcery can be spanned with good results, using elements from the two branches and uniting them into a powerful work of imagination.

Clark Ashton Smith (1893-1961) is the third of the Big Three of the magazine *Weird Tales'* "golden years" of 1928-39, the others being H. P. Lovecraft and Robert E. Howard. His works consisted of "Weird Heroic Fantasy" (another sub-branch; they come and come) that stands closer to the old Gothic school of magicians, ruins and ghosts than any other contemporary fiction. His *Zothique* stories are set in a dim and distant future, millions of years hence, in which magic has reappeared and incredibly ancient empires are slowly sinking back into oblivion as the deserts spread out, creating, to quote Lin Carter, "a dark world of older mystery, where luxurious and decadent kings and wandering heroes quest and adventure across dim landscapes, pitting their strength and wisdom against powerful wizards and alien gods, under a dying sun." The picture is painted with bold strokes and with an almost beautiful language, creating a truly alien world, in style somewhat reminiscent of *Arabian Nights*, where one is easily convinced that everything can happen. The theme was later used by Jack Vance in *The Dying Earth* (1950), a collection of interconnected short stories set in the incredibly distant future where strange science goes hand-in-hand with magic and where the ancient cities of super-science still rise toward the darkening sky in moldering splendor. But the going, I can assure you, is as rough as always in Heroic Fantasy.

Michael Moorcock (1939-) is a paradox in the field; he is well-known as one of the leading writers and advocates of the avant-garde "New Wave" science fiction, but most of his best-known and most liked novels come under the heading of the sweat-gore-and-murder Heroic Sword & Sorcery Fantasy. His hero is sometimes known as Elric of Melniboné, the unhappy possessor of a magic sword called Stormbringer. Elric is an albino and bearer of gloomy secrets that hath no name. He is of the melancholy sort. He starts the day with a hand-to-claw combat with dragons in the small hours of the morning, and sacks a couple of cities before lunch. The women are mad about him, but when Elric has butchered his last adversary for the day, he stubbornly rides away toward the sunset, completely unmoved by the rejected women's hysterical bawls. 'Tis a hard and lonely task, to be a Hero.

Actually, Elric of Melniboné stands a cut above most other heroes; he is a tragic personality possessing some traces of individuality, and his battle against the powers of Chaos is both intelligent and engrossing. Sometimes he even behaves like a human being. Every time he has killed one of his lifelong comrades or his dear wife or so, he cries a bit; I think this is a nice, human touch. He has also been caught in the act of *thinking*, which is very unusual for heroes and in fact an almost unprecedented occurrence. And in the end of the two-volume saga of Elric, *The Stealer of Souls* (1963) and *Stormbringer* (1965), everything goes to the dogs, which perhaps is the nicest and most human of all.

Since the mighty Elric lately has been butchered by his own untrustworthy sword (a very unusual finish), Moorcock has turned to another almost analogous hero, Dorian Hawkmoon, who is Duke of Köln and has an evil black gem embedded in his skull. This disagreeable jewel threatens to come alive at any moment and eat his brains, and Dorian Hawkmoon is thus as melancholy as Elric of Melniboné. The four volumes chronicling these adventures—*The Jewel in the Skull* (1967), *The Mad God's Amulet* (1968), *The Sword of the Dawn* (1968), and *The Runestaff* (1969)— are quite similar to the story of Elric of Melniboné, with lots of magic, abducted princesses, evil wizards, magic swords, monsters and so forth. I have been told that there is a great deal of allegory and hidden meaning in these stories. Knowing Michael Moorcock's other works, it would not surprise me, but I have so far been unable to detect it.

Abraham Merritt (1884-1943) was one of the foremost writers of Sword & Sorcery fantasy. He is still considered the best by many aficionados, and it is true that in his particular field he has few equals. (31)

Merritt's most well-known novels are *The Moon Pool* (1918) and its sequel *Conquest of the Moon Pool* (1919) which tell of subterranean monsters, a collection of decidedly untrustworthy creatures harboring foul plans against humanity. The idea was later readopted by a man with strong imagination, Richard S. Shaver, who in the years 1945-48 got a number of novels dealing with the monster-infested underground published in the sf magazine *Amazing*

Stories. The awed readers learned that the evil Lemurians and the Atlanteans in times of yore had gone underground and now were sending up rays toward us unknowing people. Many fell for this rubbish, and *Amazing*'s circulation rose rapidly. Loud protests from the not-so awed sf fandom and the rest of the magazine's writers put an end to the Shaver tales, however, and the Shaver fans had to go back to their flying saucers again.

The best known fantasy writer, and the one who almost single-handedly brought out the fantasy into public awareness, however, is undoubtedly the English philologist John Ronald Reuel Tolkien (1892-). His epic trilogy *The Fellowship of the Ring* (1954-55) has by now sold in the millions, and a veritable Tolkien-cult has appeared. There are Hobbit clubs everywhere, where the members appear in typical dresses, take names from the trilogy, perform rites from the books and so forth. Learned books are written about Tolkien and his world, and in sf fandom equally scholarly fanzines are published, discussing the trilogy, Tolkien's use of the Anglo-Saxon myths that form its basis, the literary shaping and so forth. How many fanzine pages that during the last years have been devoted to speculations about Tolkien's next work, *The Silmarillion*, I don't even care to guess.

Personally, I see this popularity as a very positive thing, leading, as it were, to a renewed interest in fantasy and almost forgotten fantasy writers like Mervyn Peake, E. R. Eddison, David Lindsay and James Branch Cabell. One might, however, ask why Tolkien turned out to be the catalyst that opened up the gates for fantasy literature. He is far from unique. Tolkien fans point to the grand scope of the trilogy (actually a tetralogy, *The Fellowship of the Ring* is preceded by another book, *The Hobbit*, from 1937, giving the prehistory of the magic ring). There are also many attractive traits in the traditional fairyland in which the story is laid. It is based directly on Anglo-Saxon and Nordic mythology, with Midgård (Middle Earth) as the center of the world. In this Midgård live the small peace-loving, pipe-smoking and tea-drinking Hobbits in their cozy dens in the Earth, amid elves, trolls, dragons, white and black magicians and all the other attributes of the fairy tale. The mythology is painstakingly constructed (Tolkien is the author of a number of scholarly works on Nordic and ancient Anglo-Saxon literature) and over everything hovers a gossamer veil of nostalgia, goodness and the victory of justice and righteousness over all evil forces.

This means that Tolkien's books are rather conservative in their outlook, more so, actually, than most fantasy works, as they usually are very keen in adapting new viewpoints and the new order of things and following them to their more or less logical conclusions. Tolkien's Midgård is in many ways not so much a creation of unbridled imagination as a conservative man's Utopia, where an old white-haired philologist can expect to study to his heart's delight without being disturbed by the coarse populace and their cries of justice, food, freedom, human rights and other trivialities. What we have here, is H. G. Wells's "paradise of little fat men" once again. William Ready, in his book *Understanding Tolkien,* has rightly pointed out that:

(Tolkien) is a most intolerant and conservative man, as the English are, in the end. The Hobbits are all sorts and degrees, rich and poor, upper, middle and lower classes, but Hobbit lower classes are forelock-tugging yokels as divorced from their own dreams and agony as the Irish creatures of Somerville and Ross, the grinning, bowing, house servant-slaves of the old South, the quaint little 'tween-maids of the Victorian ménage, the cottagers who hedged and thatched and plowed for the gentry while their children went into domestic service in the Big House . . . The class structure is apparent all through Tolkien's description of Hobbit life. They are nonintellectual, as he is in this day and age. He shares a lot of their tastes, or he would if he could. There is no understanding or appreciation of new-fangled ways. They would no more give house room to an abstract painting than they would read a Westron text if they didn't have to. He places them . . . his characters, in an archaic society where the song resounded:

"God bless the Squire and his relations
And keep us all in our proper stations." (32)

Catherine R. Stimpson, in her study *J. R. R. Tolkien*, goes even further, saying that:

(Tolkien's) popularization of the past is a comic strip for grown-ups. The *Lord of the Rings* is almost as colorful and easy as *Captain Marvel*. That easiness is perhaps the source of Tolkien's appeal . . . To those who pride themselves on cynicism, an adolescent failure, he spews forth a reductive, yet redemptive, allegory of the human urge to fail. For those who actually long for security, he previews a solid moral and emotional structure. His authoritarianism is a small price for the comfort of the commands: Love thy Aragorn; fear the Nâzgul. (33)

A great deal of Tolkien's appeal probably lies in a nostalgic longing for the good old days of yore when life was nice and secure and people knew their place; in other words, as I have pointed out earlier a sort of Utopia where the sun always shines and the grass is greener and the evil dragon always can be slain by a gallant knight. The story of Frodo's quest for the magic ring, together with his wiseacre servant Sam, Gandalf the magician, and a group of dwarves, is taken directly out of the old fairy tales, but yet very human and the heroics are held on a believable level. It doesn't take long until the reader is carried away and accepts it all, including wizards and dragons and the rest. It is fantasy on a high level, where black is black and white is white and Galdalf, the secure old father-figure, is always present somewhere. The small, kindhearted Hobbits' desperate longing to go back to the peace and quiet of teapot and pipe in the womblike Earth-dens stands in glaring contrast to Sauron's army of living dead and the black sky that hangs threateningly over the terrible Mordor, Sauron's kingdom in the east. This is a fitting symbol of industrialization, socialism and all the dangers of the new age that threaten to destroy the secure life of the good old days. The magic ring is science and knowledge with power over the world, and when Frodo finally overcomes himself and manages to destroy the ring, the factories of Sauron crumble to dust, the machines grind to a standstill, the horrors of industrialization are aborted. Frodo returns to his peaceful village, defeats the remainder of the revolting lower classes (aptly described as some kind of sub-human creatures) and later leaves for a place more fit for a gentleman. It is a beautiful description of the upper class's inability to face change, and the efforts of the same to fight evolution, although I am sure Tolkien never consciously meant it that way. *The Fellowship of the Ring* is the protest of an old man against everything new, and the fairy tale brings all his hidden fears out in the open.

Outside the English-speaking countries, Heroic Fantasy fiction is quite scarce; in Scandinavia indeed almost non-existent, possibly due to the fact that the Eddas are read in school and any modern Heroic Fantasy must seem rather pale in comparison. However, if I might be permitted to entertain my parochial side, I should mention the Finnish (but Swedish-languaged) writer and artist Tove Jansson, whose delightful Moomin books have been cherished by children and adults alike for more than twenty years. The Moomin books, which in later years have become increasingly adult, drop the security of the beautiful never-never land on behalf of a deeper psychological significance, and tell of the Moomin-trolls. These are humanized animals that look rather like small, furred hippopotami with long tails (except that they walk upright) that until a couple of books ago lived peacefully in the Moomin valley amid a number of bizarre creatures; the nasty and very negative Little My, the gloomy Muskrat, the not-too-bright Hemulen and some *very* unlikely acquaintances as well, such as The-Thing-Which-Lives-Under-The-Sink. It is a delightful fantasy, but in no way naïve. The world is, on the whole, good, but not altogether so. The Moomins and their friends are small and insignificant creatures, and outside the Moomin valley darkness is closing in. In some of the latest Moomin books, particularly *The Invisible Child* and *Moominpappa at Sea* the fantasy has been brought to a heightened awareness of the outside world and the forces of change. Instead of fighting change, as Tolkien's Hobbits do, the Moomintrolls face it. They leave the happy Moomin valley, venturing out into the insecurity of the outside world, shadowed by dark clouds that billow up like reflections of the darkness over Tolkien's Mordor. Moominpappa stands in the lighthouse tower, far out in the raging sea, gazing out over the endless horizon where everything can happen and where nothing is as it once was.

With the risk of evoking the wrath of every science fiction old-timer, I am including the Space Opera branch of science fiction in this chapter, as being the direct descendant of the fantasy tale. It is really the same branch, only with some of the old symbols exchanged for new. The Space Opera was prevalent in science fiction from the late twenties to the early forties, appearing in the pulp magazines of the time—*Amazing Stories, Astounding, Thrilling Wonder Stories* and others. They were crude stories, usually lacking even the simplest literary merits. People were painted in black or white, nothing else and the only thing in them more idiotic than the scientific theories was the immature handling of the compulsory love interest.

Nevertheless, they conveyed a Sense-of-Wonder, and this to an extent that probably never has been surpassed. When things started rolling, by golly, it really *started*. Whole galaxies crumbled before the atomic cannons, and the evil alien monsters were slaughtered by the quintillions by the heroes and their faithful friends. The galactic patrols roamed the void, spreading *Pax Terra* at blaster-point, and scientific miracles were as common as apple pie. Nothing, absolutely nothing, is impossible in Space Opera. It might be a lot of rubbish, but I can't resist liking it.

This branch of science fiction is, of course, closely related to the fairy tale and the Heroic Sword & Sorcery Fantasy, with the magic sword exchanged for the atomic blaster and the magic for super-science. Wizards have become scientists, with thick spectacles added to their long beards, wearing white smocks instead of the multicolored cloaks of yore. Instead of the cabalistic magic signs, we have equally meaningless formulae that, to a present-day reader, promises exactly the same things that the magic words once did. The monsters look about the same as before. The setting is somewhat more original, drawing ideas not from the ancient sagas but from contemporary science. Instead of the book of magic, we have books of mathematical tables; instead of the philosophers' stone, uranium; instead of the pentagram, the computer.

This is truly the modern fairy tale, gigantic in scope, utilizing worlds of an entirely new type, creating, in effect, something that never existed before out of time-honored materials. The basic formula is, of course, the good old traditional one, with gallant knights and evil adversaries and quests hither and thither, but the scope is decidedly brand-new. Or perhaps I should say was—forty years or so ago. It is still very much popular, though, as attested by new pocket editions of the old Space Opera novels.

The Space Opera aspect of science fiction will be discussed in the next chapter, but it is interesting to note here that the branch, together with an increasing interest in traditional fantasy, is again gaining in popularity. The miraculous adventures of E. E. "Doc" Smith's *Skylark* and *Lensman* series, Jack Williamson's *The Legion of Space*, A. E. van Vogt's *Slan* (an interesting mutant novel, aside from its Space Opera merits), Edmond Hamilton's *Captain Future* and so forth are being reissued and, apparently, very well received. It might be the old Utopian dream of man conquering matter again, and the dream of easy solutions to seemingly unsolvable problems.

In a world ridden by anxiety and fear, the exploits of star heroes and swordbearers alike must be of considerable interest. The Space Opera regards the future with hope and a positive attitude, although mostly overly naïve and sometimes openly escapist. But as a contrast to the defeatist attitude of many recent works of science fiction, it certainly serves a purpose. Perhaps this particular branch is overdoing it; but that is the prerogative of writers anywhere, anytime.

6. OUT IN THE UNKNOWN

Barchay rode into the Comanche village alone, on the back of a swaybacked horse that he had caught and broken himself, five years past. He had been traveling westward six days and six nights from the encampment on the distant eastern shore of the continent, feeding himself en route with whatever his gun could bring down.

He sat stiffly upright in the saddle, head staring forward so solidly and so massively that it might seem his neck had calcified. He had spent the whole trip in much the same posture, as the hooves of the horse carried him along, westward, and in a sense backward in time as well. It was twenty years since he last had visited this particular Comanche village, or indeed the flat lake country here in the west at all. And he was the first white man to venture out of the encampment on the ocean shore since the massacre, three months since, when the sullen Comanche had risen suddenly to claim eight hundred settlers' lives.

This run-of-the-mill Wild West story doesn't seem to be able to defend its place in a book on science fiction—and indeed it does not. But substitute the sullen Comanches for the equally sullen V'Leegs of some distant frontier planet, the horse for a "pink running-beast," the white settlers for Earthmen and the gun for a blaster, and you suddenly have the opening sequences of a "science fiction" story by a well-known sf writer (34) which tells of how the lean-hipped and broad-shouldered hero Barchay returns to the V'Leeg village to have a look at his mixed-breed son, the result of an earlier visit to the local chieftain's daughter. The story is as much science fiction as the quoted opening implies, which is nothing. Now, I don't have anything against Wild West stories, not even one based on a plot as old and feeble as this one—but I dislike badly written Wild West, and I object most strongly to having it masqueraded as science fiction. Unfortunately, this example is far from unique.

Theodore Sturgeon, one of the most brilliant writers of science fiction, has said that "a science fiction story is a story built around human beings, with a human problem, and a human solution, which would not have happened at all without its scientific content." Damon Knight, another of the living giants of the genre, has suggested that the word "speculative" should be inserted before "scientific," which would "clearly divide true science fiction from even the best imitations."

Even without Damon Knight's amendment, the quoted story is revealed for what it is: a very, very crude imitation, using the symbols of science fiction without any of their meanings. Knight's amendment makes it even more obvious: this is definitely not science fiction.

Science fiction has shown that it can accommodate itself to all possible overcoats and still exploit its unique possibilities to the fullest extent, still exist as unquestionable science fiction. There are social satires like Pohl/Kornbluth's *The Space Merchants* (1952), crime mysteries like Alfred Bester's brilliant *The Demolished Man* (1953), historical fiction like Ward Moore's *Bring the Jubilee* (1952), spy thrillers like Eric Frank Russell's *Wasp* (1957), way-out avant garde like Brian W. Aldiss' *Barefoot in the Head* (1969), military propaganda like Robert A. Heinlein's *Starship Troopers* (1959), anti-military works like Harry Harrison's *Bill, the Galactic Hero* (1965), powerful poetry like Harry Martinson's *Aniara* (1956) and even pornographic science fiction, as shown by some of Philip José Farmer's recent novels for Essex House. Not to mention religious novels like James Blish's *A Case of Conscience* (1958). And, of course, the numerous weird and horror science fiction stories, with which the genre abounds. Obviously, the genre can also accommodate Wild West yarns, dealing with the opening of new frontiers by tall, lean and sunburned (space-burned) men brandishing ugly Colts (blasters) and stealing land from the Indians (the aliens), but using the old science fiction paraphernalia doesn't make it science fiction. It still is Wild West to me.

I have already mentioned the Space Opera stories of the twenties and the thirties, which originally sprang directly from the pulp Wild West yarns, but still managed to turn out as something entirely new in pulp fiction. Their world was the fairyland of super-science, and even if the heroes were molded in the time-honored knight and cowboy formula, they nevertheless existed and committed their heroic deeds under conditions vastly different from the fiction of old. Granted, the literary quality was low, and the science was, with few exceptions, corny, but this was easily overlooked, and, I feel, with good cause. The sf writers were chartering new seas far from the well-trodden lands of predictability and security, and this was, in itself, good. The literary writers would come later on, basing their imagination upon foundations laid under a wild spree of heroic star-jumping improbability. Today, when science fiction writers are leaving "outer space" and instead concentrating on the "inner space" of man's mind, they are merely repeating the lamented pulp writers' works, treading into an unknown world where conditions are so different from the ones around us as to seem paradoxical or completely senseless to us. It is still the "strange encounter" tale.

These were the formative years of science fiction as a separate literary genre, a process started by Hugo Gernsback when he published the first real science fiction magazine, *Amazing Stories,* in 1926, and furnished the genre with a name of its own. The magazines "with their gaudy and dynamic covers which promised every reading adventure imaginable" shaped the development of the genre, providing it not only with readers and fans but with a needed and very creative "feedback" system between writers and readers through the letter columns. The Space Opera reigned unchallenged, and is now looked back on with considerable nostalgia. Alva Rogers' description of one of the Space Opera classics in his book on *Astounding* gives a good picture of the Space Opera's impact:

Who can ever forget the thrill of reading *The Legion of Space* by Jack Williamson for the first time? The first part of this classic began in the April issue and ran for six breathtaking installments. The adventures of John Star, Giles Habibula, the mighty Hal Samdu, and Jay Kalam on the evil world of the Medusae, the planet Yarkand, as they fought to save the lovely Aladoree Anthat and the secret weapon, AKKA, which she alone held in her mind and which was the only salvation of Earth, were high adventure indeed with a Sense of Wonder in ample measure. (35)

It has been pointed out that around the turn of the century, a large number of writers not usually associated with science fiction used the media as a vehicle for satire or pure entertainment, but that their numbers sharply decreased during the twenties and onward, leaving only a few accepted literary writers like Aldous Huxley and André Maurois using the versatile tool of science fiction to some degree. The reason for this might be traced down to the pulps, which at this time were shaping the science fiction genre, minting, as it were, its own coinage which was negotiable only within the field.

The genre, at this time, developed both too fast and too slow. Too fast in the respect that it used a world of super-science that didn't exist and for which conditions were not yet present, which made the genre incomprehensible for many people. And too slow in that its authors were crude and unsophisticated when it came to purely literary merits, which gave the field a reputation as simple and illiterate. This, of course, hardly encouraged mainstream writers to try their hand in the field. A story like Jack Williamson's *The Legion of Space*, while packed to the gills with Sense-of-Wonder, must necessarily seem very crude in comparison with the sophisticated mainstream writing of the time. Crit-

SCIENCE FICTION: WHAT IT'S ALL ABOUT

ics were still largely overlooking the unique merits of this admittedly crude science fiction, pointing out only the low literary standards. Myself, I suspect that this is to a large degree just a way to give the genre a blow below the belt, by criticizing a facet that doesn't have anything to do with its aims. The strong points of the early American science fiction was not beautiful language but the scope of plots and ideas.

Let me exemplify with the grand old master of the Space Opera, E. E. Smith, Ph.D. (1890-1965), or "Doc" Smith as he was called by his faithful readers, whose galactic sagas containing mile-long space ships, spectacular space battles between the galaxies, Bug-Eyed Monsters and heroes and villains literarily out of this world, has made its author the target of considerable criticism both from without and within sf circles. His exploitation of science is sheer madness, and is apt to give even the most indulgent reader headaches. It is, however, not the scientific validity that is central in E. E. Smith's space yarns. When he started writing his debut novel *The Skylark of Space* in 1915, few had dared to venture outside the solar system in science fiction. The sf writers cautiously kept themselves to the thoroughly beaten tracks of Jules Verne and the Utopian societies. E. E. Smith threw up the gates to the great unknown, the infinite universe where everything could happen, where no accepted theories held force and insecurity was at a maximum.

It was the vision that was important, not the loyalty to accepted science. Out there was an unknown universe that no one had dared to look at, and E. E. Smith, who couldn't write two sentences without becoming pathetic, gazed out into it with both eyes. Science had to bend knees for the Sense-of-Wonder, and the literary quality was a secondary matter. The sf readers willingly overlooked his nonexistent writing talents. They were looking for other things.

Since the days of E. E. Smith, the literary standards of science fiction have risen considerably. We now have great numbers of writers in the field who have the Sense-of-Wonder and literary abilities to translate this into enjoyable form. "The willing suspension of disbelief" that Coleridge designated as one of the poet's chief aims the sf writer achieves by creating worlds of illusion that are highly unfamiliar, yet made believable by a logically constructed background for the story—logical, that is, according to its own terms; and peopled by people acting logically out of the assumptions implicit in the construction of the imaginary world. This imaginary world still stands far away from our reality, but it is nevertheless there. It works in a logical way. And that, when you think of it, makes sf no more unbelievable than, say, a historical novel placed in ancient South America. There is a society, mores, rules of behavior completely unfamiliar for a contemporary Western man, yet a skillful writer can make it all seem natural enough, and, working from that, hang some facet of his plot on some assumption unique for this imagined society.

Robert A. Heinlein is the unquestioned master of this art of constructing societies as background and motivating forces for his plots. Sometimes the carefully delineated background actually gets to be more interesting than the story plot it is made to support; e.g. Isaac Asimov's complicated robot society of *The Caves of Steel* or the advertising-society background of Pohl/Kornbluth's *The Space Merchants*. This, I might add, despite the fact that the plots in question are both intelligent and of considerable value in themselves.

There are, of course, writers who don't give a fig for logic, being content with presenting the idea all by itself. The grand example of this is Ray Bradbury, who is scared to death of anything remotely connected with science and obviously doesn't have the faintest inkling of elementary scientific facts. The greater part of Bradbury's production consists of horror stories à la *The October Country* (1955) and nostalgic pictures of departed youth, like *Dandelion Wine* (1957), which literally drips with sentimentality. His science fiction works are essentially anti-Utopian, depicting, as in *Fahrenheit 451*, a society where writers aren't appreciated at all; or *The Pedestrian*, which takes place in a future where it is forbidden to walk alone at night in the city. The future is bringing science and change and, like

J. R. R. Tolkien, this scares the author. Science is bad, he seems to say; everything new is bad. Only the twenties were good.

Ray Bradbury has always been, to me, a very reactionary writer, whose strength lies in his colorful artistic handling of the prose, a prose that comes nearer to poetry than anything else in this field, and through this Bradbury has in fact made sf literarily acceptable to a degree that it probably never would have been without him. This is significant for the critics views on science fiction, as sf is a pronounced idea literature, and Bradbury is known for his weak plots and ideas. His power lies in his flowery language, and he is, in fact, a striking example of Marshall McLuhan's thesis that the Media is the Message. Behind the magnificent cathedrals of sparkling, flowing words there is usually nothing but a vague dissatisfaction with everything that the future might bring.

Bradbury's specific contributions to sf literature have been two chiefly anti-Utopian novels: the 1984-ish *Fahrenheit 451* (1953), telling of a fireman in a not-so-distant future U.S.A., where the fire brigade burns books and the antisocial people who own them; and *The Martian Chronicles* (1950), a number of short stories welded into continuity, dealing with the colonization of the planet Mars. The latter is a telling example of the American agony of the Indian massacres, a magnificent chronicle of the death of a refined culture beneath the boots of the invaders, but, as all of Bradbury's works, utterly naïve and from a scientist's point of view, crazy. Bradbury's Mars with its sweet spring evenings and blue skies belongs more to the American Middle West of Bradbury's nostalgic dreams than to the hard reality.

Bradbury is one of the few science fiction writers who have been accepted in literary circles. The reason for this indulgent attitude can be discussed, but it certainly isn't because of his plots. It is, of course, nice having the *literati* on one's side, although putting the emphasis—as in Bradbury's case—on qualities springing not from science fiction's own unique merits but on literary merits present in any

Illustration for a French limited edition of
The Martian Chronicles.

best-selling slick fiction, I think they are doing the genre a great disservice. Science fiction is a field with its own qualities and possibilities, and it should be recognized not for its handling of standard literary tools but for its handling of tools and themes unique for the field. Many sf writers of today are quite eager to push sf into mainstream literature, thus perhaps gaining a larger audience. Myself, I do not think this is either possible or desirable. It would be, I fear, to yank out its teeth, making it yet one of the many domestic house-trained fields of literature. Science fiction is not the greatest literature in the world, but it has certain valuable properties. I would like to keep those undiluted. Kingsley Amis and Robert Conquest have made some fitting observations in their foreword to their anthology *Spectrum 2*:

Science fiction, in fact, has had to grow up under its own power, developing its standards from within, from among its own writers, editors, and readers. This may have slowed it down, for self-criticism does not flourish under conditions of intellectual isolation. And yet we cannot feel that what might be called the provincial status of science fiction has been altogether to its disadvantage. To put it no higher, people like ourselves have been enabled to put in a couple of decades of stimulating reading in a field where the writ of the more portentous type of literary critic does not run. In the last thirty or forty years there has been far too much self-consciousness about "significance," self-importance about "art," self-approval about "extending the bounds of moral awareness," with a corresponding lack of regard paid to older ideas of what fiction can and should provide: entertainment as well as edification, profusion and novelty of ideas as well as technical originality, speed and suspense and surprise in narrative as well as depth of psychological probing. These older ideas have, in our own day, found an important custodian in science fiction . . . the traditional first aim of most sorts of writer has always been to please the reader, that even the most ambitious poetry, as Rosetti puts it, must be "amusing." Science fiction writers cannot but share this aim, while "mainstream" fiction, all too often, found its more intelligent writers becoming unreadable, and its more readable writers becoming unintelligent. (36)

I understand that "entertain" and "amuse" are singularly dirty words in literary circles, nevertheless I firmly believe a good story should do both of these things. Science fiction usually does; it might be the heritage from the lamented pulp magazines. The literary world is crowded with ivory towers housing unappreciated geniuses. Happily, we don't have much of this in science fiction—yet. A science fiction writer who finds it beneath his dignity to be thought-provoking and entertaining doesn't stay long in the field.

Science fiction has always been somewhat unorthodox, in this, as well as other respects. Being based mainly on the question *What would happen if . . . ?* it often has no use for the standard literary tools of mainstream fiction, and is, consequently, hard to judge by the gauges used for fiction describing familiar and predictable situations. It presents an equation that consists of nothing but unknowns.

The most commonly quoted example on this is Robert A. Heinlein's brilliant story *By His Bootstraps* (1946). Here the protagonist goes thirty thousand years into the future, is received by himself as a middle-aged man, goes back to make himself go into the future so that he can become the middle-aged man, fights with one time-version of himself that has not understood the meaning of it yet and tries to stop the first time journey, and becomes with time the middle-aged man who with diverse tricks induces himself as a young man to join him. Now, none of the values applicable to ordinary fiction can be used to judge this story—except that one about entertainment and readability. The story has no central character; no psychological depth in describing the protagonist is needed. He is merely a pawn caught in a paradox of time; in a sense, time itself and its effects is the central character. It is a dazzling show of speculative logic, based on assumptions that do not exist here and now, but still are extremely fascinating.

Time travel—to continue with the specific themes of science fiction—is one of the most versatile tools of speculation in the genre, and it has given birth to a staggering number of stories, based on paradoxical assumptions like, *What would happen if I went back in time and killed my grandfather before he had an issue?* We now even have the well-known "Guardian of Time," of science fiction, doing his noble deed of keeping past history as it is and getting grandfather-killers and Jesus-savers and the like out of the way. One of the best of these ingenious variants on the theme is a recent novel by Robert Silverberg, *Up the Line* (1969), telling of the decidedly immoral adventures of Judson Daniel Elliot III, Time Service Courier. He is far removed from any hint of heroism in the preserving of the past; actually, he conducts guided tours for the idle rich to the highlights of human enterprises, like the sack of Rome and the Black Plague and such things. One of his nice fellow Couriers is enjoying himself by tracing his female ancestors and seducing them. The protagonist doesn't do so badly either, even if he restricts himself to one female ancestor. This is probably what would happen if time travel were feasible, booming tourist trade and things. Think of guided tours to Europe with time paradoxes added.

And this is also a story without a human central character; it is still our friend the temporal paradox sitting in the high seat, reducing human heroes and villains to puppets doing as well as they can within the framework of the paradox, but still trapped. In fact, Judson Daniel Elliot III gets himself stuck in a beautifully impossible paradox at the end of the novel. The puppets are entangling themselves.

Sometimes they manage to make complete asses of themselves, too. Like in Ward Moore's *Bring the Jubilee* (1952), which is set in the 1940's in an America where the South won the Civil War—with disastrous results for the North. A time machine is invented by a group of scientists, and a historian goes back to the Battle of Gettysburg to have a look at the fun, changing the outcome of the whole war in the process and ending up creating the world as we know it. There is also a similar theme used in John Brunner's *Times Without Number* (1962, 1969) in which the Spanish Armada did not perish and went on to do its job, resulting in a vastly different world with a busy Inquisition, Time Corps and gleaming rapiers. Until the protagonist makes a mistake and the Armada perishes and here we are again.

Which takes us into the paradoxes of the parallel worlds: the probable world in which Germany won the first, or the second World War, or the one in which Jesus escaped from the cross. Philip José Farmer has written a beautiful story, *Sail On, Sail On,* set in a parallel world in which the Church has taken a more positive stand toward the sciences than it has done in our world, in which Columbus' flagship is equipped with radio, and—as a final touch—the Earth really *is* flat. Columbus flops over the edge with a bewildered splash and America remains undiscovered, because there is no America.

Next step is the big-brother of the time machine, the machine that enables one to go from one parallel world to another. It might seem like just a variation on the old journey-to-other-worlds story, but it is not. There is a whole brand-new set of paradoxes in the parallel-world theme.

Robert Sheckley has given a nice example of this in his novel *Mindswap* (1966), which, apart from an ingenious new means of traveling—by exchanging minds with some creature on the planet one wants to visit, instead of going there in person—contains a beautiful twist of the story of the man finally coming home after a wild journey through the parallel worlds. Marvin Flynn returns alive and well to his home town of Stanhope, New York, but is sometimes troubled by the thought that perhaps he has not returned to his own world after all. Perhaps he is somewhere else, and his memory and perceptions are deceiving him:

He lay beneath Stanhope's familiar green sky and considered this possibility. It seemed unlikely; for did not the giant oak trees still migrate each year to the south? Did not the huge red sun move across the sky, pursued by its dark companion? Did not the triple moons return each month with their new accumulation of comets?

So Marvin Flynn is content again, marries the daughter of Stanhope's leading real estate dealer, and stays in his home town. Nothing, he assures himself, has changed.

This is science fiction's "message" of the changing world again; that nothing should be taken at face value, that nothing will go on being what it is. We might cling desperately to the good old ways, hoping for security in conservatism, but we are only fooling ourselves. "Nothing is permanent except our illusions," Sheckley says in his novel. He is so right.

This way of regarding our everyday world as something entirely different from what we think it is, has resulted in probably the most chilling horror story I have ever read, *Mimic*, by Donald A. Wollheim. It features monsters of a particularly repulsive type, but it is not the monsters as such that makes this story so effective—it is the implications given by the story. Ghouls and ghosts and the like scarcely scare anyone nowadays, not even if they appear in a modern or futuristic setting. What Wollheim did in this story—and I believe he was the first to spot this approach—was to create a truly modern terror tale, telling of a kind of insect that adopted a protective mimicry suitable to make them survive in a modern city. They look—almost—like men. But the overcoat and hat is all part of the insect's body. This is not as farfetched as it might seem—nature has endowed many otherwise defenseless animals with a protective mimicry that makes them look like other and more dangerous creatures. It could as well happen to man, only there are no insects as big as man—as far as we know.

"Nature practices deceptions in every angle," Wollheim says in the story. "Evolution will create a being for any niche that can be found, no matter how unlikely."

If this doesn't seem grand enough in scope, we can move over to the dazzling cosmic panoramas of Olaf Stapledon, "the most titanic imagination to ever write science fiction," to quote a well-known critic. His first and most famous novel, *Last and First Men* (1930), tells the history of mankind from 1930 to the end of recorded time, two billion years in the future, in a manner reminiscent of Edward Gibbon's *Decline and Fall of the Roman Empire*. Like a history book of the future, it tells of the Americanized era and its end, the rise of Patagonia as a world center of culture and its downfall; the appearance of an intelligent race of apes that enslaves mankind until they fall and mankind builds new civilizations, creating gigantic artificial brains that first aid and then rule mankind, and finally replaces man with artificially created supermen. This revised mankind moves to Venus, evolving into winged creatures, and after millions of years farther on to Neptune, where mankind finally ends when the sun goes nova. The novel is not fiction in the usual sense of the word; it has no hero, no villain, no central character, no central theme but that of mankind's relationship to its constantly changing environment. It is gigantic in scope, creating, in effect, an entirely new type of fiction. The philosophical concepts in the book are as grandiose as the cosmic sweep—Stapledon was a Doctor of Philosophy, and the author of a number of scholarly philosophical works. It might well be science fiction's most adult and thought-provoking book, transcended only by the same author's *The Star Maker* (1937), a work which describes the history of the entire universe, reducing the cosmic sweep of *The Last and First Men* to an insignificant footnote in the books of history. In this monumental work, Stapledon also succeeds in describing a deity, something that no one has done before or after him. These two works are easily the most original works of science fiction, and their influence on later writers has been tremendous. Stapledon was not only the first to create the Galactic Empires, now so sadly common in the genre, he was the first sf writer to appreciate the thorough alienness of nonhuman creatures, and to base the plot on their alien psychological makeup instead of the usual hard action monster opera.

The theme of following mankind into the distant future

was later used by other writers, notably by Brian W. Aldiss in his collection of stories *Galaxies Like Grains of Sand* (1960) and *Starswarm* (1964). The British sf writer Arthur C. Clarke has written his own highly original variation on Stapledon's idea of the Cosmic Mind in *Childhood's End* (1953) as well as a novel set in a future one billion years hence, *Against the Fall of Night* (1953), later revised as *The City and the Stars* (1956), that obviously is heavily influenced by Stapledon. One might say that in the same way as E. E. Smith opened up the universe, Stapledon opened up time.

True, there had been stories set in the distant future before, the most notable being Camille Flammarion's *Ten Million Years Hence* and H. G. Wells's *The Time Machine*, but whereas all these earlier writers used the distant future as a background for various political or sociological ideas in the Utopian or anti-Utopian vein, or, as in the case of Flammarion, for scientific speculation, Stapledon delineated a future based on terms of its own. It had no connections whatsoever with our world, making it so strange as to be incomprehensible but still logical according to its own terms. Not necessarily good or bad, but *different*. And this might be the greatest contribution of science fiction to modern literature: the ability to appreciate an alien situation not in relation to our own political or sociological situation but to its own unique possibilities.

This is, in fact, what in my eyes makes science fiction unique in contemporary literature: the willingness and ability to step out from the familiar environment and using a more or less alien situation as the basis for a logical sequence of events that might or might not have some relevance to us. This is also what has compelled many science fiction writers to do away with the time-honored literary tools like characterization and such that—while a fantastic tool in the hands of, for example, Dostoevski—never can achieve the same usefulness in science fiction where the central character is not man himself but his environment. In order to describe new things you must have new literary tools. This is also the reason why the "New Wave" authors now find themselves in a dead end; instead of turning to new forms they have turned back to the old literary tools of surrealism, an art form that was dead thirty years ago.

In this respect, I would like to give some space to two science fiction writers who have worked in the field since the formative days, hatching more plots and superbly intelligent ideas than probably any others, as well as minting much of the literary coinage of present-day science fiction. Despite avant-gardism and "New Wave" they are still writing sf, and I believe they will go on doing so long after the most vociferous critics of this "reactionary" and "old-fashioned" science fiction have dropped out. I am referring to Isaac Asimov and Robert A. Heinlein. I can't say I like both of them wholeheartedly, but they are master craftsmen—an art that seems to be waning these days—as well as highly intelligent and original writers who have the whole wide field at their fingertips. Both have a solid scientific background, both became addicted to sf at an early age and were engaged in fan activity, and both made their debut in the same sf magazine, *Astounding*: Asimov with the short story *Marooned off Vesta* in March, 1939, Heinlein with *Lifeline* in August, 1939. (1939 was a good year for new sf writers; the well-known sf author Alfred Bester made his debut that year with the short story *Broken Axiom* in the April issue of *Thrilling Wonder Stories*, and A. E. van Vogt first appeared in sf with *Black Destroyer* in the July issue of *Astounding*.) I do not say that they are typical sf writers, but if one were to put up a gauge for what constitutes a good sf writer, Asimov and Heinlein would come very close to it.

Isaac Asimov, born in Russia in 1920 but a U.S. citizen since 1923, is associate professor of biochemistry at Boston University Medical School, although his teaching duties now are confined to occasional lectures. (His Ph.D. thesis in chemistry, written in 1948, was entitled "The Kinetics of the Reaction Inactivation of Tyroserose During Its Catalyzing of the Aerobic Oxidation of Catechol.") He is the author of well over one hundred books ranging from *Understanding Physics*, a layman's guide to physics, to science fiction. His most well-known sf work is probably the *Foundation* trilogy, already mentioned, a wide-sweeping epic telling of the decline and fall of a Galactic Empire, bearing more than passing similarities to Edward Gibbon's work on the Roman Empire, as well as obvious influence by Toynbee and other philosophers of history.

His robot stories have influenced the whole field; his "Three Laws of Robotics" can now be found wherever robots congregate, and it is indubitably thanks to him that the myriads of clanking robots that once galloped over the pages of the sf magazines now have been made much more credible.

The robot occupies a great part of Asimov's production, with collections like *I, Robot* (1950) and *The Rest of the Robots* (1964), and novels like *The Caves of Steel* (1954) and its sequel *The Naked Sun* (1957). In both these novels Asimov has used one of the most common themes of science fiction, that of the future super-city à la Metropolis; by utilizing a mass of small details he succeeds in making the city real, alive and breathing, as it were. The whole complicated city machinery is described in minute detail, focusing on the everyday routine in a city that bears no resemblance at all to our world. The plot in both novels is based on crimes carried out in this mechanized world—but crimes that are a function of the environment, not some cloak-and-dagger adventure loosely pasted on a fantastic background. The crime would be unthinkable in any environment other than this highly advanced city, and Asimov unfolds the story with murderous logic, at the same time giving a highly convincing picture of a way of life that we might be heading into right now.

Even in the way-out imaginative stories, the plot becomes credible by Asimov's accentuating of the situation's effect upon men. One example is *The End of Eternity* (1955), in which a strange temporal organization hovers somewhere outside of the flow of time, guarding time against such anachronisms as, for example, submachine guns in Caesar's time.

Asimov is, despite his thoroughness, a man of grand,

sweeping views. Robert A. Heinlein, on the other hand, is a realist, a man who never would create the Asimovian Galactic Empires. (These Empires pop up now and then in Heinlein's novels, granted, but they are light-years removed from the majestic sweep of Asimov.) Heinlein was born in 1907 in Butler, Missouri, started as an engineer, then switched over to a military career from which he retired, due to illness, as permanently disabled, in 1934. After holding a variety of jobs he finally started writing science fiction in 1939. He has never left it since.

Heinlein writes highly enjoyable and thought-out adventures set in the future, distinguished above all by the brilliantly worked-out future societies in which the action takes place. The future he delineates is practical, down-to-earth, and filled with details. His success here might be due to his technique of, to quote Sam Moskowitz, "taking the future for granted," by making his characters understand their particular environment and behave according to this. His works seem to be narrated by a skillful journalist who is there as it happens, and no sf writer can do better than that.

His political views are frequently berated, tending to be uncomfortably conservative with a lot of *übermenschen* ideology thrown in, but this is usually overshadowed by the quality of his writings. You might not like his societies, but you get interested in them. His *Future History Series* starts with the first Moon shot in *The Man Who Sold the Moon* (1950), financed by a private consortium led by a typical Heinlein hero, a space-crazy multibillionaire (Money is Might in Heinlein's world) of the John Wayne type. The series progresses with a great number of short stories and novels to the very Heinleinesque future six hundred years hence. It is a masterpiece of logical extrapolation and belongs to every true sf fan's standard reading.

The novel *Starship Troopers* (1959), with its naïve worship of the military establishment, is distasteful and excelled only by his *Farnham's Freehold* (1964), a novel of the distant future wherein the Negroes have taken power with no house-trained Uncle Toms in sight. Heinlein's archetypical hero functions as a mouthpiece for Heinlein's anti-Negro philosophy, when he doesn't stand at attention by the flag or tell his children that Charity Begins at Home and It Should Stay There, Dammit. Typical Heinlein is also the novelette *Coventry*, in which all the people in the U.S.A. who do not share the government's opinions are thrown together in gigantic concentration camps (the "love it or leave it" philosophy, worked out to perfection), where life is so bad that the protagonist soon becomes a good U.S. citizen and gets himself a job as a government spy in the camp, ratting on his buddies who are naïve enough to regard him as their friend. The story could be one of a ruthless opportunist feathering his own nest at others' expense; but it is not, at least not in the author's eyes. He is, in Heinlein's eyes, the man who sees the light of reason, and does the only sensible thing.

Heinlein is a man who believes in strict norms, God and Country, but above everything else in Holy Individualism. Socialism is worse than death, and must be fought at all costs. Dictatorships are not good either, but preferable to giving dissenters a say. Heinlein has embroidered this theme in various ways, e.g. in *Sixth Column* (1941) in which, from Heinlein's point of view, the very untrustworthy Eurasians win the World War and treat the U.S.A. to some inhuman atrocities à la Vietnam, until a group of Army men from a strongpoint beneath a mountain use religion and some devious science to scare away the ugly intruders. The novel *Revolt in 2100* (1953) describes a future religious dictatorship—a well-used idea in sf, but here more logically utilized than usual—in which the Church uses all the modern paraphernalia with mass communication, hysterical mobs and a screaming demagogue to keep the citizenry at bay.

The Moon is a Harsh Mistress (1966) describes a Moon colony where most of our accepted norms are outdated, where the patriarchate is fully developed (a typical trait of Heinlein: women are seldom considered as anything more than pieces of flesh in his worlds; in fact, there is an absolute nonportrayal of any reasonable female), and the war cry is *There ain't no such thing as a free lunch!* (TAN-

STAAFL!) meaning that charity stays at home and you can never hope to get help from anybody: goodness is weakness, altruism is treason, honesty is death. The Moon colony honors absolute freedom, the right of anyone to do whatever he wants and to hell with the weaker and poorer ones, and soon enough trouble brews with Earth. The protagonist, a tough John Wayne-ish engineer of the typical Heinlein model, straightens out the situation with the aid of an omniscient *deus ex machina* in the form of a computer, and life on the Moon goes on as before. The novel gives a terrifying picture now propagandized by, among others, the U.S. demagogue Ayn Rand.

Stranger in a Strange Land (1961) is in many respects an antithesis to most of Heinlein's fiction. It is by far his most best-selling novel, telling the story of Valentine Michael Smith, sole survivor of the first expedition to Mars, born and educated there, who returns to Earth as a superman. He carries a brand-new religious concept with him, the way of "Grok," and develops into a modern Messiah figure, ultimately killed by his fellow men. The novel is sparkling with humor, satire and wit, and is both shocking and immensely entertaining, a very mature work. We can still glimpse the auctorial Heinlein behind Valentine Michael Smith's message of love and devotion and freedom, and I distrust this novel as much as his other ones, but there is no doubt that this is a magnificent piece of work, creating a fabulous many-faceted world inhabited by real characters. It has been a magnificent "underground" best seller, probably due to its mysticism and "peace" message brought forth in the Martian religion. Also, Valentine Michael Smith is the super-hippie of all super-hippies.

Mr. Smith of Mars is yet one more of Heinlein's supermen; his heroes are always a cut above the common people. With the mind of a computer as in *Starman Jones* (1953) there is a boy who has a photographic memory and rises in ranks to astrogator (space navigator) because he just happens to have every astrogator table in his head. Or a broad-shouldered patriarchal pioneer of the old Wild West type as Mr. Farnham of *Farnham's Freehold*. They are described as human beings, with human faults, including self-pity and an ability to make mistakes, but they always stand heads above other people. They have *talents*. As a critic has pointed out, all Heinlein's protagonists are at bottom Heinlein himself, and Heinlein likes himself.

Heinlein might be a reactionary, but he is never false. He depicts the future as a function of today; it is a dangerous world, an insecure world where nothing is like ours and where nothing can be taken as certain, but it is always exciting and it promises unlimited possibilities for those who dare to grapple with it on its own terms. I believe Heinlein has done more than any other writer to prepare youth for the big adventure, the Future. Whatever can be said about Heinlein in other respects, this is enough to give him an exceptional position in the genre.

Heinlein has, of course, another side, the side that creates intellectual puzzles like *By His Bootstraps* or the malicious story *Magic, Inc.*, in which he derides the whole U.S. economic system by putting magic into everyday business life, complete with insurance against black magic, witch doctors and visits to the Devil to complain about unhealthy business methods. This is a lighthearted, witty Heinlein using a fantastic assumption for all its worth, never for a moment caring whether it is possible or not. It is great fun even if you don't believe a word of it, and this is surely a sign of successful suspension of disbelief: the art of creating improbable worlds and inviting the reader in, making him happy to join the fun.

Asimov and Heinlein as well as other "old" sf writers are today regarded by the way-out "New Wave" advocates as old-fashioned and highly illiterate. In short, they ain't hip enough. The "New Wave" of today is turning back to the old surrealism of Alfred Jarry and Boris Vian, which of course is new for science fiction, although hardly new as a literary technique. The main difference is, I think, a difference in attitudes, a basic distrust on the part of the "New Wave" in the theme of inevitable change that is the undercurrent of all good science fiction. What the "New Wave" seems to say is, in effect, that if it is new, it must be bad, and if it looks good it must surely hide a rotten core somewhere.

We have many examples of this in the "New Wave" which represents those former sf readers and writers who have given up hope for humanity and believe the world is doomed in the next thirty years, using the media to voice their distrust in anything that smacks of deviation from the old, sure ways of life and conduct. We can see this difference clearly in most experimental sf of today, as compared to the more "orthodox" sf. The "New Wave" of today is very, very pessimistic, whereas science fiction in general is not. There is of course a lot of social criticism in all science fiction, there must always be, but it is usually of the constructive kind, offering new ideas and sometimes solutions, not just death-wishes.

To take just one example, Frederik Pohl has written a number of biting and very funny stories dealing with future societies that have backfired in some way. In *The Midas Plague* (1951) it is overproduction (paradoxically a problem even today, despite the fact that most of the world is starving). The whole economic system has been turned upside-down as the result of robots taking over production and raising the output to such a degree that all human citizens have a set quota for consumption. Rich people are, of course, privileged with low consumption quotas and are permitted to live in humble houses and even apartments, while the poor people are forced to drag out their existence in magnificent marble palaces, surrounded by hundreds of robot servants, perfumed fountains, ten-course dinners and billions in the bank. The actual plot of the story (a minor part of the story, actually; here is a typical example of background idea and presentation overshadowing plot) centers around young Miss Cherry Elon, who to the accompaniment of a lot of ominous mutterings from her very rich parents, marries a poor but ambitious young man who only has a billion-dollar palace and countless robots to offer her. The marriage is on the verge of breaking up, lock, stock and barrel, due to little Cherry's inability to cope with this dreary life, when the husband finds a brilliant solution to the whole overproduction problem, and immediately gets promoted to a ramshackle hut in the most posh part of the city. The robots simply are furnished with a consuming instinct that can be varied according to need (like introducing a yearning for midi or maxi skirts when the weaving-mills want to sell more cloth). The robots start consuming like mad, and the poor humanity can return to a more natural consumption level. Happiness reigns.

This story is a wry comment upon contemporary occurrences, and yet entertaining—a good sf story in all respects. It also has the daring to treat a serious problem with humor, something we'll never find in a "New Wave" version of the same idea. I have seen a fair number of "New Wave" stories dealing with the overproduction specter, and there hasn't been one not ready to throw in the towel from the very beginning. This goes for all other anti-Utopias as well. This might be the intellectual, modern way of seeing things; I call it defeatism, and the obvious solution to the problem in Pohl's story would be to get high on booze and acid and drop out as fast as possible. Pohl doesn't see it that way. I prefer Pohl—for many reasons.

I might have given the impression that I regard everything new in sf as bad; I do not. On the contrary, the sixties have seen a tremendous rise of literary as well as imaginative qualities of science fiction, due mostly to experimentation with new ideas by old hands at the genre, such as Philip K. Dick, Robert Sheckley and Robert Silverberg, as well as new writers like Roger Zelazny and Samuel R. Delany. Zelazny in particular is a prose-poet of singular power, the unlikely combination of the dreamlike poetry of Dylan Thomas and the narrative powers of Ernest Hemingway. He is an example of the new breed of sf writers who are turning from what we might call the "hardware" of outer space and the mechanical devices exploring these frontiers to the "software" of man's mind, the "inner space" of thought and feeling, the subjective experience of the environment. His Nebula-awarded novelette *He Who Shapes* (1964), later enlarged as the novel *The Dream Master* (1966), is based on the theme of psychology engineers being able to enter a man's mind, to experience his thoughts, to live in his dreams and control them.

Typical of this new trend also is the theme of a recent novel by Brian W. Aldiss, *Barefoot in the Head* (1969), which is set in a Europe bombed back to the stone age of thought and feeling by a very new kind of catastrophe: not hydrogen bombs or robots or any of the other environment-changing machinery, but by the "Acid Head War," something that changes man's mind rather than his environment. This novel, like many other "New Wave" novels, is essentially a novel of drop-out, giving little in the way of constructive analysis of the contemporary scene or the imaginary future, but it is a promising step out from the well-trodden paths of sf, which might prove to be very rewarding. Aldiss is here, in fact, using the old catastrophe theme of sf in an entirely new way, pointing out consequences that have never before been suspected.

Significant of this is Aldiss' handling of the well-used theme of overpopulation in the novelette *Total Environment* (1968), which deals with a vast experiment in the effects of maximum population density. By furnishing this experiment with an unlimited food supply, Aldiss has drastically altered the traditional formula for stories dealing with overpopulation, creating a whole new condition and using this as the basis for sociological and psychological speculation. The changes wrought by these assumptions come in the inhabitants' minds, rather than in their physical behavior. It is interesting to note that Aldiss' experiment actually has been performed by Dr. John Calhoun of the National Institute of Mental Health, using mice and unlimited food and water. These experiments, as reported in a national news magazine (37), in fact have turned out much more horrible than those of Brian Aldiss.

So, once again we have speculative writers standing on the frontiers of actual research, looking forward. The rockets of the thirties and the forties have had their time; new symbols and themes are needed. If these new themes can be found in "inner space," then let it be so. But constructive, please.

SCIENCE FICTION: WHAT IT'S ALL ABOUT

A great deal of science fiction today consists of social criticism in one form or another, and as I have already said, it is mainly defeatist in attitude. They are, as C. M. Kornbluth has pointed out, "not statements which may be proved true or false as the reader might seem fit, but exclamations telling the reader how the writer feels and not what he thinks. Insofar as they are social criticism they are shrieks: 'Everything is bad! I'm frightened by this rotten world! I can't do anything; it's all like a nightmare! Save me, somebody, save me!' " (38)

This kind of querulousness leaves at least me rather cold, being nothing but the fear of change all over again—and this in a literary genre whose strength and fascination lies in its ability to face change and make the best of it. The inability of certain writers and editors of science fiction to face our changing world with anything but screaming fear has led to the paradoxical situation of editors to judging, to quote Damon Knight, "the quality of a science fiction novel (as) inversely proportional to the amount of science fiction in it."

Science fiction stands out by its ability to cope with the changes of environment, values and conduct, and if you take that away, you have nothing left except a literature screaming bloody murder at the slightest hint of anything new and unsuspected. This is retreating to the warm, secure womb, and I definitely do not think that it is science fiction's business to do so. The world and the human race are now faced with very real and pressing problems, and what we need are solutions or attempts at solutions, not literary drop-outs. It is, of course, easier to blame someone else (society, one's mother, whatever comes handiest) and turn anti-intellectual than to face the problems and try to take a part in the inevitable change, doing something about it. Thus we have the "New Wave," refusing to do anything but scream for help because they can't cope with the world in which they are living. This literature is, of course, significant and even interesting as a sign of the sickness in our time, but I think we've had a little too much of it during the last years.

Illustration by Tove Jansson for
the Swedish edition of *The Hobbit*.

141

SCIENCE FICTION: WHAT IT'S ALL ABOUT

At its best, science fiction is a magnificent vehicle for social analysis, as well as entertainment, pointing out bad solutions and offering new ones, speculating on the end-products of processes already at work, experimenting with entirely new concepts and their effects on man and his world. This is something that no other branch of fiction can do, and this is enough to give science fiction a unique position. The main body of science fiction is indeed doing this, and anti-future, anti-change and anti-man writings of the "New Wave" type are really nothing but a small, though extremely vociferous, footnote to the genre. Science fiction cannot but gain by experimentation with new forms and ideas, but this experimentation should be done with an adult mind, looking forward into the future rather than running away from it. The moment we lose our Sense-of-Wonder and become scared instead of interested in what we see, be it good or bad, and refuse to cope with these new assumptions to the best of our abilities, we won't have science fiction anymore.

7. WOMEN, ROBOTS AND OTHER PECULIARITIES

Science fiction is on the whole a very progressive literature when it comes to freedom and equality, but there are things in the field that can make even the most narrow-minded prelate look like a veritable light-bearer. Foremost among these dark spots stands *Woman*. Robots and green monsters are often treated in a way that is far from enviable, but robots nowadays are socially acceptable and usually described as man's best friends; and green monsters have, since the merry monster days of the pulp magazines, risen in the ranks to wise creatures equipped with all human attributes except appearance. The woman in science fiction remains what she was, a compulsory appendage. I will give a telling example from the leading sf magazine *Analog* (February 1969). The cover of this particular issue is adorned with a fair young woman, holding a cute little baby in her motherly arms. The picture relates to the novelette *A Womanly Talent*, written by Anne McCaffrey (a woman, mind you!) considered one of the best sf writers of today. The novelette contains an illustrative picture of a space woman's everyday life. Lajos, the hero, has come to Ruth to get some consolation after a failure:

Ruth transferred her attention to his muscular back. She loved the line of him, the broad double plateau of his shoulder blades with the small mounds of hard muscle, the graceful curve that swept down to the narrow waist, the hollow of his spine, the Grecian beauty of his buttocks. She quickly suppressed a flare of desire. This was not the time to intrude sex on his personal anguish. And she knew that her intense sexual

143

hunger for him stemmed from a yearning for the child of his seed. A daughter, tall and fair, with Lajos's dimples in her cheek. A son, strong-backed and arrogant, with thick black straight hair.

This hunger for his child was so primal, it paralyzed the sophistication overlaid by education and social reflexes. Nowadays a woman was expected to assume more than the ancient duties required of her. Nowadays, and Ruth smiled to herself, the sophists called those womanly talents Maintenance, Repair and Replacement, instead of housekeeping/cooking, nursing and having babies, but the titles didn't alter the duties nor curb the resurgent desires. And when you got down to it, men still explored new ground, even if it were alien ground, and defended their homes and families. (39)

This is, in a nutshell, the most modern view on womanhood in science fiction. The holy cry seems to be "Woman, know thy place!" and even though women usually are present in the space ships, they are generally treated like some kind of inferior creature. Love scenes between hero and heroine are generally not encouraged, even though some sort of marital bliss usually is hinted at as a reward for faithful service. Here is an example from one of the Space Opera classics, Edmond Hamilton's *The Comet Kings* (1942), a Captain Future adventure, in which we find the brave Captain in a moody scene with Joan, his faithful yes-woman:

"Why Joan, what's the matter?

"Oh, nothing—I'm just foolish," she muttered. "But I can't help feeling a little sorry to leave the comet."

He did not understand. Joan looked up at him with deep emotion in her fine eyes.

"Out there, Curt, you belong to the whole System. I know you love me, but duty comes first—your obligation to use your scientific powers to help the System peoples.

"But if we'd been forced to remain on the comet world, cut off forever from the outside, nothing else would have come between us. It could have been a paradise for us. But it's lost now."

Curt Newton bent and kissed her.

"Joan, don't feel like that. Someday when our work is done, we'll find our own paradise. I know a little asteroid that's waiting for us. It's just like a garden. Someday."

With chintz curtains in the living room and Colonial furniture, no doubt. Anything to make the little wife happy. The sex roles are as unyielding as the metal in the space ship's hull; emancipation is an unknown word. In a world where women at last are beginning to be recognized as human beings, science fiction still clings to the views of last century. If a daring member of one of the current women's liberation movements stepped out into the men's world of the future, she'd probably be shot on sight. The Gothic writer Horace Walpole once dubbed the suffragettes "hyenas in petticoats," and while the sf writers of today are not that bad, they still hold to the old mother-children-and-kitchen image as far as women are concerned. They might be bright and look like *Playboy* bunnies, but don't let that fool you. What they really want is home and husband and kids, and their bodies and occasional brains are nothing but the bait to lure the man into the trap. If she persists in being a career woman, she must be queer in some way like, for example, Dr. Susan Calvin in Isaac Asimov's noted robot series, who loves robots more than men.

The classic function of the woman, as depicted in gaudy colors on the covers of the pulp magazines, was to follow the hero as a kind of reverentially listening Dr. Watson. By her obvious ignorance of the most elementary things she would give the hero the opportunity to launch into long explanations as to why the devious Hrrgians had invaded the Solar System, or the workings of the new Space Warp. Betweentimes she should be abducted by some horrible green monster with lots of fangs, which lovingly wound its tentacles around her appetizing form and disappeared with her. The hero himself only grudgingly wound his tentacles around the heroine, who, notwithstanding, loved him with a hopeless (and virtuous) passion, longing for the sweet moment when the mighty man would give up his toil for the Universe and retire with her to the already mentioned paradisal asteroid.

In her private life, the female appendage usually was daughter to some ancient professor with long white hair and thick spectacles who earned his keep by inventing curious machines now and then. In practice, she mostly served as an eye-catcher on the magazine covers, dressed in some very curious and decidedly unsafe transparent spacesuit and some scant lingerie. The artist Earle Bergey was especially noted for his seminude cover girls. One of his covers for *Startling Stories* (Winter 1945) shows the fair-haired girl looking on at some sort of robot gathering, dressed in nothing but boots, a bikini and a space helmet. Without air tubes, it should be noted. The hero must be more shy, or just more intelligent, because he sports a bulging spacesuit that covers everything except his lecherous hands.

So much for the pulp science fiction. It has been about the same ever since.

It has always been a constant source of surprise to me that science fiction, which has given so much attention to understanding and respecting other races and life forms so utterly, seldom has seen fit to be just a teeny-weeny bit progressive when it comes to the sexes. Probably this indifference to females as being anything other than decorative appendages has its source in the early sf that, above all, concerned itself mainly with scientific adventures and speculations, not human beings. The hero/scientist was important, as were the usual standard equipment of robots, space ships, aliens and so on. The woman, except as a concession to the demand for some puerile love interest, was not. Perhaps some of the younger readers of the magazines appreciated the sight of the scantily dressed females on the magazine covers, but that was about all. Women were purely decorative, period. That the woman's position in the society could be discussed and used as a basis for speculative fiction never occurred to the otherwise progressive writers. It has hardly

Although women occupy minor roles in most science fiction, they often show up idealized on the covers of fan magazines, as the above example indicates.

occurred to some of them yet. Robert A. Heinlein, who still firmly believes that women are fit only for the harem, is a striking example of this. Even a progressive writer like H. G. Wells, who had firm opinions regarding woman's right to personal and sexual freedom, kept his sf writing free of any ideas to this end. The debate around women's liberation was reserved for novels like *Ann Veronica*.

This, of course, led to making the woman in sf into a piece of furniture, to be admired and—perhaps—used, but never to be taken seriously. "An embracing machine without any trace of either intellectual life or creative talent," as the Swedish artist Siri Derket has put it. One of the most prominent sf writers, Isaac Asimov, voiced some years ago many sf writers' attitude toward the female, in *Startling Stories'* letter column:

> There is a great deal of significance, I think, in the fact that the four stories in the September issue of *Startling Stories* did not contain a single female character. Of course, I would be the last to claim that all females be abolished. Women, when handled in moderation and with extreme decency, fit nicely in scientifiction *at times*. However, the September issue goes to prove that good stories can be written even with the total absence of the weaker sex.
>
> There are some fans that claim "human interest" a necessity in stf, since otherwise stories degenerate into uninteresting scientific or semi-scientific recitals. That is a very correct stand, or would be if it were not that these one-track-minded fans know no other form of human interest than the love interest. (40)

It should be pointed out that this was said thirty years ago; but it is significant that the attitude in science fiction as a whole has changed very little since then. During these thirty years, science fiction has changed in every respect: the blasters have made room for penetrating psychological criticism and debate, and of the sf writers of that time, only a handful are active today. Yet the woman is the same now as she was then. She shouldn't be in sf in the first place. If she nevertheless manages to get into it, she shall know her place. Period.

Of course, I am not demanding that all science fiction should contain women or even treat them as human beings —I am decidedly against stock characters, and those sf writers who think that women should be kept in the harem should of course be allowed to keep them there—in their fiction—but I find it curious, to say the very least, that only a very small number of sf writers have bothered to base stories upon the assumption that the woman's position might be different in another society. And I mean *entirely* different, not just some reactionary viewpoint taken up and used all over again, like the walking and talking wombs of Edward Bellamy's *Looking Backward* or Robert A. Heinlein's *The Moon is a Harsh Mistress*.

Frederik Pohl and Cyril M. Kornbluth devote a part of their novel *Search the Sky* (1954) to a wry, tongue-in-cheek account of a world run by women, the result of an interstellar colonization that has lost contact with Earth. The result is an upside-down society in which men are regarded as a sort of inferior creature, fit only for procreation purposes and the like. They have no voting rights, and career men are frowned upon, even though there are radical women around who have "got nothing against men in business; that's old-fashioned prejudice." Nevertheless, the (male) protagonist is regarded as little more than a talking parrot when he starts to explain things to a leading businesswoman. She admires not him, but the heroine. "You've got a right to be a proud woman, believe me," she says. "The way he got through it, without a single stumble! Never saw anything like it in my life."

It is Earth all the way down to the last little detail, just with the roles of man and woman exchanged. Women always try to seduce some poor young man, and, if pregnancy results, he is forced to pay her a monthly allowance. The protagonist is even subjected to an attempted rape by a drunk (female) truck driver. And suddenly he isn't a hero any longer—he's just a decorative piece of furniture, to be admired and used. If this seems farfetched, look around you. You have it everywhere here and now, only it is the other way around.

Robert Sheckley has taken up another aspect of woman vs. society in a short story, *A Ticket to Tranai* (1955), a story which, apart from giving some intelligent comments upon man's love/hate relationship with his machines—the protagonist gets a job disimproving robots, because they're so good they're causing inferiority feelings in their human operators—shows the ultimate in man-wife relationship. Wives are kept solely for entertainment. Betweenwhiles they are kept in a stasis field that makes them nonexisting until the husband decides he needs company; then she is available at the flick of a switch. This also makes the women very long-lived, as they do not age while in the stasis field. The hero, a young, innocent man with the significant name of Goodman, fresh from Earth and on his way to marry a young woman, finds the idea disgusting. "It hardly seems fair to the woman," he says.

> Melith laughed. "My dear friend, are you preaching the doctrine of equality of the sexes? Really, it's a completely disproved theory. Men and woman just aren't the same. They're different, no matter what you've been told on Terra. What's good for men isn't necessarily—or even usually—good for women."
>
> "Therefore you treat them as inferiors," Goodman said, his reformer's blood beginning to boil.
>
> "Not at all. We treat them in a *different* manner from men, but not in an *inferior* manner. Anyhow, they don't object." (41)

They surely don't. One of the reasons for this might be that they can be sure to outlive their husbands by a couple of hundred years; and of course they are spared the toil and drudgery of everyday life, being taken out of stasis only on special occasions: romantic moonlit evenings, parties and the like. Young Mr. Goodman, refusing to see the merits of this system, disconnects the stasis generator immediately

150

after the marriage ceremony, giving his dear young wife in return the wonderful life of a suburban housewife. It ends, predictably, in catastrophe, when she meets the traveling salesman who promises to take her out of the stasis field once a week at maximum. Exit good intentions.

The late British sf writer John Wyndham (John Beynon Harris, 1903-1969) takes up the problem in his novel *Consider Her Ways* (1961). Here, all men have died after being exposed to a deadly virus, originally intended as a rat poison. Women, however, turning out to be immune, create a peculiar world, reminiscent of an ant-community, with queens, workers, soldiers and so forth. Procreation is done by way of parthenogenesis. A woman in our time gets in mental contact with one of these future women. The ensuing dialogue, which takes up most of the novel, might not give much new blood to the debate, but it is still a healthy sign of science fiction recognizing the problem.

At the beginning of the twentieth century women were starting to have their chance to lead useful, creative, interesting lives. But that did not suit commerce: it needed them much more as mass-consumers than as producers—except on the most routine levels. So Romance was adopted and developed as a weapon against their further progress and to promote consumption, and it was used intensively.

Women must never for a moment be allowed to forget their sex, and compete as equals. Everything had to have a "feminine angle" which must be different from the masculine angle, and be dinned in without ceasing. It would have been unpopular for manufacturers actually to issue an order "back to the kitchen," but there were other ways. A profession without a difference, called "housewife," could be invented. The kitchen could be glorified and made more expensive; it could be made to seem desirable, and it could be shown that the way to realize this heart's desire was through marriage. . . .

The air was filled with frustrated moanings. Women

maundered in front of microphones yearning only to "surrender," and "give themselves," to adore and to be adored. The cinema most of all maintained the propaganda, persuading the main and important part of their audience, which was female, that nothing in life was worth achieving but dewy-eyed passivity in the strong arms of Romance. The pressure became such that the majority of young woman spent all their leisure time dreaming of Romance, and the means of securing it. They were brought to a state of honestly believing that to be owned by some man and set down in a little brick box to buy all the things that the manufacturers wanted them to buy would be the highest form of bliss that life could offer. . . .

You see, the great hopes for the emancipation of women with which the century had started had been outflanked. Purchasing-power had passed into the hands of the ill-educated and highly-suggestible. The desire for Romance is essentially a selfish wish, and when it is encouraged to dominate every other it breaks down all corporate loyalties. The individual woman thus separated from, and yet at the same time thrust into competition with, all other women was almost defenseless; she became the prey of organized suggestion. When it was represented to her that the lack of certain goods or amenities would be fatal to Romance she became alarmed and, thus, eminently exploitable. . . . Thus, she became, in a new, a subtler way, more exploited, more dependent, and less creative than she had ever been before. (42)

From this female point of view, there is a short step to the male one, brilliantly exemplified in the before-mentioned Sheckley story. It is obviously written in jest, but it carries a good deal of truth, using as well the science fiction media to its fullest extent. A piece of advice given to Mr. Goodman at the wedding is especially revealing of the prevalent male attitude. Compare this to the quote from John Wyndham's novel:

ADVICE TO A NEW HUSBAND

You have just been married and you expect, quite naturally, a lifetime of connubial bliss. This is perfectly proper, for a happy marriage is the foundation of good government. But you must do more than merely wish for it. Good marriage is not yours by divine right. A good marriage must be worked for!

Remember that your wife is a human being. She should be allowed a certain measure of freedom as her inalienable right. We suggest that you take her out of stasis at least once a week. Too long in stasis is bad for her orientation. Too much stasis is bad for her complexion and this will be your loss as well as hers.

At intervals, such as vacations and holidays, it's customary to let your wife remain out of stasis for an entire day at a time, or even two or three days. It will do no harm and the novelty will do wonders for her state of mind.

Keep in mind these few common-sense rules and you can be assured of a happy marriage.

> — By the Government
> Marriage Council. (43)

Robert Sheckley is an exceptional man in many respects; this is written as a satire. Most other sf writers apparently believe that this way of treating women not only is sound but also desirable.

Then we come to sex in science fiction. This is easily dealt with, because it occurs very, very seldom, and then in a very immature way. Sex in science fiction is for procreation purposes only, and as such merely hinted at. Sex for sheer pleasure is almost unknown. Granted, science fiction has come a long way since the pulp age when Theodore Sturgeon seemed to be the only sf writer to understand that man (and even woman) was equipped with a sex drive. Most sf writers haven't realized this yet; it will be a stunning

153

shock for them when they do. One of the utterly few sf works that I know of, dealing with heterosexual sex for the pleasure of it, is a short story by Frederik Pohl, *Day Million* (1966); and that is a mighty strange love story by any standards. The young lovers use machines to do the job for them. It should also be noted that this particular story first was published in *Rogue*, a men's magazine, not in an sf one.

And if you, against all odds, should get a perfectly normal couple to do the thing without the aid of sophisticated machinery, you can bet it is described in a way that changes the tender love act into some revolting parody of human love. In Anne McCaffrey's already-mentioned novelette *A Womanly Talent*, we find a love scene described, not as one would expect, as a tender act of love, something to be cherished and to be happy for, but reduced to the vibrations of a couple of needles in a "coital graph," supervised by a couple of white-smocked, bored voyeurs:

> Op Owen glanced at the two graphs, the needles reacting wildly in response to the sexual stimuli mutually enjoyed. Lajos's graph showed the normal agitated pattern; Ruth's graph matched his except for the frenetic action of the needle, trying valiantly to record the cerebrally excited and conflicting signals its sensitive transistors picked up. The needle gouged deep into the fragile paper, flinging its tip back and forth. . . .
> (44)

"That was most incredible. The most prodigious performance I have ever witnessed," one of the white-smocked voyeurs gasps when the meter dance has subsided. I agree with him, but for quite different reasons: I think it's sickening.

Anne McCaffrey is in every respect a thinking woman and an intelligent writer who surely can do much better than this, and I am inclined to regard this example as what I would like to call the sf contamination, for this way of reducing the sex act to a mechanical, emotionless electronic copulation is an attitude found everywhere in the genre. It might be partly attributed to the genre's preoccupation with mechanical devices and a subsequent disregard for everything human and emotional, but the main reason is that the genre as a whole is so puritanical that it runs away and hides, screaming with fear, at the sight of a penis. Not that there aren't exceptions, but they are extremely scarce. As for realizing that love and sex are motivating forces of man, handling the theme with tenderness, not as a gimmick but as something beautiful, there's only Theodore Sturgeon and perhaps one or two more. And Sturgeon's stories of this kind are very marginally science fiction.

William Tenn has described the very complicated sexual system of a species that has no less than seven sexes in *Venus and the Seven Sexes* (1949), a hilarious story that depicts a truly alien way of propagating the species, and the same author's *The Masculine Revolt* (1965) is set in a not so future U.S.A. where the women rule and resistance starts with the introduction of the codpiece as a part of men's attire. "MEN ARE DIFFERENT FROM WOMEN!" say the ads. "Dress *differently!* Dress *maculinist!* Wear Polyglow Men's Jumpers with the *Special Pollyglow Codpiece!*" This leads immediately to the war of the sexes, in which the men strengthen themselves with slogans like "Behind every successful woman there stands an unsuccessful man!" and "A man who enjoys no power during the day cannot be powerful at night. An impotent man in politics is an impotent man in bed. If women want lusty husbands, they must first turn to them as heroic leaders."

This story is an intelligent satire on the heavily enforced sex roles of man and woman today, done with a great deal of humor, but it is one of the very few works of science fiction to use the theme of sex vs. society.

Philip José Farmer, the only U.S. writer I know of that ever has seriously mixed science fiction and pornography, jumped into prominence in the sf field with his (decidedly unpornographic novel *The Lovers* (1952) which dealt with sexual relations between a human male and an extraterrestrial insect that had developed a protecting mimicry exactly like a woman. The moral aspects are interesting, but the story is weighted down by the usual monster and blaster ballet. Farmer later wrote a number of short stories dealing with sexual relations between extraterrestrials as well as between humans and extraterrestrials, that might be the most intelligent and mature stories of this kind in science fiction. They were later collected in book form as *Strange Relations* (1960).

Kurt Vonnegut, Jr., the most biting satiricist of science fiction, has based a short story, *Welcome to the Monkey House* (1968), originally published in *Playboy*, on the curious sexual mores of a very near future. The story is set in a future in which overpopulation is acute, seventeen billion human beings are squeezed together on Earth and procreation is the greatest sin possible. Women are organized in desexualized murder patrols—equipped with leather boots, whips and the other usual sado-masochistic paraphernalia—which carry out euthanasia by request. The moral problems of birth control are solved in an ingenious way, which is worthy of describing more closely. It turns out that it is a crime against Nature to use preventives; it must lead to Hell, immortality, the ruin of civilization and so on and so on. The answer to this is a pill that doesn't in any way impair the ability to procreate. It just makes the citizen completely numb from the waist down. The pill is so effective that "you could blindfold a man who had taken one, tell him to recite the Gettysburg Address, kick him in the balls while he was doing it, and he wouldn't miss a syllable." Thus science and morals go hand in hand.

This marvelous way of ethical birth control was thought up by a man who was shocked at seeing some apes copulating in a zoo, and immediately went home to invent a pill that "would make monkeys in the springtime fit things for a Christian family to see." In Vonnegut's story, the savior comes in the form of the depraved Billy the Poet who starts abducting women, taking them off the pill and teaching them the facts of life. This is a good satire on contemporary morality, and I would like to see followers to it.

WOMEN, ROBOTS AND OTHER PECULIARITIES

Homosexuality is a theme that science fiction has kept its hands at a good distance from, even if cautiousness now seems to lessen here as well as in other literary fields. Theodore Sturgeon, one of the utterly few sf writers who isn't afraid of stepping outside the nice, solid and secure parameters of accepted sexual mores has described a smooth-functioning space ship team of two men, bound together by a homosexual relationship of a rather complex nature, in the short story *The World Well Lost* (1953). He included as well a pair of extraterrestrial homosexual creatures, which gives a new, almost tender and (for some people) shocking picture of this type of sexual bond. Predictably, Sturgeon became the target for much attention after writing this story. "I wrote an emphatic sort of tale about some homosexuals," he says, "and my mailbox filled up with cards drenched with scent and letters written in purple ink with green capitals."

Sturgeon has for some years been taking love apart in his stories, to see what makes it tick (love, not Romance; that's quite another thing), and this has resulted in a number of short stories and novels in which the plot is nothing more than a background, a way of making the characters express themselves. Many of his best stories are not science fiction even in the broadest sense of the word. I have an uneasy feeling that this is what makes Sturgeon great: that he doesn't care about gimmicks and environment at all, just the characters themselves. He is the absolute antithesis of Robert A. Heinlein, to whom environment is all and the characters just a part of the overall picture.

Sturgeon has, however, written one undiluted sf novel dealing with different sexual mores: *Venus Plus X* (1960) takes place in a Utopia of sorts, created and inhabited by people who are neither men nor women but something else, who reproduce by grafted uterus and surgery, a kind of artificial parthenogenesis, if you like. It turns out that these people, the Ledom, are people of Earth, ordinary humans who are born as males and females, but artificially altered to their new physical status. In this society, in which sex as we know it does not exist, men court and marry men.

157

Only there are no men or women, just a kind of neuter. The protagonist is broad-minded enough to overlook all this, but when it is disclosed that these people willingly have changed themselves into something that, to him, seem like homosexuals, revulsion immediately takes indulgence's place. "You're the rottenest pack of perverts that ever had the good sense to hide in a hole," he cries.

A sort of rustle went through (the Ledoms)—movement, not sound. Finally, "What changed you, Charlie Johns? You thought very well of us a few hours ago. What changed you?"

"Only the truth."

"What truth?"

"That there is no mutation."

"Our doing it ourselves makes that much difference? Why is what we have done worse to you than a genetic accident?"

"Just because you do it." Charlie heaved a deep breath, and almost spit as he said, "Philos told me how old a people you are. Why is what you do evil? Men marrying men. Incest, perversion, there isn't anything rotten you don't do."

"Do you think," said Mielwis courteously, "that your attitude is unusual, or would be if the bulk of mankind had your information?"

"About a hundred and two percent unanimously." Charlie growled.

"Yet a mutation would have made us innocent."

"A mutation would have been natural . . . We'd exterminate you down to the last queer kid . . . and stick that one in a side-show. That's all I have to say. Get me out of here." (45)

In other words, Sturgeon seems to say (and this makes me fear that the seeming open-mindedness of sf toward the habits of extraterrestrial creatures might not go so deep after all, nor be so spectacular) that alien ways of conduct are all right, as long as those performing them are alien

158

enough, e.g. obviously nonhuman creatures. But if some being resembling you behaves in a way that is revolting to you, then good-bye indulgence and broad-mindedness. The attitude toward extraterrestrial creatures in science fiction during the last thirty years has changed from open hostility to indulgence and sometimes to something bordering on self-contempt, as I will show later on, and I wonder when the habits of man himself will be met with the same open-mindedness.

The more exclusive variants of sex like sadism, masochism, necrophilia, fetishism and so forth can be found in ample measures in the Sword & Sorcery Heroic Fantasy. Despite the cries from some advocates of this type of entertainment that it is pure and virginal and clean, there is sex to be found everywhere; sublimated in various ways, but still there, and in fact the overshadowing ingredient. There is sex—but an immature, infantile sex where the copulation is the sword-fight and the orgasm is the death of the opponent. Women are invariably beautiful, desirable and, beneath their exquisitely sculptured bodies, completely sexless. The symbols of sex (breasts and so forth) are there, but sex itself can be found only in a grotesquely sublimated form. Like in the Wild West story, the sex urge has been transformed into violence and death in the manner of the Marquis de Sade and Leopold von Sacher-Masoch. It is interesting to note the close correspondence between the numerous maltreatments of heroes in Heroic Fantasy by various exotic goddesses, queens, etc., and Krafft-Ebing's description of masochism as:

> . . . a peculiar perversion of the mental Vita sexualis consisting in its victim being overmastered in his sexual feelings and thoughts by the concept of being completely and utterly subjected to the will of a person of the opposite sex, being treated *de haut en bas* and humiliated and even maltreated by that person . . .

After giving the reader his money's worth of masochism, however, the hero can be found getting the upper hand, making the woman obedient and subjective by the power of his penis.

The hero's sword-penis is used a lot, although mostly on other males. The conclusion of Michael Moorcock's saga of Elric of Melniboné even goes as far as to give a beautiful example of auto-eroticism coupled with sex fright:

> He turned his head to one side and saw (the sword) leave the ground, sweep into the air and then rush down on him.
>
> "*Stormbringer!*" he cried, and then the hellsword struck his chest, he felt the icy touch of the blade against his heart, reached out his fingers to clutch at it, felt his body constrict, felt it sucking his soul from the very depths of his being, felt his whole personality being drawn into the runesword . . . Elric of Melniboné, last of the Bright Emperors, cried out, and then his body collapsed, a sprawled husk beside its comrade, and he lay beneath the mighty balance that still hung in the sky.
>
> Then *Stormbringer's* shape began to change, writhing and curling above the body of the albino, finally to stand astraddle it.
>
> The entity that was *Stormbringer* . . . looked down on the corpse of Elric of Melniboné and smiled.
>
> "Farewell, friend. I was a thousand times more evil than thou!" (46)

Philip José Farmer, the unorthodox chronicler of man's hidden desires, has in a recent novel, *A Feast Unknown* (1969), amused himself by taking up all these tendencies and collecting them into one single, morbid and on the whole quite terrifying story dealing with the sex deviations of a Heroic Fantasy Hero.

Farmer is unique in science fiction—for many reasons. There exists—to return to the more everyday kind of sex— a striking example of the results of an attempt to inject some sex in sf. The example is from 1938, but could as well be from a much more recent date. At that time, a new magazine *Marvel Science Stories* tried to jazz up science by a pinch of sex. For that magazine Henry Kuttner, later on one of sf's most influential writers, wrote four stories with a sexy angle. They were published in the first two issues of the magazine, and the unanimous howl of wrath that followed this unprecedented proceeding resulted in the magazine dropping the subject as a hot potato. Kuttner was scandalized for a long time afterward. Science fiction's foremost chronicler, Sam Moskowitz, attempts to account for this phenomenon in his book *Seekers of Tomorrow* (1967), in which he says that:

. . . science fiction is a literature of ideas. The people who read it are entertained and even find escape through mental stimulation. Sex, vulgar or artistic, is available to them in countless forms if they wish it, but the type of intellectual speculation they enjoy is presented only in science fiction. (47)

Which is seductive enough, if you are of the opinion that sex and related activities never can be of any interest from a speculative/intellectual point of view. I do not share this opinion. Neither apparently does Sam Moskowitz, who in a sudden volte-face comes to the conclusion that Philip José Farmer's novel *The Lovers* not only is brilliant science fiction, but that its sex content is what makes it brilliant.

There can be many reasons to this underdevelopment of sex as a serious subject in science fiction, but one of the most important, I believe, is the overshadowing interest in purely scientific innovations that have for so long formed the basis for hard-core science fiction. Psychology and speculations in sexuality didn't belong to the sciences that were fostered by writers and editors.

Also, a great part of the readership of sf has, and is, composed of adolescent boys who regard sex as something filthy (a view shared by many adults as well), and this can't encourage any digressions in sex. To all this is added the fact that most science fiction is written in the U.S.A., and the U.S.A. is perhaps the most puritanical country in the world. With its dread of sexuality, where extravaginal copulation in some states means twenty years in jail for the participants and where fornication is a criminal offense, you can't hope for much open-mindedness regarding sex anywhere, least of all in science fiction.

There are now promising signs of particularly European sf writers recognizing sex as a permissible theme for science fiction, and I hope they will prove to be the start of a new and more human attitude in this respect. Unless, of course, the sf writers all have sublimated away the sex urge into the virile space ships and super-cities of the future.

If we turn to the plight of robots and alien creatures in science fiction, we will immediately find a positive and humane attitude of a kind that very seldom is shown toward females. This has, of course, not always been the case. The precursors of the robots of today's sf—from the mechanical men of the *Arabian Nights* and the Finnish *Kalevala* to the chemically created men like the legends of Golem and Mary Shelley's *Frankenstein*—have invariably turned out to be either machines of war and destruction (Sinbad the Sailor's encounter with robots in the *Arabian Nights* takes place in a tomb, where the robot cuts off the heads of a couple of grave-robbers) or monsters turning against their creators, like the Golem and Frankenstein's monster. The robots of Karel Čapek's play, from which the word *robot* originated (actually, these figures were not what we now call robots, mechanical men, but chemically created creatures, *homunculi*, now known in science fiction as androids) even went as far as to try to wipe out mankind. The opera lover also remembers the female robot Olympia of Jacques Offenbach's *The Tales of Hoffmann* (based on three stories by the German horror master E. T. A. Hoffmann, who decidedly belongs to the anti-man league. These robots were undoubtedly of the anti-scientific type, the anti-development, See-what-a-hell-on-Earth-science-and-progress-is-creating monster.

In present-day sf the robots are mostly depicted as utterly humanitarian creatures with all human virtues and then some. The danger comes from the giant computers or the social system which never can be completely trusted. The robots are often maltreated and subjected to aggression of all possible kinds, but they are always willing to turn the other steel cheek. Unless, of course, they have been programmed wrongly, in which case it obviously is man's fault, not the robot's.

The reason for this sudden change from fear to deep friendliness and esteem for our mechanical brethren can be traced largely back to one single person, who practically single-handedly has mapped out the guiding lines for the specific science fiction science known as Robotics, which now is included in every true sf writer's handbook in future societies. The man is Isaac Asimov.

During the forties Asimov wrote a number of short stories dealing with robots, in which he disarmed the dread of robots so effectively that it never since has been able to show its ugly head again. The robots of Asimov's world were so programmed that they never could do anything unexpected, as distinguished from the women and the androids, who were equipped with all too much of a will of their own. This was accomplished through the Three Laws of Robotics that was—and is—the robot's equivalent to the Ten Commandments. With the significant difference that the robots are constitutionally incapable of breaking their laws:

1. A robot may not injure a human being, or, through inaction, allow a human being to come to harm.
2. A robot must obey the orders given it by human beings except where such orders would conflict with the First Law.
3. A robot must protect its own existence as long as such protection does not conflict with the First or Second Law.

These laws cover all robot activities, with the anxiety for man's safety first and the robot's last. Armed with this feasible precautionary measure, Asimov got to work, writing a number of now classical robot thrillers, usually following the same basic formula:

1. Robot inexplicably violates the First or Second Law.
2. U.S. Robots & Mechanical Men Inc. puts their foremost expert on robots, the robot psychologist Dr. Susan Calvin, on the case.
3. Dr. Susan Calvin proves that the robot has been acting according to programming all along, and in fact not violating the Laws of Robotics.

Sometimes Dr. Susan Calvin is not present, and the formula of the stories might vary somewhat, but the basis is always the same: The robot starts to act peculiarly because it is physically or psychologically stuck, and the human protagonist uses the Laws of Robotics to get it unstuck again. It might seem like a weak formula, but it is decidedly not. Asimov's razor-sharp logic has worked wonders with these stories.

Asimov's collected stories of Susan Calvin and her infallible robots (*I, Robot*, 1950, and *The Rest of the Robots*, 1964) have proven remarkably vigorous, and have to my knowledge never been out of print. This might be due to the fact that Asimov's robots are extremely dependable creatures, almost the only dependable things that exist in science fiction. They bring about a feeling of paternal confidence. And Susan Calvin, the super-intelligent old spinster (sic!) is so genial that you can't dislike the robots she loves so dearly.

Other writers have had much more sordid experiences with robots: e.g. Robert Silverberg with the short story *The Iron Chancellor*, wherein a sturdy household robot is subjected to reprogramming by the dexterous son of the family and ends up beating the whole family to death—but such mishaps are rare.

The robot dread, such as is brought forth in anti-science, anti-Utopian Faustian novels like *Frankenstein* or *R.U.R.*, comes from a time when the Machine still was the thing to fear, and the exploration of nature's darkest secrets still was supposed to take place in the engineer's chromium-shining workshop. Today the fear manifests itself in other forms. Robots never do any harm; they rather resemble nice, friendly St. Bernard dogs. We have a beautiful example of the old, wise, man-loving robots doing their good deeds in Clifford D. Simak's brilliant, award-winning novel *City* (1952). Here we find the robots taking over man's duties when man leaves Earth for a new existence on Jupiter, serving as mentors for the new rulers of Earth, the dogs. Jenkins, the old, old robot, sits before the crackling fire in the old, old mansion of the Websters, absently stroking the silken fur of a dog, dreaming of mankind as the night closes in. The robots don't even behave like man any longer. They *are* man.

Lately we have also seen the appearance of a completely new kind of robot—the machine that is guided by a human brain in such a way that the machine *is* the human being, with the whole human body exchanged for a mechanical one that not only tries to imitate the human body but is made for a specific use. A truck, a tank, a space ship. These *Cyborgs* (which I gather should mean Cybernetic Organisms) are human beings in every respect save appearance; they have an identity, they live, they die, they have hopes, they make mistakes. Some of them even love. (A kind of mechanophilia, I guess.) The U.S. sf writer Anne McCaffrey has written a series of short stories dealing with "Helva, the singing ship," a girl born so deformed that her parents were given the choice of euthanasia for her, or a future as an encapsuled "brain" with a mechanical body. She becomes a star ship, using the ship in exactly the way she would have used her human body, and in time she even falls in love with her captain. The love interest could have been lifted right out from the pages of *True Romance,* but it nevertheless is encouraging to see some human emotion displayed. In fact, Helva must be the most individual character of all the pseudo-humans to turn up in science fiction since the loving robot women of Lester Del Rey's *Helen O'Loy* (1938), who ended up marrying her inventor and lived happily ever after.

But if man has succeeded in taming his robots, this is not the case with the androids. They are disagreeably like man in all respects save the ability to procreate. The androids are manufactured in android factories and are sent out into the society with a production number stamped on the forehead. This number is the only thing that tells them apart from human beings; they even have a sex urge, and they are, like human beings, utterly undependable.

If you liken the robot to a big, nice dog, the android resembles an intelligent, untamable cat. The android's attitude to the commandments is the same as man's: an amused indulgence. The android is.

The android is, in short, the incalculable factor in the equipment that belongs to the sf writer's workshop, and is in this respect filling a function reminiscent of the first robots. He is man's creation, but not his slave. While the rest of man's environment is clearly recognizable as his own creation, a product of his own work, the android is a highly independent being, a constant bad conscience, that desperately tries to break free of man's grip, toward an identity of his own.

It is the guilt for the Negroes, the Indians, the Jews, the Vietnamese, the people of South America and mankind's rape of weaker individuals that comes back in the android. We have a typical example in Algis Budry's cynical story *Dream of Victory*, in which a sizable part of Earth's population consists of androids after an atomic war that has killed most of humanity. After the catastrophe the androids were needed to keep the wheels of civilization going, but with the birth rate soaring, they are eased out from jobs that are needed for humans. The androids, who have built up civilization almost by themselves after the war, are getting desperate at the prospect of being exterminated. The story describes the gradual degradation of an android, Stac Fuoss, from office boss—a position taken over by a human employee—to alcoholic, part-time worker and murderer. Fuoss's tragedy lies not in his debasement but in the fact that his victim is a human being, his mistress. This becomes the start of hate campaigns directed against the androids, as the human's hate, based on guilt feelings, bursts out in the open.

The android functions as sf's contribution to the race debate. The robots pose no problem, because they just obey, and the extraterrestrials are so different from us that some kind of understanding must be found in the end. But the androids—that's another thing. Just like Negroes, Indians, Mexicans and what-have-you, they must be kept down at all costs, never for a moment being permitted to regard themselves as equals to The White Man. Because if they did, they might get it into their heads to demand equal rights, and that would mean the end of White Man's supremacy.

In a postscript to his novel *Venus Plus X*, Theodore Sturgeon quotes the results of a U.S. poll dealing with the equality of humans with differently colored skin. Equality is written into the U.S. Constitution, but this belief is apparently not embraced by many U.S. citizens. Sixty-one percent thought that all men were equal. The same people then were asked if Negroes were equal to whites . . . "and with the very next breath four percent said Yes—and this without the sound of a shifting gear." Now, what would the reaction be if the same question was applied to androids—a creature that in some ways might be superior to man? The instinct for self-preservation demands that these beings are considered inferior, no matter what logic says, and exterminated as soon as possible. If we had androids, the whole world would turn into a gigantic Selma, Alabama.

Clifford D. Simak has written an sf novel, *Time and Again* (1951), in which the androids are waging a sort of guerrilla war against mankind, asking for nothing but the right to stay alive. And the (human) man who thinks that all living creatures have a right to live is hunted by various "Man First" organizations. In a recent novel by Philip K. Dick, *Do Androids Dream of Electric Sheep?* (1969), the androids turn out to be somewhat less than friendly toward mankind, indeed suffering feelings of resentment and inferiority toward the world of organic life. In the world of 1992, when the third world war has left precious little animal life left, this is grave. So there we have a special corps of bounty hunters, particularly the hunter Rick Deckard with the full-time job of tracing and killing androids.

If the sf writer nowadays is inclined to take the side of the android against his tormentors, this is even more the case when we come to the human mutations, usually depicted as being superior to man in some respect. Mutations usually manifest themselves as physical or psychical deformations; but evolution is a chain of mutations, and it seems probable that a new type of man (perhaps suited to an environment polluted by atomic fallout, DDT, detergents and so forth) will evolve and take over the world with the same right as *homo sapiens* took over the world from Cro-Magnon. This would obviously mean trouble.

One of the grand classics of science fiction dealing with this theme is Olaf Stapledon's *Odd John* (1935), which tells of a boy born with super-intelligence, as far removed from man as man is from the apes. He tries to create an ideal state, but is hunted down and ultimately killed. Stapledon later wrote another novel using the same theme, *Sirius* (1944), in which a dog is equipped with human intelligence. It does not work out.

To take other examples, we can take the plight of telepaths in a world of nontelepaths. The classic here is A. E. van Vogt's *Slan* (1940), in which a group of telepaths, the result of a psionic experiment, fight for their existence against the rest of humanity. They win (of course) but not because mankind approves of their gift. Wilson Tucker's *Wild Talent* (1954) is another novel based on this theme. Van Vogt's novel is weighted down by the usual Space Opera paraphernalia and a vague *übermenschen* ideal. Tucker describes his protagonist Paul Breen as an utterly alone, uncertain man, exploited because of his talent by people who hate and despise him. He is possessed by doubts of his right to live in a world that isn't his.

In John Wyndham's novel *The Chrysalids* (1955; also published as *Re-Birth*), the mutants are a couple of children who grow up after the Great War, when large parts of Earth still are deadly wastes, and where the fear of deviating individuals finds typical expression in religion. The Norm is man in God's image, no deviation from the Norm is permitted. *Keep Pure the Stock of the Lord* and *In Purity Our Salvation* are some of the cries with which the clergy fortifies itself for the heretics' fire, murder and other atrocities. A child born with an extra finger or toe must be killed, women who give birth to deviating children are regarded as unclean and are punished. The novel is an indictment of biogtry and a denunciation of conformity, as well as a moving plea for sanity in a world that has seen precious little of sanity when it comes to people behaving differently from ourselves.

Brian Aldiss has used the theme of superman with a difference in a short story, *Visiting Amoeba,* which retells the story of superman succeeding man. This theme has been used many times before, notably by Olaf Stapledon in his magnificent *Last and First Men,* but Aldiss' treatment of the idea is rather different, placing the event in a dim and distant future in which our universe is old and tired, the power is ebbing and humanity lives a ghostlike existence on its millions of worlds. Man's chapter is finished, and beyond the galaxies a new world is created, a young and vigorous world, whose sole inhabitant makes his way to man's central world, followed by chaos and destruction. As the end approaches the central world, he explains the inevitable for the last Emperor:

"I wanted man to be aware of what is happening to him," you said at last. "That much was owed him. I —*we* owed it. You are—our fathers. We are your heirs . . ."

He touched you gently, asking in a firm voice, "What should be told to the people of the Galaxy?"

You looked out over a city now pricked with lights, and up to the evening sky. You found no comfort there or in yourself.

"Tell them again what a galaxy is," you said. "Don't soften it. They are brave. Explain to them once more that there are galaxies like grains of sand, each galaxy a cosmic laboratory for the bold experiments of nature. Explain to them how little individual lives mean compared to the unknown goals of the race. Tell them— tell them that this laboratory is closing. A newer one, with more modern equipment, is opening just down the street." (48)

From this the step is short to our friends the extraterrestrials, lovingly referred to as BEM's, Bug-Eyed Monsters, who without question are the most common denominator of science fiction since the days of Lucian. BEM's mean not only carnivorous monsters of all kinds and sizes, but any extraterrestrial that has the bad luck to come into contact with man. We know them from thousands and thousands of lurid magazine covers adorned with nubile females being menaced in gaudy colors by slimy, drooling, fanged and constantly hungry monstrosities that, inside the magazine, inevitably get blasted to atoms by our other friend the good ol' hero. Lately, the alien has changed somewhat, from the old murderous creature to a being with some curious habits but still a fascinating personality. Sometimes the BEM is the hero, and man is the monster. Things have changed.

The classic BEM appeared in 1897. This was the year of the Stockholm Fair, organized to commemorate King Oscar II's twenty-five-year reign, "the ultimate manifestation of Swedish genius and taste," to quote a panegyric brochure. These were good times, at least for some, and the bourgeoisie partook their table d'hôte at Hufvudstadshotellet at the reasonable price of seventy cents, or a bottle of Muscato Passito at Taverna degli Artisti in the "Old Town" of the Fair. The lower classes could get a plate of "tasty, nourishing soup" at simpler eating-houses for five cents. Such was life in Stockholm. But in England great things were happening: the Martians landed in Surrey.

Those who have never seen a living Martian can scarcely imagine the strange horror of their appearance. The peculiar V-shaped mouth with its pointed upper lip, the absence of brow bridges, the absence of a chin beneath the wedge-like lower lip, the incessant quivering of this mouth, the Gorgon groups of tentacles, the tumultuous breathing of the lungs in a strange atmosphere, the evident heaviness and painfulness of movement, due to the greater gravitational energy of the earth—above all, the extraordinary intensity of the immense eyes—culminated in an effect akin to nausea. There was something fungoid in the oily brown skin, something in the clumsy deliberation of their tedious movements unspeakably terrible. Even at this first encounter, this first glimpse, I was overcome with disgust and dread.

This description is, of course, taken from H. G. Wells's novel *The War of the Worlds* (one of the most one-sided wars of science fiction) which first was published as a serial in the London *Cosmopolitan Gazette* in the secure year of the Stockholm Fair. Wells was not the first writer to make use of hostile extraterrestrials, but he gave them the physical appearance that later on became so sadly notorious. Long after the last of Wells's monsters put its slimy tentacles down to rest, its brothers, sisters, cousins and close friends marched on over the book pages and the movie screens in a never-ending stream. Some looked like overgrown frogs or cabbage-worms, others belonged to the families of insects or snakes or were of some nondescript amorphous shape. Most of them had tentacles which they used to strangle some of the less important members of the space ship's crew. Some BEM's ate humans, others were content just to kill them. All were decidedly anti-human. The future was depicted as a jungle through which man must fight his way, always on guard against hostile aliens of all kinds.

The basic idea, particularly during the years of the pulp magazines, was that the outer world—whether it was space, other civilizations or the future—was hostile toward man, that man must fight against this hostile outer world with all his ingenuity, changing it to suit his needs. The BEM's were a part of the picture, just like interplanetary space and the insecurity that always follows scientific innovations. The friendly aliens were few and far between, and when they appeared it was only to help man against some other bestial creature with wily plans against mankind. Early science fiction almost without exception started from the assumption that we, the human race (usually we, the White Anglo-Saxon Protestants) were in the right, and everything else were ogres.

The reason for all this, I believe, can be traced back to the specific American pioneer romanticism, when the European settlers were opening new frontiers, fighting the aboriginal inhabitants who, understandably enough, resisted being invaded and killed. In America, the aboriginal inhabitants were slaughtered and their civilization raped and looted and destroyed. The new Americans didn't intend to let anyone do the same to themselves. By depicting these aliens as monsters, they can find excuses for the slaughter. The Wild West genre is a typical example of American guilt for the Indian massacres being sublimated into pride of the extermination of these red-skinned monsters, these savages, these maniacs. The science fiction of the pulp era has many similarities with the Wild West stories. The White Man is coming to take over, and if the original inhabitants resist, then exterminate them.

The War of the Worlds is interesting as an example. The British Empire has a history almost as bloody as that of the U.S.A., and the guilt feelings of an intelligent and sensitive Englishman are as heavy as those of an American. The Martians had obviously set their minds to conquer Earth in the same way as the British conquered India, and the result would probably have been as disastrous for the British as it had been for the Indians. The superior war machinery of the British had its counterpart in the Martian's heat rays and robots. Man doesn't stand a chance. When the miracle occurs, it appears in the form of an inconsiderable microbe which is deadly for the Martians. Earth is saved—but not by man. Rightly, we should have been killed just as the Indians were.

Since Wells, mankind has been subjected to a veritable

torrent of monster invasions featuring every conceivable monstrosity and then some, from the usual slimy-tentacled green BEM's from some distant planet or another to the armies of Terran's mutated or prehistoric or just plain impossible beasts, type King Kong, which seem to adorn every movie screen in sight. Most of these creatures belong more to the improbable world of the hard-core horror or fantasy story, giving very little of what I would call the constructive monster approach—that of using the aliens to convey an idea. It should be noted that when the BEM appears in serious science fiction, the emphasis is not put on the horror angle, but on the alien's way of reacting to our environment, or man's attitude to the alien.

The French writer André Maurois has taken up an interesting side of the monster theme in his short story *Fragments of a World History* (1926). This takes place in the world of 1963, which is toppling on the brink of a new world war. The war hysteria is spreading and the war seems inevitable—then someone remembers H. G. Wells's novel. The leading newspaper trusts pool their resources and start to spread bits of mystic news over the world—news of aggression from some unknown source. The carefully worked-out technique in doing this has been used many times since:

1. They evoke fear and belief in mystical and fatal phenomena.
2. They explain that these phenomena are caused by one or more knowingly acting beings, and try to find them.
3. They expose the aggressors, and the war starts.

After a long cogitation it is decided to appoint the inhabitants of the Moon as aggressors, as the Moon obviously is devoid of life, and one month after the "exposing" of the wily aggressors, the propaganda machinery goes at full blast. Carols like "Man first" and "Death to the Moon" echo in the streets, and in Berlin the crowds sing the new chorale *Hate Against the Moon*. In London, the hysteria takes somewhat different outlets, and the most popular ditty is *Oh, Stop Tickling Me, Man in the Moon, Stop Tickling, Stop, Oh! Stop!* A weapon is invented in the form of a heat ray, and "retaliation" is undertaken with a lot of patriotic noise and flag-waving. Then it turns out that the Moon *is* inhabited, and three days later the Selenites strike back. The dreaded war is a fact, but now with an incredibly more dangerous adversary. Exit the good idea.

Maurois depicted his extraterrestrials as thinking creatures that acted logically and in fact were as worthy of respect as any human being; this he brought forth in a number of short stories during the twenties. Maurois was, however, a representative of the European school of speculative fiction, and it took a long time before these ideas got a handhold in the U.S. sf magazines. The breakthrough came with Stanley G. Weinbaum (1900-1935), who during his short life managed to change the prevailing attitude toward the BEM's as cruel monsters to that of seeing them as definite personalities, acting not out of malice, but of a logic of their own; sometimes incomprehensible, but always there. His debut story, *A Martian Odyssey* (1934), was originally written as a parody of science fiction, featuring a number of very curious BEM's. The planet of Mars of Weinbaum's story was furnished with flora and fauna that would have given a scientist ulcers, but it was not the scientific accuracy that was important: it was the fact that for the first time in science fiction, BEM's acted as individual beings. They were mighty strange in all respects—few sf writers have, in fact, managed to create alien beings as strange as Weinbaum's—but they were definite personalities. You could reason with them. At least with those that had the physical abilities of reasoning with someone outside of themselves.

The attitude toward BEM's didn't change overnight as a result of Weinbaum's story, but they have never been the same since, either. They still entertain grave misgivings toward man, sometimes open hostility, but there are always reasons for their attitudes, and perhaps they can be put right without blasters.

A typical example of this attitude is Harry Harrison's novel *Deathworld* (1960), which is set on a planet inhabited by monsters of the most horrible kind possible. Every animal, every insect, every growth on this planet seems to be possessed by one single thought: to kill as many human beings as possible. The colonizers have dug themselves down behind impenetrable steel barriers and venture out from these forts only in armored tanks fitted with flame-throwers, machine guns and cannons. The children are taught to handle guns at the age of four years, and are ruthlessly drilled to act quicker than quick when attacked. One second of inattention means certain death. The colonists arm themselves to their teeth as the attacks become more fierce and harder to repel.

Actually, the planet is not particularly hostile; but all living things are very, very sensitive to aggressive thoughts. And show me the man who isn't aggressive. . . .

This question of communication has been used as the theme for a good many science fiction stories, one of the most far-reaching being a novel by Brian W. Aldiss, *The Dark Light-Years* (1964). An interstellar expedition is confronted with an alien species, the Utods, that possess physical and mental powers greatly above man. They are also quite amiably inclined—but there is one catch. They literally wallow in filth. Their own filth, that is. The prospect of acknowledging these creatures as man's equals or even superiors is too much. Also, the Utods are so alien in their concept of life and logic that no communication is possible. Aldiss is here giving yet another example of the problem stated by Theodore Sturgeon in his *Venus Plus X*: the inability to grant to another being the right to act in a way that is abhorrent, by faith or by custom, to yourself. In our culture, the most despised sexual perversion is the one in which sexual pleasure is derived out of the fetish of feces. Think of an alien race of coprophiles . . . I admit the thought is rather grisly, but it is not impossible. (Coprolagny is actually one of the most widespread sexual perversions.) The man who thinks himself unprejudiced because he has black, yellow, brown or pink-colored friends, should search himself for his reactions to an openly coprophilic being.

This problem of seeing the inner qualities of a being fundamentally different from ourselves is exemplified in a somewhat less grisly way by the Irish sf writer James White in the novel *All Judgment Fled* (1968). This takes place in a near future, thirty or forty years from today, when man is just beginning to push out to Mars and Venus in small six-men space ships. The story starts with a gigantic alien space ship coming into the solar system, completely out of control, and going into orbit. A research team is sent out to investigate the ship, and is faced with a number of alien creatures. The crux of the plot is that out of the life forms found on the ship, only one is an intelligent agency, but because no communication is possible, the problem is to find out which of the species is the intelligent one, and which are the animals. This is a story of logical deduction, but also a highly suspenseful story and, in all, an example of good science fiction at its best.

James White is well-known in science fiction for a number of extremely intelligent and humanitarian short stories dealing with confrontations with extraterrestrials, particularly his stories set in a kind of orbiting hospital where alien beings are given medical help. Some of these stories have been collected in book form as *Hospital Station* (1962). He explained the background for his stories dealing with the man-alien confrontation in a TV program I produced for Swedish TV at the British sf convention in Oxford, 1969:

I am, of ocurse, preaching a little bit by having extraterrestrials as well as human beings living and working together. . . . We are having difficulties enough living together when we just have slightly different colored skins, and I want to show a future where people with six eyes can live together peacefully and cooperate with people with two. That's the way I hope it will be, and that's the way I hope it will be on Earth before we meet the extraterrestrials.

This is a remarkable change from the monster philosophy of the pulp magazines, and an attitude that the science fiction field should be proud of. In the above-mentioned TV program, John Brunner mentioned a scale for assessing the value judgment in fiction, worked out by an American sociologist. In the original project, this scale was applied to magazines like *Colliers, The Saturday Evening Post,* the *Ladies' Home Journal* and so forth, and it was discovered that the ideals implicit in fiction of this kind were comfortable, conservative to the point of being reactionary, bourgeois, middle-class, and if not intolerant toward minority groups, at least patronizing toward them. A young woman in California decided to do her doctorate thesis by applying the same standards to one month's samples of science fiction magazines, and she came up with the interesting discovery that the implied values tended to be humanitarian, progressive, forward-looking and, as for minority groups, she said, in science fiction even the robots were treated like human beings.

Which, of course, is an encouraging thought. Thus we now have the paradoxical situation in which the debased monster suddenly has been elevated to Nice Guy, putting man into the role of the evil monster, or at least into the role of the obtuse country hick faced with the splendid Galactic Empire that runs the Galaxy and treats man like some amusing pet animal. The men who think they are just different are quickly put straight again, as in this example from a short story by William Tenn, *Betelgeuse Bridge* (1951):

"Not only that. Superior. Get that, Dick, because it'll be very important in what you have to do. The best engineering minds that this country can assemble in a hurry are like a crowd of Caribbean Indians trying to analyze the rifle and compass from what they know of spears and windstorms. These creatures belong to a galaxy-wide civilization composed of races *at least* as advanced as they; we're a bunch of backward hicks in an unfrequented hinterland of space that's about to be opened for exploration. Exploitation, perhaps, if we can't measure up. We have to give a very good impression and we have to learn fast." (49)

"Whew! 1492, repeat performance!" comments Dick, and not entirely without reason. It turns out, however, that the snail-like aliens actually are decadent and quite stupid, even if they manage to swindle Earth out of every ounce of fissionable material. They are "the profligate, inadequate and sneak-thief heirs of what was once a soaring race." And soon enough man steps in to take up his rightful place as the leader of the Galaxy. Hurray.

Tenn's story can be seen as a sort of intermediate link between the time-honored monster philosophy and the attitude which seems to be gaining strength in sf today, that of considering man as one of many races, with his own unique possibilities, neither animal nor superman, just one thinking being among others. James White's *Hospital Station* is, I think, a splendid example of this attitude, light-years removed from the patronizing views implicit in, e.g. Ray Bradbury's *The Martian Chronicles* wherein the Martians are depicted as some kind of degenerate creatures, unable to keep their civilization going when the Terran immigrants come; or the kill-and-kill attitude of novels like Robert A. Heinlein's *Starship Troopers* in which the only good extraterrestrial is a dead extraterrestrial and cold-blooded murder is the word of the day.

Today we even have a fair number of sf stories bordering on self-contempt in their attitude toward man vs. extraterrestrials, e.g. *The Genocides* (1965) by Thomas M. Disch, in which malignant extraterrestrials have taken over Earth, farming it for their own purposes, with man living as vermin in the fields, hiding from his new masters; or like William Tenn's highly intelligent novel *Of Men and Monsters* (1968), wherein mankind is reduced to the role of rats living in the walls of the alien colonizer's houses. This is often no more than a reversing of the coin of yore, but it is still a step forward.

At the moment, science fiction seems to be in a somewhat

178

monster-free period, concentrating more on man's own achievements than confrontation with more or less malignant extraterrestrial BEM's. However, the monsters come and go, and we will probably have them back again before long. The latest real monster period occurred in 1958, when the U.S. sf expert Forrest J. Ackerman started the horror magazine *Famous Monsters of Filmland* with gory stills from Hollywood's extensive monster repertory accompanied by texts dripping with Ackermanian irony. The first issue sold 300,000 copies, and some sf magazines fought with hands and claws and tentacles to be first to the smorgasbord. First of them all was W. W. Scott, editor of the now defunct sf magazine *Super-Science Fiction,* who immediately changed the policy of his magazine, telling his writers that monsters now was the word of the day and start writing about them, please. (50)

The monster craze soon faded away, leaving the BEM's where they belonged, as one useful tool of sf among others. *Famous Monsters* is still being published, larger and sicker than before, but this magazine, as well as its imitators, is predominantly aimed at kids of eight to twelve years old. The letter column of *Famous Monsters*, with its photos of horribly dressed-up boys, is pathetic and unpleasant. Working miniature guillotines can be bought by postal order, and monster-minded kids are encouraged to join the magazine's club, chairman of which, according to the illustrations, is a putrid corpse with an unpleasant leer. *Famous Monsters* has very little to do with science fiction, but it seems to be popular. As distinguished from science fiction, which usually holds very humanitarian views toward alien creatures, this type of monster magazine consistently puts a sign of equality between physical and mental deformities. Wherever this might lead, it will obviously not be toward a greater understanding of differently shaped creatures, human or non-human.

8. THE MASS-CULTURE STRIKES

I might have given the impression that science fiction is strictly reserved for the printed word. It is not. *Superman* has wandered about in space and future since 1938, in company with *Buck Rogers* and *Flash Gordon* and the *Fantastic Four* and some fourteen thousand other curious creations of the comic strip. The green monsters and a good assortment of ghouls, etc. make life merrier for their young readers, and the film industry is beyond all description. In volume, the printed word only occupies a small portion of the veritable torrent of more or less probable, intelligent or enjoyable science fiction that can be found today. Even the largest sf magazines seldom manage to climb over 100,000 copies in circulation; in fact, they are more likely to stay around 50,000. Even the sf pocketbooks, which are printed in first editions anywhere from 40,000 to 150,000 copies, seem small in comparison to the circulation of the comics. This is, of course, not unique for science fiction; every literary field finds itself deluged under the mass of comics and TV. That comics, TV shows and films almost always are crude to the point of being idiotic, is part of the mass culture, and is surely not science fiction's fault. It has given the genre an undeservedly bad reputation in certain circles, though.

To start with the comics, the most well-known science fiction comic strip was manufactured by a U.S. artist who had learned the trade by doing *Blondie* and similar ones. The artist was Alex Raymond, known for his *Secret Agent X-9* and *Rip Kirby* strips, and the sf strip was, of course, *Flash Gordon*, "the Prince Valiant of outer space" as an enthusiastic chronicler has put it. The first installment of the adventures of this broad-shouldered and very Aryan hero among green monsters, beautiful space women and hateful fiends with clearly Asiatic countenances, was published on January 7, 1934. Since then he has been giving his money's worth in magazines and newspapers around the world, in the company of his slightly doting fiancée Dale Arden and the mad scientist Dr. Zarkov. Flash Gordon usually occupies himself fighting with an extraterrestrial (but very human) Emperor called Ming, a baddie of no mean resources, who must be even more feeble-minded than Flash, because he always is outwitted in the end.

During the years that Alex Raymond drew *Flash Gordon*, its greatest asset was its crisp and clean style and its skillful use of shadow, but it has since become quite simpler. Raymond died in 1956 in a car accident, but the strip had been taken over already in 1951 by one Dan Barry. Barry's attitude toward his job doesn't differ much from any sf writer's. "The scientist's job," he says, "is to get men into space and on the planets. Mine is to presume he is already there and to carry on with the uses and misuses of the accomplishments." (51) Unfortunately, very little of these good intentions can be found in the strip.

Those readers who were young at the time probably remember the Flash Gordon radio series, the novels (at least six of them, to my knowledge), the pop-up books, the coloring books and the last but not least the curious films featuring Buster Crabbe, who played Tarzan before he dropped the loincloth in favor of Flash Gordon's trusty blaster. These films now have gone on to camp fame, being featured in museums and moon-ins. And as for the comic strip, those who want to recapture the nostalgic feelings can get the old Flash Gordon adventures in book form from the Nostalgia Press at $12 a copy. The same publisher has also, by the way, brought out the old *Buck Rogers* strips at $12.50. Take your pick.

Flash Gordon is still going strong, with an estimated readership of sixty million persons. The same does not apply to *Buck Rogers*, however. He first appeared in a novelette by the U.S. sf writer Philip Nowlan, *Armageddon 2419 A.D.*, in the August, 1928 issue of *Amazing Stories*. The story dealt with the adventures of Anthony Rogers, an engineer who is overcome by some kind of radioactive gas in an abandoned coal mine in Pennsylvania, and subsequently sleeps into a future five hundred years hence, where world domination is in the hands of Mongolians, and the center of world power lies in inland China, with the inhabitants of the U.S.A. one of the few people unsubdued. These rulers of Earth are called the Han Airlords, and are—for a North American—a singularly obnoxious Oriental race that actually comes from outer space (shades of the BEM again). In *Armageddon 2419 A.D.* and its sequel *The Airlords of Han* (1929, Anthony Rogers leads the resistance against the invaders, much in the same way as the American Indians fought against the European settlers, only with the significant difference that in this case the natives win.

These novelettes, brought together and published in one volume by Ace Books, are justly considered classics of science fiction, not due to their purely literary merits—they are indeed very few—but because of the grand Sense-of-Wonder that pervades them. The openly racist attitude can easily be overlooked (it is the old Yellow Peril all over again, as infantile as ever before or after), and what we have is actually an sf story of merit, featuring a number of interesting scientific innovations that, in one form or another, actually are among us today: like the bazooka, the jet plane, the walkie-talkie. It is still readable, which is more than can be said about most pulp fiction of that time.

The idea was picked up by John F. Dille, president of the National Newspaper Syndicate, who hired Philip Nowlan to write the continuity of a comic strip based upon these novelettes. Dick Calkins, a cartoonist on his staff, was assigned to draw the strip, and it appeared under the somewhat changed name of *Buck Rogers 2429 A.D.* in 1929. Each year the strip's title was updated by one to keep up the five hundred years' difference, until finally the name was stabilized as *Buck Rogers in the Twenty-Fifth Century*. During the first two years, the strip followed the original novelette quite closely, but with time new characters and new adventures were introduced until it bore virtually no resemblance to the original work. When *Sputnik I* went up in 1957, it provided a temporary circulation boost for Buck, but eventually the strip died. During the last ten years or so *Buck Rogers* had changed so much that it held no resemblance at all to the original strip; in fact, it was little more than a poor copy of *Flash Gordon*. Yet *Buck Rogers* during the first twenty years was a highly original sf comic strip, possibly the best of all the space strips of the time. During the thirties, *Buck Rogers* also appeared as a highly successful radio series, sponsored by Cocomalt and written and produced by Jack Johnstone, who also wrote and produced the *Superman* radio shows. This was ages ago, though, and *Buck Rogers* now occupies that special niche of sf reserved for particularly cherished objects of childhood nostalgia. Buck's creators are now dead as well.

What made *Buck Rogers* unique among science fiction comic strips, and in fact makes it readable to this day, was its sense of humor. Buck himself appeared as a lanky youth, devoid of the most obnoxious heroic traits, who wandered about in a highly improbable interstellar space in the company of the beautiful Wilma, old Dr. Huer (Heh! Heh!) and a broad-shouldered hero, encountering all kinds of curious civilizations and grave perils, including (during W.W. II) some remarkably malignant Mongolian aliens, and an evil robot emperor who rebuilt the whole company to robots.

The fantasy was wild unto the borders of insanity and close on the heels of our heroes, the local villains Killer Kane and his beautiful companion Ardala followed. Killer Kane differed favorably from the traditional comic strip baddies, though. He was a pathetic, henpecked boob, who was constantly pushed around by Ardala, who had all the brains of the outfit. One could always count on Killer Kane to make an ass of himself, either through sheer clumsiness or chicken-heartedness (he could not stand the sight of blood). The unhappy villain was time and again caught and brought to the Rehabilitation Center of the Solar System, but this kind of treatment always seemed to fail miserably where Kane was concerned, and he was always willing for a new try and a new failure. The strip, in fact, seldom seemed to take itself seriously, and this quality, together with its obvious entertainment value, made it into something rather special in the comic strip department of science fiction.

The greatest of all comic strip heroes, both inside and outside of science fiction, however, is the mighty *Superman*, who has delighted mankind with the sight of his gaudy underwear since 1938. In that year, two enthusiastic sf fans named Joseph Shuster and Jerry Siegal after five years of hard efforts succeeded in syndicating the super-strong overman. *Superman* broke like a bombshell on the comic market, and put its imprint on the whole field. Tightly-dressed and cloaked supermen appeared immediately from every conceivable nook and cranny, and National Periodical Publications, which owned the hero, had to work overtime suing the plagiarists. One of the most well-known imitators, *Captain Marvel*, is interesting as one of the super-stars of the time, Eando Binder, used to write the bold captain's merry adventures—alternating with Mickey Spillane.

Superman quickly became the declared hero of all kids, and during World War II, he also was distributed to the fighting troops, who probably needed all the encouragement they could get. *Superman* magazine rose to a circulation of 1,400,000 copies, and the *Superman* films, now decidedly more camp than suspenseful, spewed forth, together with radio shows ("Faster than a speeding bullet! More powerful than a locomotive! Able to leap tall buildings in a single bound! Look! Up in the sky! It's a bird! It's a plane! It's . . . SUPERMAN!"). The Man of Steel became the foremost figure in U.S. mythology. He is still there.

The story of Superman's origin on the planet Krypton, how the planet was threatened with disaster and how he was put into a small rocket and sent away to Earth seconds before the whole planet exploded, growing up on Earth and assuming a false identity as newspaperman Clark Kent, spending most of his time doing various good deeds in the most complicated way possible, has been told so many times in the strip that I don't have to go into any greater detail. It should be noted, though, that the Man of Steel has grown increasingly mightier during the years, and whereas he in the old days grunted and sweated considerably as he lifted a small house or drained a lake, he can now be found moving whole cities, destroying small planets with his fists ("WHAMM!") and jumping through time without even getting slightly flushed by the effort.

He is still extremely vulnerable to the super-radioactive element Kryptonite, though, a fact that is being used again and again and again as an excuse to get a new adventure rolling. He can always get help from his old friends Batman and Robin, though. And occasionally his feeble-minded friends and well-wishers, the reporters Lois Lane and Jimmy Olson of *The Daily Planet*, have to help him out. As a reward for long and faithful service, Lois Lane finally was granted connubial bliss with her hero *Superman* in 1969, but apparently the deal fell through; they were divorced after one day. I guess a superman is more fun to admire at a distance than to live with. This short union never produced any offspring, which is a pity in a way. We would have got a super-superman with Lois Lane's brains and Superman's build. On the other hand it could—ghastly thought—have turned out the other way.

The science fiction slant of *Superman* has always been strong, and this not without a cause. The creators of the figure were enthusiastic sf fans, and in sf fandom they are, in fact, known more for the fact that they did publish the first sf fan magazine, "fanzine." It was natural that they stayed within the sf field with *Superman* as well. They were, however, not permitted to go on working with their figure for long. Joseph Shuster drew the daily strip up to 1947, after which he was eased out, and then did strips for *Action Comics, Superman, World's Fair Comics* and *All Star Comics* alternating with ten other artists up to 1948. After that, both the creators were kicked out.

That the sf motif nevertheless stayed strong was due to the editor who took over *Superman* and its many sister magazines after the war—Mort Weisinger, once a noted science fiction fan. With the aid of storywriters like Edmond Hamilton, Eando Binder and Jerry Siegal, he filled the

Superman magazines to the gills with everything from time travels to parallel worlds, and became in practice the editor of the biggest sf magazine that ever existed. The magazines were, to be sure, aimed at a rather low age level, but the boundless imagination should have influenced these readers to not a mean degree.

Entertaining Comics' science fiction magazines *Weird Science* and *Weird Fantasy* belong rightly among the real science fiction magazines, as they mainly published science fiction and fantasy stories in comic strip form. These comic magazines were published from 1950 to 1956, in the end as one magazine under the name *Weird Science-Fantasy*, using stories by Ray Bradbury and other sf writers of the time, drawn by artists like Al Williamson and Wallace Wood. They were of a remarkably high quality, compared to other comic magazines, and are now real collector's items. These magazines are, in fact, the only ones which ever have tried to inject some quality, sf-wise, in the comic field in the U.S.A. It is perhaps significant that they did not last long.

Among the new sf comics that now are deluging the market, Marvel Comic's curious super-heroes are the most interesting. *The Amazing Spider-Man, The Iron Man, Fantastic Four, The Mighty Thor, The X-Men* and all their innumerable friends, well-wishers and foes, which in their utter lack of any pretense of credibility and logic are something unique in the comic industry. The man behind all these bizarre creations is one Stanley Lieber, commonly known as Stan Lee, who now spends much time addressing university audiences. In these circles, Marvel Comics is, according to a college student quoted in *Esquire*, considered as "the twentieth-century mythology and (Stan Lee) as this generation's Homer."

Stan Lee himself sees his grotesque fantasies as fulfilling the same function that myths, legends, tales of romance and fairy stories did for earlier generations. His heroes are supermen and superwomen in the worst meaning of the word, but they still have very human weaknesses and faults.

The Mighty Thor is a very American variation that Snorre

Sturlasson probably would have much trouble recognizing, despite the headgear and the constantly battle-ready Mjölner. Actually, this Thor is a crippled doctor whose nurse despises him but is in love with his broad-shouldered alter ego. *The Amazing Spider-Man* is privately an insecure, guilt-ridden teenager who has no luck with girls and catches a cold every time he goes out in his hero tights. The majority of the members of the *Fantastic Four* range from feeble-mindedness to outright imbecility. In all, Marvel Comics' heroes are highly original and, in their best moments, quite refreshing.

Lately the science fiction comics have been given a new slant with the introduction of the Frenchman Jean-Claude Forest's sexually outstanding heroine *Barbarella*, renowned through Roger Vadim's film with Jane Fonda in the role as the sex machine of the future. *Barbarella* first appeared in 1962 in the French magazine *V*, and can now be bought in book form. *Barbarella* is interesting especially from a pornographic point of view. She cohabits with robots, fallen angels and green monsters without discrimination, and is in this way an interesting departure from the usual sexless sf comic. Nowadays, Barbarella is quite passé, and her place has been taken over by even more unbiased space women with constantly battle-ready bodies, e.g. the U.S. sado-masochistic *Phoebe Zeit-Geist*, the French *Jodelle* and the Italian *Satanik*.

In the nice, carefree days of yore, the heroine was abducted by the monsters; today she hunts them up and rapes them.

Aside from the comics, the unflagging search for the lowest common denominator in science fiction entertainment has been the time-honored privilege of the TV industry which, in this respect, has scored beautiful hits in bad judgment and extraordinary low quality. The TV version of science fiction only seldom manages to reach beyond the crudest Space Opera, and it is significant that the most popular U.S. TV series, *Star Trek*, which has created a fandom all its own, stubbornly held to the standards current in the pulp magazines of the thirties. This despite the fact that the

Panel from *Barbarella*.

writers included Big Names of science fiction like Robert Bloch, Richard Matheson and Harlan Ellison. One of the programs, *The Menagerie*, even won a Hugo Award, a constant source of wonder to me.

"*Star Trek* was a gourmet's dream to a land full of starving science fiction fans," an enthusiastic fan recently wrote in a fanzine (52). "Originally, a virgin thought in the mind of its creator, Gene Roddenberry, this personification of class took root in the unlikeliest of fields—network television." And, fired by mounting enthusiasm, the writer went on to say that, "Indeed, if Shakespeare had been alive today he might very well have written for *Star Trek*—the thinking man's *Buck Rogers*."

This description is perhaps more significant of the enthusiasm shown by *Star Trek's* superfans than for the actual qualities of the series. Having had the dubious pleasure of seeing a fair number of the *Star Trek* programs in the line of duty, as a producer at Swedish TV (I did not buy the series), I can only say that if Shakespeare were alive and kicking today, he just might find some more rewarding field to work in.

This sf series, brought out by NBC, has, however, given birth to an unparalleled following, in the wake of which comes the usual offers of icons and holy objects—at a price. For $2.00 you can get a set of three "Genuine space ship insignia, exactly as seen on TV, worn by the crew of the *Enterprise* on their uniforms!!!" $1.00 brings you eight frames from the film discarded in the film company's cutting-room, featuring "climactic moments of crisis, suspense & decision" or "monsters & alien beings" or a host of other equally interesting things. There are insignia stickers, two-color watermount decals, *Star Trek* letterheads, *Star Trek* memo pads, "official biographies" of the various characters of the series (" 'Fascinating . . .' says Mr. Spock"), Flight Deck Certificates (Standard and Deluxe), color postcards, bumper stickers and an "Official Newsletter," all of which can be obtained for a healthy price. If you are a superfan you can even buy all the scripts for the first *Star Trek* season—for

SCIENCE FICTION: WHAT IT'S ALL ABOUT

$150.00 There is a whole industry catering to the needs of the fans.

It appears that *Star Trek* isn't grabbing European fans in the same way as the U.S. ones; nevertheless, Mr. Spock recently managed to be voted England's No. 2 TV personality, with Jim Kirk of the same series as No. 5. In Germany, an earlier TV series similar to *Star Trek*, the *Space Patrol*, proved to be a success, but not such a great one as its U.S. counterpart.

TV seems to have taken a liking to Space Opera. We have *Time Tunnel*, *Land of the Giants*, *The Invaders* and a host of other quite similar creations. A look in *TV Times* shows that during a typical summer week (June 26 to July 4, 1969) the ten big TV networks showed not less than sixty-five science fiction programs, about half of them feature films of the usual horror type, with the rest Space Opera serials like *Star Trek*, *Thunderbirds* and the like. In Japan, a country almost more Americanized than the U.S.A., there is an abundance of local Space Opera super-heroes, including the grinning and samurai-swinging *Kyaputen Urutora* (Captain Ultra), who leads the Space Patrol toward new victories aided by his trusty pals Joe and Hack. Another of the popular Japanese Space Opera series, *Reinbo Sentai Robin*, features the "Rainbow Space Association," composed of Captain Robin; Professor, the brain of the outfit; Wolf, a crack shot; Lily, a robot nurse; Benkei, a superstrong robot; Pegasus, a ridable robot that can operate on land, in the sky and undersea; and Bell, who has ears three thousand times more sensitive than any human being. None of these series are particularly good—to say the very least.

British TV shows a fair amount of science fiction, ranging from *Star Trek* and the home-manufactured *Doomsday Watch* and *Dr. Who* to more serious series like *The Prisoner* and *Out of the Unknown*, the latter featuring dramatizations of stories by John Brunner, Robert Sheckley, Clifford D. Simak, Isaac Asimov *et al*. This particular sf series could perhaps best be compared with the U.S. *Twilight Zone*, whose producer, Rod Serling, has been awarded the coveted Hugo Award twice for his outstanding TV works.

THE MASS-CULTURE STRIKES

The real villain is, however, the movie industry, with its flood of monsters and broad-shouldered space heroes. It has done more to give the genre a bad reputation than all the literary critics in the world. Good science fiction films have been done, to be sure, but the great number of sf films are nothing but monster operas of the worst possible kind, slapped together for the benefit of malignant kids.

The first feature films ever made were actually science fiction—I am thinking of films like George Melies' *A Trip to the Moon* (1902) and *An Impossible Voyage* (1904), both based on stories by Melies' fellow-countryman Jules Verne. George Melies, owner of the Théâtre Robert-Houdin in Paris, was a popular magician and specialist in electro-mechanical marvels. He saw the movie as an entirely new media in which he could achieve effects never before conceived. Buying a camera from the father of French movies, Louis Lumière, Melies set about discovering the possibilities of this new media, and within a few years he had invented almost the entire repertory of the trick film as it is now, from double exposure to stop motion, fades, dissolves and animation. Until the war ended his career as a producer in 1914, he made a great number of "transformations, tricks, fairy tales, apotheoses, artistic and fantastic scenes, comic subjects, war pictures, fantasies and illusions." He usually appeared himself in these films, together with girls from the Folies Bergère.

Melies' films were pure fantasy, absurd dramas played out in a never-never land of imagination where everything could happen and invariably did. He was, in fact, a product of and the foremost filmatic example of the belief in the unlimited possibilities that the new time promised—the old magic coupled with the science of the new time to form a universe of new worlds. World War I not only put an end to Melies' own excursions into these worlds of unbridled happy imagination, it was also the source of the neo-romanticist "Gothic" horror film that, in a manner reminiscent of the written science fiction, has created the modern science fiction film.

To make a long and rather complicated story very short,

it began in a way with Robert Wiene's classical expressionist film *Das Kabinett von Doktor Caligari* (1919). Originally it was to have been directed by Fritz Lang, and, telling the story of Doctor Caligari's use of a sleepwalker to commit nocturnal atrocities, gives a horrifying insight into the German psyche: the wish to create Führers whom one could follow blindly. It is a magnificent piece of nightmarish absurdity, using horror elements of "inner space," if you like, strengthening the effect by the ingenious use of unrealistic decor.

The theme of man creating his own masters from within was again brought forth in Paul Wegener's *Der Golem, Wie er in der Welt Kam* (1920), based on Gustav Meyrink's novel, which in turn was based on the old Jewish legend of the homunculus, the artificially created man. The Golem turned against his creator, destroying him, as did man's own subconscious in John S. Robertson's *Dr. Jekyll and Mr. Hyde,* based on Robert Louis Stevenson's novel.

The scars left by W.W. I were clearly to be seen in the German films of the time, like W. F. Murnau's *Nosferatu* (1922) based on Bram Stoker's novel *Dracula,* in which an inhuman monster seeks world domination with the aid of volitionless victims; and particularly in Fritz Lang's classic film, *Dr. Mabuse der Spieler* (1922) and its sequel *The Testament of Dr. Mabuse* (1933). Dr. Mabuse is in many respects another Caligari, who seeks power through terror, the creation of fear and anarchy from which he will emerge as the undisputed leader.

It has been said that these two films were aimed at the Nazis, but this is a matter of considerable doubt. Lang's wife, Thea von Harbou, who wrote the scripts for his films, was an avowed Nazi and a member of the Nazi Party, and Lang himself was on the most cordial terms with the ruling Nazi elite. *Dr. Mabuse der Spieler* was actually an attack on the destroyed Communist Party. As for its sequel, Goebbels suppressed it (at the same time offering Lang the job as head of the German film industry) and Lang fled to the U.S.A. to make, among other films, the classic *Fury* (1936). In many respects this is an antithesis to his earlier films, in which an innocent man is made the victim of credulity, ignorance and hate which grows into a lynching. He had, to be sure, already looked at this side of the coin in *M* (1932), in which a sexually perverted man, ridden by fear for himself yet unable to break himself free, is hunted down by police and gangsters alike. Perhaps *M* and *Fury* are portraits of the society envisaged by Lang as the result of Dr. Mabuse's dreams, had they become reality.

The themes of the German horror film were reflected in the U.S.A. by films like James Whale's *Frankenstein* (1931) and, more notably, by Tod Browning's *Freaks* (1932), probably the most chilling horror film ever made, featuring not the usual cosmetic Hollywood monsters but real human beings, malformed and mutilated, who played the highlights of a traveling freak show. These "monsters" were portrayed as human beings, despite their appalling appearances, and the film was made with a sensitivity, almost tenderness, that lifts it high above the crude monster operas of the time. It should be noted that the film immediately was suppressed by the film company and subsequently banned in most countries until the mid-sixties. Werewolves and green monsters are one thing, apparently; the real thing must never be shown.

E. B. Shoedsack's *King Kong* (1933) actually conveyed glimpses of something like an understanding of this inhuman creature in its theme of "Beast betrayed by Beauty," the monster as a victim of circumstance in about the same way as an earlier Frankenstein's monster had been, but this is on the surface only. Underneath, it is Monster vs. Human, nothing more. In the gloomy years of the Depression, we still had Dr. Mabuse around, though larger and with considerably more hair on his chest. And with *The Werewolf of London* (1935) we have the monster craze going full blast.

Aside from a few optimistic films like Alexander Korda's and H. G. Wells's *Things to Come* (1936), which actually offered a glimpse of hope to humanity, the science fiction film seemed to be obsessed by the destruction envisaged by the German film of the twenties. It deluged the market with monsters of the most curious kind and offered futures with no future at all, a trend that is as strong today with films like Joseph Losey's *The Damned* (1961) Jean-Luc Godard's *Alphaville* (1965) and Francois Truffaut's *Fahrenheit 451*. The Japanese film directors like Inoshiro Honda devoted much of their efforts after W.W. II to films depicting the horrors of the atomic war, in the guise of spectacular monster films, *Rhodan, Godzilla, et al.*

Lately, there has been an interesting departure from the gloomy predictions, with films like Roman Polanski's delightful *Dance of Vampires* (1967), an elegant and witty parody on Hollywood monster films; and Stanley Kubrik's and Arthur C. Clarke's magnificent *2001: A Space Odyssey* (1968), "the first ten-million-dollar religious film," to quote Arthur C. Clarke. *2001* is not the only sf film to use hard technology as the basis for metaphysical speculation, but it is surely one of the very few to even try to be intelligent and mature. Mostly, the sf films are a sorry lot, content with using the symbols of the German horror films of the twenties without the meaning, creating horror for its own sake, conveying nothing, saying nothing, meaning nothing. We have the Monster, the Hero, the Heroine. Apart from that, and a lot of gore, there is nothing to be found. No meaning, no wit, no intelligence, no nothing.

American science fiction films are, with very few exceptions, synonymous with Monsters. The slimier, the better. The cinema-goer lives happily in a curious world of vampires, zombies, werewolves, mutated giant insects, robots, androids and assorted extraterrestrials. We have masterpieces like *Attack of the Giant Leeches, Earth vs. the Giant Spider, Zombies of the Stratosphere, The Creature With the Atom Brain* and so on and so on *ad nauseam*. The film industry still revels happily in the over-simplified world that written science fiction was grateful to leave thirty years ago, and the poor cinema-goer thinks that this is the way it should be. This is decidedly not the way it should be, but try to explain that to a film producer.

The horror film (and science fiction is equivalent to horror in ninety percent of the films), since the thirties, has been based on certain clichés that seem changeless. The Mad Scientist (a kind of Americanized Mabuse or Caligari without the brains) is still running around in his foggy castle—or, if he is modern, in a chrome-shining laboratory with lots of gadgetry, somewhere in the Mojave Desert—constantly attended by his ugly creations and the hunchbacked assistant, traditionally named Fritz, Karl or Ygor. (These creatures usually speak broken German; a nice linguistic touch.) This assistant, who like his mad master is a pronounced sadist, usually dedicates his spare hours on moonlit stormy nights to whipping the Heroine, a shapely young woman with blonde hair and cow eyes. When no heroine is at hand, he hunts her up, alleging that he carries tidings from her lover (the Hero) or her father, a nice old man who usually experiments with the Forbidden Secrets of Nature and expires before the movie ends. The Heroine then sheds a couple of glycerin tears over his mangled body, but soon finds solace in the hairy arms of the Hero. Like the Heroine, the Hero is as close to being a moron as you can get without being locked up, and it is a constant source of wonder to me that they manage to stay alive for even a couple of minutes.

The Mad Scientist and the Monster are half-brothers, and go privately under the name of Boris Karloff. Sometimes, however, he is portrayed as a slightly depraved and depressed nobleman harboring Dark Secrets in the best Gothic Romance and Eugène Sue manner, in which case he calls himself Vincent Price. If he becomes a monster as a teenager (an advanced puberty problem, unknown at the time of Freud) he can be found singing in the Swedish Folkparks during the summer, using his spare time being a cowboy star, name of Michael Landon. The scientists dispute which of these is the most horrid one.

Close on the heels of the Monster comes the film about the Son of the Monster. This son is a disreputable creature with a number of atrocities and starving film producers on his conscience. Probably he was created on a dark night, while the werewolf Moon shone over the cozy crypt, and Dracula played the violin in the churchyard. The unhappy mother keeps herself out of sight, as well she might. Perhaps she is at work making another son, because this one won't last more than a couple of hours, at the most.

When at last the whole family has done its duty, from sisters, cousins, nephews, grandsons and little Orphan Annie, the situation becomes so desperate that Abbott and Costello end the epic with *The Monster Meets Abbott and Costello*, whereupon everyone concerned gratefully forgets about the whole thing. The Monster changes tights and starts a new career as *The Monster From the Black Lagoon*, and there we are again.

Lately we have seen significant changes in the monster film, due to the scientific miracles of our time. Thus the Monster more and more often comes to Earth in cute little flying saucers, calling himself Mxtrwpqtrl. The more intelligent extraterrestrials dress themselves up as humans, calling themselves Fritz, Karl or Ygor, whereupon they immediately wheedle the scantily-dressed Heroine out to the desert, maintaining that Love or something is involved. The Heroine willingly follows the handsome Monster, who, however, harbors evil plans and only wants to use her to Conquer the World. The Heroine gets mad, and is saved by her boyfriend who is a scientist and almost unbearably nice. After some clumsy heroics, during which the Monster almost laughs himself to death, letting himself be killed without further ado, the Hero blasts everything to pieces and escapes with his Heroine toward the sunrise while the studio orchestra plays like mad in the background.

Sometimes the Hero is aided by a Nature-catastrophe. He gets very moved by this, and utters some wise comments about the Fugitiveness of All Evil and the Results of Tampering With Nature. Whereupon he smiles melancholically with his blinding white teeth and marries the Heroine.

Sometimes the Hero comes to the Monsters. This is an entirely new move in the genre, and the film producers are rightly proud of themselves. The only difference is, actually, that here we have the Hero going on like a maniac on the Monsters' homeground, not the other way around, which makes a fantastic difference. An extraterrestrial who visits

Earth is always a Monster, and should be treated as such. A Hero who comes to another planet with his faithful Heroine at his heels is on the other hand worth both admiration and obeisant reception, and if he doesn't get this, it is bad for the extraterrestrials. Why, the Hero says, should I waste my breath on nice words when an atomic bomb gives the same result and more definitely?

In these days of space race and cold war, the Hero sometimes lands on the distant planet only to find that another ship has beaten him. Its crew members have clearly Asian features and go by names like Fritzky, Karlsky and Ygorsky. They are both wily and spiritually hunchbacked, and can't even play baseball. They are also in agreement with the monstrous inhabitants of the planet. Civilization is obviously in grave danger, and the situation is saved only when the nice Heroine with a regretful giggle presses the atomic blaster into Ygorsky's back and (by mistake) presses the trigger. Thereafter she collapses into the Hero's arms and is carried back to the ship which thunders away through space seconds before the planet explodes with a very loud bang that almost drowns out the string-band.

Cabbage-worms, grasshoppers, spiders, etc. are also very popular in these films. They are then *mutations,* and considerably larger than the tiny creatures that in summertime skid around inside the reader's shirt. Often they have mutated with the aid of radioactive radiation, but they are as often the result of the Heroine's father's horrible experiments in the desert. This is very scientific, and gives the film producer unsought opportunities to babble about science and technology and $E=mc^2$ and other things that neither he nor the moviegoers know a thing about.

The father usually dies early in the film, and the experiments are continued by his hunchbacked assistant by name of Fritz, Karl or Ygor, who is a bad 'un with evil plans vis-à-vis the world. The overgrown insects now give the public their money's worth in destroyed cities, massacred people, a ruined Empire State Building, etc., whereupon the Hero comes charging in, looking for his beloved, the Heroine, who has been abducted by the perverted assistant.

The Hero mobilizes some bald professors and the U.S. Army, and then the story is about ended.

When the last explosion has died out, the Hero and the Heroine stand amid the smoking remains of the Monster and the hunchbacked assistant, spreading pieces of pungent wisdom around, accompanied by the string-band. This unexpected happy ending makes the moviegoer mad with joy, and verifies once again cinema's undisputed value as the giver of good, wholesome and clean entertainment. As the advertisements so truthfully say: Go to the movies—and give your life a new meaning!

9. THE MAGAZINES

Talking to a hardened old-time sf buff about the old pulp magazines is likely to induce a near-religious misting around the eyes as the great names are invoked—E. E. "Doc" Smith, Edmond Hamilton, Murray Leinster, Jack Williamson, Stanley G. Weinbaum and others of the "golden years" of *Amazing Stories, Astounding, Startling Stories, Weird Tales, Thrilling Wonder Stories, et al.* Often, to the accompaniment of nostalgic sighs, the sacred tablets are hauled out: the cherished magazines printed on coarse, cheap yellowed paper with its characteristic smell; the stock illustrations depicting as many hackish science-fictional situations as you could care for; the old stories; the letter columns with all the Big Names, then only loudmouthed cubs; the illustrations by Finlay; the gaudy covers by Paul, Schneeman, Wesso, Bergey and Brown. There is nothing like them, and the magic of these names are equal to those of New Orleans and Jelly Roll Morton, King Oliver and Johnny Dodds for an old-timer jazz lover. Indeed pulp age sf is as different from present-day science fiction as is the old New Orleans jazz from John Coltrane or the subtle lyrics of the Beatles. "True, we now have the paperbacks, and a great thing they are, too," writes Alva Rogers in a study of the pulp years of *Astounding SF,* "but they are not the same as the pulps, nor will they ever be." (53)

For an outsider, these magazines and the writers of the time must seem rather crude, compared with the slick and literary magazines of today, presenting writers handling the media with an increasing skill that was unheard-of thirty or forty years ago. Science fiction has indeed changed immensely since the pulp era, as has all literature, and I think it would only be fair to use a somewhat different yardstick

199

for these admittedly crude magazines of the past, than for those published today. They are like vintage cars, which were tops in their field once-upon-a-time and still are cherished by the aficionados even though they compare very unfavorably with the four-wheeled dinosaurs of today. They show their age, but they were nevertheless instrumental in starting the science fiction field as we know it today, creating to a large degree not only its readership but its authors as well, and, of course, guiding the genre's development.

Without the science fiction pulps, we would now have no organized sf fandom, no sf conventions, no fan magazines and pretty few sf writers. I doubt if there would be much American science fiction at all. For the hard-core science fiction magazines, i.e. those wholly devoted to science fiction, first appeared in the U.S.A., with the result that the U.S.A. is the country where most science fiction is written and published now. The British magazines of the turn of the century, like the *Strand Magazine* and others which habitually published science fiction, were as their European counterparts mainstream magazines with a more or less pronounced sf slant.

The beginning came around W.W. I, when the new science showed its most ugly face, and the grandiose dreams of the affluent future became more realistic. Popular scientific magazines spewed forth, from the venerable French *La Science et la Vie* with its many editions in various countries, to Hugo Gernsback's *The Electrical Experimenter, Science and Invention, Radio News, Modern Electrics* and so forth. Many of these magazines speculated in future scientific developments. *La Science et la Vie* devoted much of its space to articles about communications with the Martians and descriptions of the Moon voyages to come. Many of its covers could actually have been taken from any self-respecting science fiction magazine of a later date.

Hugo Gernsback's magazine *Modern Electrics* was enlivened with science fiction serials between the scientific articles, from *Ralph 124C41+* to Jacque Morgan's *The Scientific Adventures of Mr. Fosdick*, the latter appearing as a serial until the magazine folded in 1913. These magazines did not actually create modern science fiction—H. G. Wells, the first modern science fiction writer had already been writing mature sf for many years, and he was far from alone in Europe doing this—but whereas these authors primarily had been writers concentrating upon the impact of change on man, the new American magazines brought forth a new breed of science fiction writers. These were technicians and scientists with a negligible literary talent, who developed their theories of the probable scientific advances in literary form. True, there had been scientists writing before, the most notable being the French astronomer Camille Flammarion, but these scientists saw themselves primarily as popularizers of science, and were careful not to speculate too freely. Also, these speculations had been limited to books, and rather scholarly ones, at that. The specialized magazines, dealing more or less exclusively with science fiction, brought a great change to the whole field. Unorthodox U.S. scientists like Hugo Gernsback and Ray Cummings, once the secretary of Edison, worked on in the time-honored Utopian tradition. They wrote stories that were far less subtle than the works of, for example, H. G. Wells, François Maurois or the Swedish sf writer Claes Lundin, but were typical of the new type of Scientific Romances that was to become something specially American. All this happened in the U.S. sf magazines.

Besides these magazines representatives also appeared for fantasy, in the footsteps of the Gothic tale, e.g. the U.S. *Thrill Book,* which started in 1919, and *Weird Tales,* which started in 1923 and for many years was the starting point for many of the great names of the genre, from H. P. Lovecraft to Henry Kuttner and Ray Bradbury.

At this time, Sweden had a Hugo Gernsback of its own, by the name of Otto Witt, who in practice was more Gernsback than Gernsback himself. His magazine *Hugin,* which appeared with its first regular issue on April 7, 1916, can with good reasons be regarded as the first attempt to make a science fiction magazine. In the premiere issue of *Hugin,* Witt writes an introduction that is quite revealing of his particular brand of Sense-of-Wonder:

SCIENCE FICTION: WHAT IT'S ALL ABOUT

You have seen the fairyland of science. Everything in this country is a scientific romance. The forest is simple and real, the paper is the fantasy. The waterfall is trivial and ordinary; the turbine, the dynamo and the generator—*they* are the poems . . . And (Hugin) knows well what types of language it must use to make itself understood in our age. They are:

> The Scientific Fiction
> The Technical Causerie
> The Idea-stimulating Sketch
> The Adventure Story and
> The Scientific Fairy Tale

Which seems well enough. Actually, *Hugin* was a rather sorry thing to behold, filled to the gills with patriotism and a "Sweden right or wrong" philosophy that was outdated even then. Witt's propensity for obscure "scientific" innovations like the "electrolite" (a kind of super-fertilizer working with "animal electricity") that made him the target for considerable ridicule, didn't make things better. Altogether eighty-five issues of *Hugin* were published up to the last issue at Christmas, 1919. The literary quality was pitifully low, and Witt's sense of logic seemed to sleep around the clock (he wrote every word in the magazine himself), but the honor of having published the first sf magazine undoubtedly belongs to him.

The first pure science fiction magazine of the type we are used to, i.e. a story magazine in which writers other than the editor/publisher were allowed to appear came in 1926, three years after Otto Witt's death. Publisher and editor was, of course, Hugo Gernsback, and the magazine was *Amazing Stories*. Already in 1923, Gernsback had published a "Scientifiction Issue" of his popular technical magazine *Science and Invention* (August, 1923), containing half a dozen science fiction stories. Originally, he planned to publish his specialized sf magazine under the title *Scientifiction*. An inquiry among the readers of *Science and Invention* in 1925 did not give any encouraging results, however, and when the sf magazine finally materialized in April,

Hugin's standard format.

1926, it was under the more forceful title of *Amazing Stories.* The success of this particular name is best attested to by the subsequent flood of sf magazines with rather similar titles, like *Astonishing, Astounding, Stirring, Fantastic, Startling* and so forth.

Jules Verne and H. G. Wells appeared regularly for a time, until Gernsback had managed to get together his own group of writers, mostly scientists with good imaginations but painfully lacking in literary talents. This was the beginning of the "pulp era" of science fiction, the name derived from the low-quality paper on which *Amazing* and its contemporaries were printed. Under Gernsback's guidance the Space Opera writers appeared, and the circulation rose rapidly to a top of 100,000 copies, according to an editorial in the September, 1929 issue.

At this time, however, Gernsback had already been separated from *Amazing,* which now was published by Teck Publications under the editorship of T. O'Conor Sloane, another scientist, who carried on in Gernsback's footsteps with wild interplanetary adventures until 1938, when the editorial chair was taken over by a sf fan named Raymond A. Palmer. Palmer had a weakness for mysticism, and the magazine promptly became filled with stories set in Atlantis and Mu and the subterranean worlds. The latter were usually written by Richard S. Shaver, a welder who produced his stories as facts, alleging them to be transcriptions of voices from the underworld, etc. This whole affair raised quite a furor in sf circles, but it is nevertheless reported to have raised the circulation of *Amazing* to a peak. In 1950, Palmer left *Amazing* for flying saucer magazines like *Other Worlds* and *Imagination.*

In his place came Howard Browne, who immediately came under attack from the sf fans but nevertheless raised the circulation of the magazine to new peaks. After many ups and downs, *Amazing* is now little but a shadow of its former self, filling much of its space with reprints from a happier time.

Long before this, a number of other sf magazines had seen the light of day. Hugo Gernsback went bankrupt at the end of 1928, losing all his magazines, his radio station and his home. He was totally ruined. He had kept the list of subscribers, though, and in the beginning of 1929 he sent out a circular letter to all his former subscribers, asking for subscriptions to a new magazine resembling *Science and Invention*. He still had the reputation as the best editor and publisher in the field, and he is said to have received 20,000 subscriptions of one dollar each. Gernsback was back in business again, and in June and July the same year he started two new sf magazines, *Science Wonder Stories* and *Air Wonder Stories*.

The competition hardened, especially after *Astounding Science Fiction* (now *Analog Science Fact—Science Fiction*) appeared in January, 1930. Originally titled *Astounding Stories of Super-Science*, it was published by Clayton Magazines under the editorship of Harry Bates until March, 1933; then in October, 1933, it was bought by Street & Smith, Inc. which published it as *Astounding Stories*, edited by F. Orlin Tremaine. In December, 1937, the legendary sf fan, writer and editor John W. Campbell took over. Probably no other editor has influenced the science fiction field as much as John W. Campbell; he was, at any rate, the undisputed king of the "golden years" of American science fiction. He was, and is, a man of many varied interests and one can, in fact, follow the ups and downs of these interests in the sf field as a whole.

From 1926 until the mid-thirties, Gernsback was the undisputed master of the sf field, and Gernsback's god was the Machine. During his reign science fiction was a matter of *super science*, magnificent scientific innovations that played the leading part in the stories. Heroes and villains alike were reduced to beauteously ringing voices that sang the praise of the Machine.

Campbell changed the genre by demanding science fiction in which the effect of the innovation or the occurrence on man was the principal thing. Scientific correctness came in second place. Campbell put the emphasis on the relations between man and his environment, with environment the variable factor: *What would happen if . . . ?* During the course of some years science fiction changed into something new, and the new writers who Campbell discovered and encouraged—Isaac Asimov, Clifford D. Simak, Robert A. Heinlein, A. E. van Vogt, etc.—set about spreading the message to the other magazines.

Even the old *Weird Tales*, which traditionally had kept itself to the horror fantasy branch of science fiction, was influenced, although the Lovecraft-school was predominant until the magazine folded in 1954. It is possible that Campbell's accentuation of man's situation in a changing world was one of the reasons for the discontinuation of *Weird Tales*. There simply wasn't any need for it any longer.

The circulation of the science fiction magazines rose as a result of the new trend. The genre even began to be accepted by mainstream literary critics. Orson Welles's famous radio dramatization of H. G. Wells's *The War of the Worlds* on October 30, 1938, gave a boost to the whole field; people who hitherto never had given the genre much attention bought the magazines featuring the type of monsters that briefly had terrified a whole nation. Within the next eight months seven more science fiction magazines were launched. (54)

In 1943, Donald A Wollheim, one of the front-rank personages both in sf fandom and the professional sector, edited an anthology of science fiction short stories, *The Pocket Book of Science Fiction*, featuring works by the "new" sf writers, which became thereby the very first science fiction anthology.

World War II brought a new dimension to science fiction; with the end of the forties, social criticism became more frequent in U.S. sf magazines. Two new sf magazines, that soon were to be leading in the field, appeared: *The Magazine of Fantasy and Science Fiction* (1949) and *Galaxy* (1950). The sociological satire was foremost represented by Frederik Pohl and Cyril M. Kornbluth's stories about the advertising-industry-or trust-ruled future. Time for the grand views again, with the emphasis on the change of society on account of a certain stimuli: unlimited power; religion coming into full undisputed power; and the colonization of other planets; the American Way of Life *in absurdum*. The writers created their societies with great care, incorporating the characteristics they needed, stocking them with people and examining the result.

Galaxy's editor Horace L. Gold's interest in social criticism and satire as well as lighter literary standards influenced the direction of science fiction as much as *Astounding's* John W. Campbell had influenced it ten years earlier. This time the change was not that great—as the writers who Campbell had discovered now stood on their own feet and worked within the field according to their own private views—but the trend toward social criticism was there. It became more pronounced as Frederik Pohl, at the beginning of the sixties, became editor of *Galaxy*.

Galaxy has now slipped behind somewhat, and the foremost U.S. sf magazine of today is commonly considered to be *The Magazine of Fantasy and Science Fiction*, a serious magazine with high literary standards and the recipient of a number of Hugo Awards for outstanding achievements in the sf field. *Analog*, still edited by the indestructible John W. Campbell, is of course still in the front ranks.

England has for the most part followed the signals from the U.S.A. The first British sf magazine, *Scoops*, came in 1934, a juvenile magazine of few merits that was discontinued after twenty issues. Walter Gillings, a noted British sf fan, later edited sixteen issues of the first adult British sf magazine, *Tales of Wonder*, 1937-42, chiefly using U.S. material. *Authentic Science Fiction Monthly*, which was published in eighty-five issues from January, 1951 to October, 1957 under the editorship of H. J. Campbell (not to be confused with John W. Campbell) was actually a pocketbook series with a letter column, etc. These magazines mostly reprinted stories from U.S. sf magazines, however—even if British writers like John Russell Fearn, E. C. Tubb and Kenneth Bulmer appeared regularly.

England still lacked a focal point for science fiction, where new writers could be published. This focal point came as four magazines, the most noted being *New Worlds*. *New Worlds* started as a mimeographed amateur magazine

207

published by John "Ted" Carnell during the pre-war years. In 1946, *New Worlds* was transformed into a professional magazine, published by Pendulum Publications Ltd., still edited by John Carnell, and three issues were published before Pendulum went out of business in 1948.

After that, Nova Publications was formed primarily by a group of London fans headed by Leslie Flood, John Wyndham, Frank Cooper, Eric C. Williams, G. Ken Chapman and Ted Carnell. This successfully launched *New Worlds* again from No. 4 in 1948; started a sister magazine, *Science Fantasy*, in the summer of 1950, the first three issues under the editorship of Walter Gillings, after which John Carnell edited both magazines. Both ran bimonthly until the end of 1953 and were financially very successful; *New Worlds* had a circulation of 18,000 copies during this period, the highest any British magazine had ever attained.

Printing problems arose at the end of 1953 when the publisher wanted to make both magazines monthly. At this time another publishing company, Maclaren & Sons Ltd., became interested and eventually refinanced Nova Publications, making it possible for John Carnell to enter the field as full-time managing editor in March 1954; *New Worlds* became a monthly. The first issue of the reconstituted company's *New Worlds* contained, among other things, Arthur C. Clarke's short story *The Sentinel* from which, many years later, the basic plot of Stanley Kubrick's film *2001* was to be taken.

Science Fantasy remained a bimonthly and ended with No. 64 in April, 1964, the same month in which *New Worlds* ended with No. 141. During these long, highly successful ten years, *New Worlds* and *Science Fantasy* had proven the starting point for a number of now well-known British sf writers like John Brunner and J. G. Ballard, and in fact created a serious and intelligent science fiction of a truly British type. The fact that Britain today boasts some of the best and most influential writers of science fiction in the world can largely be traced back to John Carnell and his magazines.

Nova Publications during these years had also published

another sf magazine, *Science Fiction Adventures*, on a bi-monthly basis from March, 1958 to No. 32 ending in May, 1963. It started originally as a straight reprint from the U.S. edition, then from No. 7 onward it published British writers. A U.S. edition of *New Worlds* was published briefly in 1962 (five issues), but the venture didn't prove too successful.

In 1964 it was decided to cease publishing the magazine, partly due to the loss of the Australian market. The title rights of *New Worlds* and *Science Fantasy* were sold to Roberts & Winter Ltd. in London. They subsquently published them as paperback-sized magazines, but they never attained their former glory or circulation. The title of *Science Fantasy* was changed to *Impulse SF* but this did nothing for its image and it was finally discontinued. Michael Moorcock, the foremost of Britain's "New Wave" advocates, edited and published *New Worlds* as an avant-garde magazine with some sf connections, with the assistance of a grant from the London Arts Council. Michael Moorcock's *New Worlds* published a number of highly original science fiction avant-garde stories; most notably, Brian Aldiss' *Barefoot in the Head* and Norman Spinrad's *Bug Jack Barron*, both as serials. This particular brand of avant-garde science fiction did not appeal to large groups of readers, though, and the magazine has now been discontinued. The title of *New Worlds*, after a run of twenty-four years, has ceased.

Meanwhile John Carnell, who is far from "New Wave," has continued as an editor of sf, with a difference. He edits a book series called *New Writings in SF*, published in Britain by Dobson Books Ltd. (hardcover) and Corgi Books (paperback), while Bantam Books publishes them in the U.S.A. *New Writings in SF*, which can be considered a sf magazine of sorts, has been phenomenally successful, the total British editions up to No. 16 passing the half million mark in paperback. The idea of new stories in paperback format was of course, not new. It had originated with Frederik Pohl's *Star SF* series in the 1950s, and since then we have seen a number of book series devoted to publishing new stories of science fiction. They have editorials and sometimes even interior illustrations, and it would not surprise me a bit to see letter departments included as well. They don't accept subscriptions, though. Not yet, anyway.

The fourth sf magazine of those playing a principal part in the development of British science fiction was the Scottish magazine *Nebula Science Fiction*, edited and published by Peter Hamilton. It went on for forty-one issues, from Autumn, 1952 to June, 1959, presenting some of the best British sf writers, including E. C. Tubb, Kenneth Bulmer, John Brunner, Eric Frank Russell, William F. Temple etc., whilst Brian W. Aldiss, now a science fiction superstar, made his first appearance here with *T*. U.S. writers were reprinted, although infrequently. There was an attempt at an American edition beginning with No. 30 dated September, 1958 that ran monthly to No. 39, June, 1959.

The most recent addition to the British sf magazine market is *Vision of Tomorrow*, published originally by the Australian Ronald E. Graham Pty Ltd. and edited and produced in England under the editorship of Philip J. Harbottle. At the time of this writing, the Australian publisher has discontinued the magazine, and it is doubtful whether a new British publisher will be found. Originally conceived as a reprint magazine, inspired by the editor's and publisher's wish to reprint works of the late John Russell Fearn, it appeared with its first issue in August, 1969, with a policy to publish new stories only, limited to British, Australian and Commonwealth, and European contributors. The editor is noted for contacting British sf writers of the fifties —who published in *Nebula* and the old *New Worlds,* and who faded out with the advent of the "New Wave" and slump in British sf magazines—and encouraging them to return to writing.

Sweden, being a small country, has nevertheless managed to support sf magazines with circulations close to those of the British and U.S. ones. I have already mentioned Otto Witt's curious magazine *Hugin.* It was obviously an early try in the field, but it left few marks. The first hard-core science fiction magazine in Sweden did not come until 1940, when AB Nordpress in Stockholm launched the weekly pulp magazine *Jules Verne-Magasinet*, featuring short stories and serialized novels from the U.S. pulps. At its peak it had a paid circulation exceeding 80,000 copies a week, which is quite a lot for a country of less than eight million people. All the great names of the contemporary U.S. sf magazines appeared regularly: Henry Kuttner, Isaac Asimov, Alfred Bester, Robert A. Heinlein, Robert Bloch, Ray Bradbury, and Edmond Hamilton's *Captain Future* novels were serialized.

Unfortunately, the literary quality was low, to a high degree resulting from crude translations, and when reading through the magazine now, one often has to agree uncomfortably with a contemporary critic's judgment on the magazine's contents as "blood-dripping drivel."

The sf hegemony didn't last long in this magazine. Already at the end of 1941 the first sport and mystery stories appeared, together with comic strips with no connection whatsoever with science fiction. A new subtitle of the magazine, *Veckans Äventyr* (The Adventures of the Week) also appeared in the logo, and within some years the magazine had changed its name to this new title. The magazine existed until 1947, when it finally drowned in a flood of Wild West, sport and mystery stories and was discontinued, mourned by none except a handful of aficionados. A check shows that in the 332 issues of the magazine were published 770 short stories and installments of serials, and of those 537 can be considered science fiction.

The title *Jules Verne-Magasinet* has now been brought back to life by a Swedish sf fan, Bertil Falk, who publishes it as a small, semiprofessional magazine.

Jules Verne-Magasinet never put a mark on Swedish science fiction, mainly because it did everything to discourage Swedish sf writers and fans—probably stories were cheaper when bought from the U.S.A., so the Swedes had to keep their stories to themselves. The genre did not get a break until two sf fans in Jönköping, Karl-Gustav and Kurt Kindberg, launched a monthly sf magazine that took the genre seriously, and encouraged Swedish writers and fans as well. The magazine was *Häpna* (Be Astounded).

The first issue came in March, 1954, and even though it started reprinting British and U.S. science fiction, it soon began publishing Scandinavian writers as well. *Häpna*, in fact, started Swedish fandom in the same way as Hugo Gernsback's *Amazing* started U.S. fandom, giving the fans a steady supply of good contemporary sf as well as the opportunity of contacts via the letter column. When *Häpna* finally folded in January, 1966, the fandom and the writers it had nursed were able to stand on their own feet. Without *Häpna*, I strongly doubt there would have been much sf interest to speak of in Sweden today.

At the time of this writing, plans are under way to start *Häpna* again, under the new name of *Tidskrift för Science Fiction* (Magazine of Science Fiction), with Sam J. Lundwall as editor.

Galaxy had a Swedish edition from August, 1958 to June, 1960. Nineteen issues were published in all—as compared to the 130 issues of *Häpna*. The Swedish *Galaxy*, published by Classics Illustrated, was largely a copy of the U.S. original, with few—very few—original stories thrown in. For some reason, it never caught on with the Swedish readers, and the publisher turned his interest elsewhere, notably to Swedish editions of *Mad* and *Help*.

A Norwegian edition of *Galaxy*, *Tempo-Magasinet*, appeared briefly in 1953-54, and a short-lived Finnish edition of *Galaxy* also appeared in the late fifties. Apart from that, no other Scandinavian sf magazines have appeared outside Sweden.

As for the rest of Europe, Western Germany has been rather active, sf-wise, particularly through the publishing of German editions of U.S. magazines. *Galaxy* appeared for some years in a German edition called *Galaxis Science Fiction*, and *The Magazine of Fantasy and Science Fiction* has also appeared in a German edition. The Germans seem more interested in book series than magazines, though, and a magazine like *Anabis* with its circulation of 1,000 copies is more like a fanzine than a magazine.

Germany has a lively sf fandom (as attested by the 1970 World SF Convention at Heidelberg), brought to life by

Utopia Magazine in 1953, but to this date this fandom apparently has been unable to produce any science fiction writer of quality. The local Big Names, Walter Ernsting and K. H. Scheer, devoted their efforts wholeheartedly to the type of Space Opera yarns that were popular in other countries twenty or thirty years ago, and it seems likely that both book series and the few short stories produced will stay at the monster-and-blaster level. Germany's Herr Science Fiction Walter Ernsting, who more or less dictates German science fiction, is now responsible for a kind of weekly Space Opera magazine featuring the *übermensch* Perry Rhodan. These magazines sell at a rate of 300,000 copies a week, and have now been published in more than 450 issues. They have reportedly sold more than 60,000,-000 copies (!) and have now appeared in the U.S.A. as well.

Austria's foremost sf magazines have been *Uranus* and *Star Utopia*, both published by Josef and Maria Steffek in Vienna, using mostly U.S. material.

Science fiction has also filled much of the space in the French magazines *Fiction* and *Galaxie*. *Satellite*, another French magazine, has used a good amount of French material, resulting in a number of very promising native writers, e.g. Michel Ehrwein and Pierre Versins. There is also a fine printed and illustrated semi-professional fanzine, *Horizons du Fantastique*, which uses entirely French material, critical and also short stories. France boasts a large number of journals and magazines devoted to the supernatural, some of which with some stretch of imagination can be considered fantasy (except that the readers consider this particular fantasy the gospel truth).

The leading sf magazine in Spain, *Nueva Dimension*, lives a somewhat insecure existence, lately attested to by the seizing of all copies of its No. 14 issue on June 26, 1970, by the Spanish Political Police, on the grounds that the issue in question contained material dangerous to the security of the Spanish State. The offending piece of science fiction turned out to be a story by an Argentinian writer, dealing with the Basques and a time machine. *Nueva Di-*

mension has been described as "perhaps the most distinguished sf magazine in the world in typography, selection, world coverage, and artistic taste." It has, moreover, published a good number of U.S. sf writers, including Harry Harrison and Theodore Sturgeon, as well as European masters of the avant-garde, like Boris Vian.

Spain is not the most sf-oriented country in the world; and from the official reaction to an in all respects innocent sf story, I would guess that the genre doesn't stand too much chance to reach its full potential.

Science fiction in Italy thrives under a much more benevolent political climate, boasting two magazines: the excellent *Nova SF*, published and edited by Ugo Malaguti; and the Italian edition of *The Magazine of Fantasy and Science Fiction, Oltre il Cielo*, edited by "Ingenier Silvestri," which now has been published in more than 150 issues and is in the process of creating a rather lively sf fandom. *Oltre il Cielo* has developed a number of promising young sf writers, e.g. Lino Aldani, Sandro Sandrelli and Roberta Rambelli. Lino Aldani might be the most interesting. His stories often deal with sexual and moral problems, and this with an open-mindedness that one very seldom finds in sf elsewhere. A good number of his stories have been translated, most of them into French. In 1963, eight issues of a magazine called *Futuro* were published, wholly devoted to Italian sf writers.

The Soviet Union, as well as other East-European countries, although having a fair number of sf writers and traditions in science fiction, has not yet produced a science fiction magazine, to my knowledge. The closest thing to a sf magazine that I have encountered is a fan magazine, *Sci-Fi*, published in Hungary by a youth club. A Russian literary magazine aimed at the foreign market, *Soviet Literature*, devoted a complete issue (No. 5, May, 1968) to science fiction, printing among other things a novelette by the Polish sf writer Stanislaw Lem, *Cor Serpentis*, and this might be a hopeful sign.

So much for the magazines. It should be added that science fiction is a pronounced short story literature, whose ideas and treatment of ideas to a large degree are best suited for the concentrated short story format—something that has been clearly shown by a great number of long-winded, verbose novels that would have been much better off with their wordage cut in half.

To paraphrase Alva Rogers' observation in the beginning of this chapter, we now have the paperbacks, and a good thing they are, but the magazines are something else entirely. During the last thirty-five years science fiction has changed completely, from a crude and naïve pulp literature into a sophisticated tool for entertainment and good, intelligent speculation, developing its standards from within with very little or no help from the outside mainstream literary world. This is a magnificent feat, and the principal part of the honor belongs to the magazines. Them, and no one else.

10. FIAWOL!

The somewhat cryptic heading above is the most enthusiastic sf fan's war-cry when it comes to explaining the happiness of being a sf fan, and especially a sf fan in sf fandom. Translated into plain English it means *Fandom Is A Way Of Life*, and as a motto it isn't entirely unrealistic. This fandom encompasses the international sf movement, comprised of all sf and fantasy readers who are active and interested enough to seek contact with like-minded people in one way or another, through amateur magazines (fanzines), clubs, letters or conventions. SF fandom is unique in the way it has grown continuously and spread over the world, since its beginning in the U.S.A. in the twenties. As I have mentioned earlier, there are now even sf clubs and fanzines in the East Bloc. The main reason for this is probably the fact that sf fandom is not anything like an organization with central offices and so on. You gain entry by being interested enough to write someone a letter or subscribing to a fanzine, and you can't get kicked out again unless you do it yourself—a not uncommon thing, called *Gafia* (Getting Away From It All). During the forty-plus years of sf fandom, only a couple of persons have managed to make such complete asses of themselves that they have found themselves outcasts. The sf fans are generally very broad-minded.

A diligent fan might rise in the ranks to BNF (Big Name Fan); an honorary title that means absolutely nothing except that he is known to a sufficient number of people, through fanzine publishing or letter-writing or whatever it might be. The fans of the thirties—now lovingly referred to as "First Fandom"—are to a great degree still active in the field as well-known writers, publishers and editors, e.g.

Isaac Asimov, Donald A. Wollheim, Ray Bradbury and John Carnell, who now play an important part in the evolution of the genre.

Practically all sf writers of today come from sf fandom. They discovered it through the letter columns of the sf magazines, participated enthusiastically in the sf conventions and published mimeographed or offset printed fanzines with circulations of perhaps a hundred copies, in which they (at least sometimes) discussed science fiction, fought innumerable feuds and polished their talents until the day they were accepted in the professional sector. The contact between professional writers and their readers has since the beginning of sf fandom been maintained via the fanzines.

Writers, editors, etc. write regularly (and gratis) in the fanzines, participate in the discussions in the letter columns and visit the conventions as ordinary members. (There are, of course, conventions limited to professionals in the field, like the Science Fiction Writers of America's annual awards dinner.) The democracy is absolute, and there are very few signs of submissiveness toward the Big Names to be found.

Emblem of Hugo Gernsback's
original Science Fiction League.

SCIENCE FICTION: WHAT IT'S ALL ABOUT

The Big Names contribute to the fanzines on the same conditions as other contributors.

This has created a fruitful feedback system which, as Kingley Amis has pointed out, has kept most sf writers away from the ivory towers of the mainstream writers. We have an interesting example of this in the fierce debate regarding the pros and cons of the "New Wave," that is waged not between critics but mainly between writers and readers. Which, in my opinion, is the only way a debate should be handled. The writer, after all, is writing for his readers—or he should be, anyway—not for his critics.

The Hugo Award of science fiction is another example of the democracy of this field, whereby the readers are permitted to voice their opinions regarding the science fiction published during the past year. For once, the literary critics are equal with the readers, and the results of the Hugo votings give, I believe, a much more truthful picture of a science fiction work's impact than all the professional critics in the world.

When *Amazing Stories* started modern science fiction forty-five years ago, few norms of the genre existed. Since then, the field has developed into a highly complex literature with obvious literary qualities that to a great extent are the result of the exchange of ideas and the criticism voiced in sf fandom. This is also the source of the U.S.A.'s dominance in the sf field. Fandom started in the U.S.A. as a result of *Amazing Stories* and other early sf magazines. The first pronounced sf writers came from this U.S. fandom, and when this modern science fiction appeared in other countries, good science fiction was written only in one place, the U.S.A.

In England, where sf fandom appeared after the U.S. one, readers and writers had the advantage of writing in the same language as the U.S. fans, and were thus able to participate in the internal debate in a way that wasn't possible for aficionados in other countries. Today, following a rise of interest in science fiction over the world, writers find it easier than before to get published in their native languages, and the magazines that during recent years have appeared both in Europe and South America promise a development similar to that of the U.S.A.: first a local fandom, and then writers who know how to use the tools of the trade. As in the U.S.A., European mainstream writers turning to science fiction mostly seem to repeat the themes of yesterday's science fiction. There are innumerable painful examples of this.

The beginning of this sf fandom was due to—as almost everything in modern science fiction—Hugo Gernsback's magazine *Amazing Stories,* notably the letter column *Discussions.* The mass of letters streaming into sf magazines has always been a source of wonder for people outside the field. During the pulp era, the magazines often contained ten to fifteen pages of letters, discussions and more or less private feuds between writers-editors-readers. The sf fans have always kept their contacts mainly through letters, and the large readers' departments of the magazines have been the traditional meeting-places for readers and writers alike. *Discussions* became a natural center for debates, contacts were established between readers, and only a couple of years after the start of *Amazing Stories,* the first fanzine appeared.

First of all were *Cosmic Stories* and *Cosmic Stories Quarterly,* carbon-copied fanzines produced by two young fans who had met through the letter department of *Amazing Stories.* They were Jerome Siegal and Joseph Shuster, later famous as originators of *Superman.* At about the same time the *Science Correspondence Club* was formed under the benevolent guidance of Hugo Gernsback, as a club for sf fans. It was later reorganized as the venerable *International Scientific Association.* The club published a mimeographed fanzine called *The Comet,* to which the Big Names of the day contributed regularly. The department of rockets and space was written by an unknown German sf fan named Willy Ley. *The Comet* devoted, however, most of its space to the new science, and perhaps this was not exactly what the sf fans hungered for.

A club called *The Scienceers* was formed in New York; and in July, 1930 the first "pure" sf fanzine was published,

The Planet, featuring short stories written by members of the club, reviews of films and books, and news and gossip from sf fandom. Similar fanzines appeared from other clubs and fans: *The Time Traveller, Science Fiction, SF Digest, The Fantasy Fan,* etc. The fans got into contact with each other through these fanzines, new clubs appeared all over the U.S.A., and in the beginning of the thirties a sort of loosely organized sf fandom appeared in England as well, with the founding of The British Science Fiction Association. The first British sf convention was held in Leeds on January 3, 1937, only three months after the first U.S. convention.

U.S. fandom got its first Cinderella tale in November, 1933, when old Uncle Gernsback suddenly employed the publisher of the fanzine *The Fantasy Fan* as editor for his magazine *Wonder Stories.* The new editor was a seventeen-year-old boy named Charles Hornig, and Hornig immediately started to encourage new writers from sf fandom. This was later repeated by other sf fans who after years as fans and fanzine publishers became professionals in the field, e.g. Donald A. Wollheim, one of the super-fans of the time, now a recognized writer and a leading publisher in the genre.

The first great sf organization in the U.S.A., *The Science Fiction League,* was founded in 1934, again with Hugo Gernsback as the father; and later the New York branch of a sf-slanted organization called *International Scientific Association* (ISA) started planning for a national gathering of sf fans. The convention, instigated by Donald A. Wollheim, took place in Philadelphia in October, 1936, with about forty attendees. Three years later the first "World SF Convention" was held in New York, coinciding with the New York World's Fair. This "World Convention" originally was to have been sponsored by the ISA with Donald A. Wollheim as chairman. Later, due to feuds and the breaking-up of the ISA, a group of fans including Isaac Asimov, Frederik Pohl, Dirk Wylie, Robert Lowndes and Donald A. Wollheim founded *The Futurian Society of New York* to handle the convention. More feuds started, another group known as *New Fandom* appeared, and when the World SF Convention finally started on July 2, 1939, *New Fandom* had been given the run of the show. Far from being the unifying factor in a feud-ridden fandom, this "World" convention actually started more feuds than any other event of the time. Feuds still are common in sf fandom; they make for interesting happenings, at any rate.

The U.S.A. is, if I may say so, a rather provincial country in many respects, and even though "World SF Conventions" were held every year from 1939 onward, the first real World SF Convention wasn't held until 1957, in London. U.S. fandom slowly began to understand that there actually existed a world outside the borders of the U.S.A., and at the 27th World Science Fiction Convention, held in St. Louis, U.S.A., over Labor Day weekend, 1969, a motion was passed (to the accompaniment of loud protests from the conservatives present), affecting the future of the Conventions and the Hugo Awards. It reads as follows:

1. The name of the sf convention now held in North America and styled the "World Science Fiction Convention should be changed to the North American Science Fiction Convention (NASFiC).

2. A true World (or International) Science Fiction Convention (or Congress, etc.) being desirable, it is recommended that a committee be set up at St. Louis to confer with similar committees and individual fans in Europe, the Pacific, etc. to suggest suitable mechanisms for holding such conventions.

3. To maintain the continuity of the name "World Science Fiction Convention" the following interim plan is suggested. The World Science Fiction Convention title shall rotate through continental zones in a prearranged manner. One of these zones shall be North America. The fans of each zone shall determine as they see fit which convention in their zone shall assume the title "World Science Fiction Convention" when the title is resident in their zone. In North America the NASFiC would automatically assume

the title when the title is resident in North America.

4. The numbering of the NASFiC shall continue the numbering from the former World Science Fiction Conventions in order to preserve continuity when dealing with hotels.

The Hugo Award, a counterpart to the Oscars of the film industry, was first presented at the 11th World SF Convention in Philadelphia, 1953. Willy Ley received an award for excellency in fact articles, Philip José Farmer as best new author, *Galaxy* and *Astounding SF* as best magazines, Forrest J. Ackerman as No. 1 fan personality, and *The Demolished Man* by Alfred Bester as best novel. The Hugo (so named in honor of Hugo Gernsback, who later was presented with a Special Award at the 18th World SF Convention in Pittsburg in 1960) is an English language award, that can be given only to materials presented in English and first translations into English. The categories are Best Novel, Best Novella, Best Novelette, Best Short Story, Best Dramatic Presentation, Best Professional Magazine, Best Professional Artist, Best Fan Artist, Best Fanzine, Best Fan Writer and Special Award (the latter in 1969 presented to astronauts Armstrong, Aldrin and Collins "for best Moon landing ever"). There are usually a couple of special awards, like Big Heart Award, First Fandom Award, etc. The Hugo Award has now been recognized by publishers also, and an award-winning novel can be sure to have this fact advertised in bold letters on the covers of forthcoming editions.

The recipients of the Hugo Award are voted for by the members of the World SF Convention. This is also the case of the British Fantasy/Science Fiction Award, which was instituted by the British Science Fiction Association and first presented at the British SF Convention at Yarmouth at Easter, 1966, on the basis of a poll taken amongst the Association's members. The winner (on his general record rather than for any specific book) was John Brunner. John

Sample of the Heicon promotion.

Brunner won another British SF Award in 1970, for his novel *Stand on Zanzibar*.

The Australian *Ditmars* award and the Swedish *Alvar* award are presented to recipients of the respective countries in about the same way, by the members of the national convention.

The Nebula, the award given to worthy recipients by the Science Fiction Writers of America at their annual convention, differs somewhat from the Hugo and its sister awards. It is given by professionals in the field to other professionals as a token of estimation, and it appears that these professionals sometimes have quite different views on what has been the best sf published during the preceding year than the fans have. The award, which consists of a spiral nebula made of metallic glitter and a specimen of rock crystal embedded in a block of clear lucite with a black base, as different from the Hugo space ship, is given to the Best Novel, Best Novella, Best Novelette and Best Short Story. An annual collection of Nebula award-winning stories is published both in hardcover and paperback.

During the last decade, science fiction fandom has begun showing signs of developing into a truly international occurrence in which aficionados from all parts of the world might find friendly souls. The 28th World Convention in Heidelberg, Germany in 1970 became a meeting-place for readers, writers and editors from all parts of the world, and this, in my opinion, can't help but broaden the understanding between rivaling groups within this microcosm. Fandom as a whole has been a far from homogenous body, constantly racked by feuds, as attested to by Sam Moskowitz's very revealing account of the unbelievable state of U.S. fandom up to W.W. II, *The Immortal Storm* (Atlanta: ASFO Press, 1954, 269 pp.). Harry Warner, Jr., another sf fan who has been in fandom since its beginning, has written another book dealing with U.S. fandom in the forties, *All Our Yesterdays* (Chicago: Advent, 1969, 359 pp.).

I do not believe that fandom suddenly has become all nice and friendly and working together toward some future goal of science fiction for everyone, but fandom has obviously matured a lot since the tumultuous prewar years. The personal feuds between some fans in the U.S.A. also must seem quite uninteresting when seen against a backdrop of an international sf fandom. After all, sf fandom is composed of a number of people who happen to be interested in science fiction, and even if there are some people in it who appear to be more interested in the paraphernalia of clubs, fanzines and conventions than in the actual literary media, the overall picture is one of a large number of individuals devoting themselves to a common interest. No one pretends that theirs is the best of all possible interests or mankind's salvation, but they are wholeheartedly involved in this fandom of intelligent and readable literature that gives a lot of food for thought and the possibility of meeting like-minded people.

For many years there has existed a number of fanzines which specialize in news about occurrences in fandom, book reviews, professional news and the like. The most venerable of these, the U.S. *Science Fiction Times* has not been seen for a long time now, but until it ceased it had published more than 460 issues. At the moment, we have the U.S. *Luna Monthly, SFWA Bulletin, Science Fiction Review, Locus,* etc.; the British *Vector* and *Speculation;* the German *SF Times;* The Swedish *Science Fiction Nytt;* the French *Le Sac a Charbon, Horizons de Fantastique,* and so forth.

Emblem of the
Scandinavian S.F. Union.

Added to this are all the fanzines, these mimeographed or offset printed publications that sometimes have all the attributes of the professional magazines except the circulation; e.g. Tom Reamy's *Trumpet* and Leland Sapiro's *Riverside Quarterly.* Not to mention all the specialized fanzines that are devoted to certain writers, like the James Branch Cabell Society's *Kalki,* edited by James Blish, and the numerous E. R. Burroughs and J. R. R. Tolkien fanzines. These fanzines are hard to obtain for the uninitiated, but they are usually well worth the trouble.

The literary quality of the fanzines is much higher than would be expected from amateur publications, many of their contributors and publishers being professionals in the field. The debates in these are far more unprejudiced than those carried on in the largely circulated magazines' letter or editorial departments; actually, most of the debates in science fiction are carried on in these fanzines. And there are a number of highly original writers and illustrators working in these fanzines, whose works probably would have much trouble getting published in the large magazines. And this is not because the quality is inferior.

Poster for the 1st "European SF Convention".

The sf fanzines are labors of love—many of them, as I have mentioned, having a true professional look—not only as regards the quality of the contents but also from their outside appearances. They range all the way from the unsophisticated single-sheet fanzine written out in ten copies by way of carbon copies, to 200-page mammoths written out on an IBM electric typewriter with "executive" differential type spacing and carbon paper tape, printed in four-color offset with glossy covers. The contents vary from the letter-fanzine, consisting of little but letters to the editor and his more or less witty comments, and up to the scholarly literary magazine with articles by Robert A. Heinlein, Isaac Asimov and John Brunner and a letter column that is graced by every Big Name of sf that can be imagined and then some.

Some of these fanzines are so staggeringly intellectual that one hardly dares to read them. A Swedish fanzine, *Science Fiction Forum*, appeared in 1969 with an issue (No. 40) of 240 mimeographed pages, closely written with even right margins, and printed in an overall circulation of one hundred copies. I shudder to think of the work put into that monster of a fanzine.

In a field which has been met with precious little understanding by outside critics, science fiction fandom has created its own standards of quality. Via the fruitful feedback system between readers, writers and editors it has succeeded in transforming an admittedly crude literature into a suitable tool both for entertainment and social criticism as well as a literature of no mean literary qualities. The editors of the magazines have always been predominant in influencing the development, but the readers always have known their preferences as well—and they have had the chance of making themselves heard. This is democracy to a degree that never has occurred in any other literary field, and it has given remarkable results. Whatever the faults and shortcomings of this sf fandom, it has succeeded in improving its literature throughout the years—and who can hope to do better than that?

11. THE FUTURE

And what can be expected of the science fiction to come? "It's difficult to prophesy, especially about the future," the Danish artist Robert Storm Pedersen once said, and I am certainly not prophesying. Certain tendencies can be traced in present-day science fiction, though. Twenty years ago, science fiction devoted itself mostly to the probable effects of man's contact with the outer world, extraterrestrial creatures and so on. Even the Moon shot was as much sf as it could be. Today the speculative element in the Moon shot is obviously gone, a story dealing with the first landing on the Moon is science *fact*, not fiction (at least not in the sf sense of the word), and within the next decade, stories dealing with the first Mars landing will probably meet the same fate.

I believe science fiction will go farther out—but in a speculative rather than a distance sense. Inter- and extragalactic voyages have been commonplace occurrences in science fiction since the days of E. E. Smith. I believe that the next decade will witness a change in the science fiction field as great as that of the preceding forty years. A new breed of science fiction writers are on their way in, as attested to by, for example, Ace Books' excellent *Ace Science Fiction Special* series. Here we, interestingly enough, not only find writers of singular power who were completely unknown ten years ago, but also a number of names well-known in sf who are experimenting with new forms, minting the sf coinage of the next decade as it were.

The traditional action-story will, of course, be with us, spreading its particular form of Sense-of-Wonder in a way that no kind of "new" sf can hope to encompass. But apart from that I see two distinct directions for science fiction, directions that, each in its own way, can enrich the genre, giving it a new vitality and a new meaning. The first is the avant-garde "New Wave" science fiction that hopefully will find its own vernacular before it drowns in its own four-letter words or loses itself in the surrealistic cathedrals of words that it has created itself. The second is the fantasy-slanted, very absurd and often very funny brand of science fiction represented by, among others, Robert Sheckley.

Sheckley, according to himself, no longer writes anything that doesn't amuse him, and what amuses him—and a growing number of readers—is a highly improbable world where absolutely nothing works as one would expect it to work. Sheckley uses the old Sense-of-Wonder philosophy with all the traditional gimmicks attached, but in his peculiar never-never land the machines live a life of their own, and the result comes actually much closer to wild fantasy than the thundering space ship armadas of E. E. Smith.

In two of his latest books, *Mindswap* (1966) and *Dimension of Miracles* (1968), Sheckley has placed very ordinary men in a universe where none of the usual natural laws work, where black is white and planets are built by greedy cosmic building-contractors, where the machines act like resentful and petty human beings, and the dizzying views fall flat to the ground at the first inquisitive examination. They are cosmic revues with the common man as the bewildered common denominator. Even if Sheckley's obvious delight in his ideas sometimes tends to degenerate into pure idea acrobatics, his stories and novels are consistently original, and Sheckley's grand sense of humor—an all too seldom found commodity in present-day science fiction—sometimes elevates his fantasies into the bizarre universes of Franz Kafka and Boris Vian. Because underneath the absurd humor, Sheckley is deadly serious. He has something to say, an idea, a meaning, and he uses absurdity to put it across to the reader.

This absurdity, or whatever you would like to name it, can also be found in the comparatively new type of mature fantasy that has become increasingly popular in the U.S.A. during recent years. I don't just mean black humor like

Joseph Heller's brilliant *Catch-22*, but more the symbol-laden mysticism of, for example, Hermann Hesse, whose novel *Steppenwolf* in 1969 sold 360,000 copies in thirty days in the U.S.A. This is encouraging, because Hesse is human and wise, but one of the principal reasons for his popularity must be his inclination toward mysticism. *Siddhartha* alone is a kind of new gospel, while his *Steppenwolf*'s denunciation of the social contract and strong emphasis on the individual's eternal divine nature is obviously attracting millions of people.

We find this mystical experience in many science fiction works of today, notably in the works of Roger Zelazny and Samuel R. Delany—not to mention Philip K. Dick. Along with those come works like Avram Davidson's highly personal treatment of the literary Vergil figure in *The Phoenix and the Mirror* (1966), a powerful metaphysical experience placed in a strange never-never land of classical time. The mysticism of this work is again brought forth quite differently in a recent work of Roger Zelazny, *Damnation Alley* (1969), a cruel novel set in a future after the catastrophe, in which Hell Tanner, the last survivor of the exterminated cycle gangs, fights his way across a blasted continent teeming with symbols of guilt and failure.

The sf stories belonging to this group that John Carnell calls "medieval futurism"—future technologies with heavy overtones of the feudal systems of the Middle Ages, sometimes with accompanying magic, etc.—would seem to fit in here as well. Although to me this particular sub-branch of science fiction seems more of an offshot of mysticism, being essentially action-stories built on the fronts of the mystical experience.

One of the curious occurrences of science fiction today is the sudden rise of interest in fantasy, particularly on campuses. It started with J. R. R. Tolkien, but is rolling on with a renewed interest in Mervyn Peake, James Branch Cabell and a number of more modern fantasy writers as well. Personally, I am inclined to see this as yet another example of the attraction of mysticism—fantasy is appearing in exactly the same circles that have been embracing the

Transcendental Meditation fad, among others—and if it is so, we will probably see much more fantasy coming during the next decade. Kenneth Bulmer, a well-known sf writer, says in a letter that:

> As to why I think (a fantasy magazine) is needed these days, I see the disarray into which the sf magazines are falling and feel that fantasy will be the medium in which what we sf people have been for so long trying to do can be successfully carried on. There is also a tremendous interest in fantasy at the present time, not just in sword and sorcery, and this probably stems in part from a rejection of scientific materialistic values, due to the obvious and many times rammed home reasons even the Sunday color magazines are aware of. I think that many of the values being rejected are still capable of viable use in the present world and in the future; but they need to be restated and this is where fantasy can come in with fresh methods of presentation, new slants and a whole modern and up-dated format of entertainment. The messages will then continue to get through . . . I'm all for the modern world and whilst I deplore a great deal of what is being done and allowed to be done, and omitted, in the name of progress, I am still completely convinced that the values of the past cannot all be tossed aside—the old baby and the bathwater syndrome again—and that examples of conduct and thinking will indicate where we need to look for guidance of and from the future.

The "New Wave" is, of course, another offspring of Hermann Hesse's mysticism, only as yet more crude and lacking the understanding of the symbols used. The "New Wave's" brand of mysticism is known as "inner space," and J. G. Ballard, one of the "New Wave's" most well-known advocates, and the author of a number of brilliant excursions into the universe of mytsical experience, as early as 1962 stated his aims as:

SCIENCE FICTION: WHAT IT'S ALL ABOUT

I would like to see more psycho-literary ideas, more meta-biological and meta-chemical concepts, private time-systems, synthetic psychologies and space-times, more of the remote, sombre half-worlds one glimpses in the paintings of schizophrenics, all in all a complete speculative poetry and fantasy of science.

In other words, a denunciation of the real world, a return to the abstract, the incomprehensible, the metaphysical. That this can be done while retaining the powers of communication between writer and reader, offering an insight into the dream world of abstractions and mysticism, has been proved not only by the early writers of the absurd such as Alfred Jarry, but also by J. G. Ballard himself in novels like *The Crystal World* (1966). Here, a crystallitic disease engulfs Earth, transforming the eternal forests into shimmering caverns of diamonds where men run, arms stretched out like ruby crosses, and the trees raise their flaming cathedrals up toward the unmoving, shimmering sky.

Ballard has, together with his fellow "New Wave" writers, been subjected to fierce criticism from the old sf garde who do not think this is science fiction. I do not agree with this wholeheartedly, as the "New Wave" is a sign of change within the field, and if the field is incapable of change it would surely be extinct before long. However, it is certain that few "New Wave" writers have found their vernacular; instead they retreat into some kind of impotent absurdity that says nothing, conveys nothing and means nothing.

There is also a marked rise in the use of obscenities in the "New Wave," which strikes me as completely unnecessary. A recent novel by Norman Spinrad, *Bug Jack Barron*, is practically a collection of obscenities. And Spinrad is far, far from alone in this. Now, I am far from being a prude. I was born and reared in a country where tolerance toward sex in all its forms is considered important. I consider myself open-minded as far as sex is concerned. Yet I find it curious, to say the very least, the way certain "New Wave" writers can't write three words without using one or two obscene words. Frequent use of obscenities might shock some people, but in the long run this is more childish than effective. Samuel Mines, a well-known editor, has observed that:

> I expect this in low intelligence and crude tastes. When I find reasonably well-educated individuals afflicted with the same compulsion I am forced to either of two conclusions: that they are so immature they are still trying to impress by shock value, or they are in need of therapy. Look it up in a good psychiatric textbook—Tourette's syndrome is well-known to psychiatrists: The obsessive need to employ obscenities in speech . . . I am not arguing for a lily-white phoniness in writing. I'm for realism, not euphemism. I'm not shocked by four-letter words. I simply think they debase our style and our level of expression. I'm complaining about the *needless* overdone vulgarity which some writers without taste apparently think is realism. (55)

The "New Wave" science fiction is filled with a general sense of defeat, a wish to turn away from the hard realities of this world, and perhaps this obsession with vulgarities is just one result of this. It does not make for great literature, though, and it certainly does not take the sf genre forward. This, of course, also goes for all the literary tools that have led this "New Wave" into a dead end with no way out. The Polish sf writer Stanislaw Lem recently observed that the "New Wave" authors:

> . . . feel that all the "realism" in "serious" sf was but a myth gone to the dogs and that there should be a *change* in the future, but they do not know how to effect such a change, and therefore eagerly seize upon such literary paradigms as surrealism, which is only an indication of their intellectual poverty. For new things require new forms and surrealism has already become a historical factor in the stream of art. (56)

So much for the new directions in the English-speaking countries. Outside England and the U.S.A., the sf writers are naturally far less sophisticated, and most local Big Name sf writers actually belong more to the pulp era of sf than to the present-day field. Swedish attempts at science fiction are often interesting, but far from original, e.g. Sven Delblanc's *Homunculus,* which is the old Frankenstein story told again in a modern setting. There are, however, a number of Swedish mainstream writers, like P. C. Jersild, Ann-Margret Dahlquist-Ljungberg and Arvid Rundberg, who often use science fiction as a literary tool with exceptionally good results, and more are appearing. It should be noted, though, that none of these writers ever have had any connection with sf or sf fandom previously to their writing sf, and the themes employed are thus often old hat for the aficionado.

A quality sf book series exists, published by Askild & Kärnekull Förlag AB and edited by Sam J. Lundwall. Actually, with close to forty sf novels published in Sweden during 1970, science fiction is doing better than ever in this country.

Denmark has been remarkably well-furnished with sf during the latest years, much due to the efforts of Jannick Storm, the editor of a sf book series, published by Hasselbalchs Förlag. Jannick Storm is an advocate of the "New Wave" in science fiction, and many of the new sf works published by native writers are also quite New Wave-ish, e.g. Knud Holten's recent *Suma-X.* Other interesting recent Danish sf novels include Sven Holm's *Termush* and Anders Bodelsen's *Frysepunktet* (The Freezing Point).

Norway has no less than two diligent "New Wave" advocates, Jon Bing and Tor Åge Bringsvaerd, the authors of a number of short stories and plays, as well as editors of anthologies of way-out science fiction. A recent Norwegian sf novel, Axel Jensen's *Epp,* was awarded the Abraham Woursell European Literature Award in 1966.

Germany, although with literary progenitors in sf from E. T. A. Hoffmann, Kurd Lasswitz and Hans Dominik, has yet to produce one single sf writer of class. Sf in Germany means usually Perry Rhodan; there are Perry Rhodan comic strips, Perry Rhodan films, hundreds of Perry Rhodan clubs, Perry Rhodan conventions, anything you can name and then some. This Captain Future-copy apparently is just what the Germans like, and other German sf is about on the same level as this Cosmic Hero. There are two dime novel series, Moewig's *Terra Nova* and Zauberkreis' *Zauberkreis SF*, both principally featuring translations, as does the Heine, Moewig and Goldmann *Space Pocket Books*.

Italy has advanced during recent years with a number of interesting sf writers, e.g. the already-mentioned Lino Aldani, Sandro Sandrelli and Antonio Belloni, the latter unquestionably of the old school of sf. Among the sf fans who lately have emerged as writers are Luigi Naviglio, Riccardo Levehgi and Carlo Bordoni, all three publishers of fanzines. Italy has traditions since the turn of the century with the old Jules Verne-follower Emilio Salgari and his collaborator Luigi Motta, who among other things produced a plagiarism of Bernhard Kellerman's *Der Tunne* called *Il Tunnel Sotto il Mare*. Later Italian writers have shown considerable more independence, for example Italo Calvino, a bizarre writer of quality on a level with the best written in the U.S.A. today. The publishing house Adrian in Rome publishes a sf book series called *Alpha Centauri;* while Ugo Malaguti, the editor and publisher of the sf magazine *Nova SF,* is the editor of a series of sf classics published by Libra Editrice, as well as one series of contemporary sf, *Mondo di Domani.*

Austria recently witnessed a science fiction first, when the Austrian Volksbuchverlag published a book on science fiction, *Spuren ins all—Science Fiction—Das Seltsame Fremde* (Trails into Space—Science Fiction—The Strange Alien One), written by Winifried Bruckner, editor of the Austrian Workers Union's magazine *Solidarität.* The book was given away free by the Chamber of Workers as a gift to all young workers in Austria.

The interest in science fiction is also growing in the East European countries, where science in all forms is encouraged and science fiction sort of comes along. Russia has traditions from Konstantin Tsiolkovskij, the original inventor of the three-stage rocket, who wrote a number of quite heavy novels in the field. Ivan Yefremov's *Andromeda* has been translated into a number of languages, and Egen Zamyatin's *We* is one of the classic anti-Utopias of science fiction. Among the publishers that habitually publish science fiction, Molodaja Gvardija, Mir, Detgiz, Znanije and Mysl are the leading ones, with Mir being the publisher that translates most American and European science fiction into Russian, as well as Russian science fiction into other languages. Popular Soviet writers like I. Lukodianov, Gueorgui Martinov, Boris and Arkady Strugatsky, Anatoly Dneprov, Ilya Varshavsky and others are habitually translated into a number of languages including English, Spanish, Italian, German and so on.

In 1967, Molodaja Gvardija published a book of analyses of science fiction and presentations of certain sf writers, *Fantastika-67*, that dealt with, among others, Ray Bradbury, Stanislaw Lem, Boris and Arkady Strugatsky, Isaac Asimov, Robert Sheckley, Arthur C. Clarke and Clifford D. Simak. In 1970, the Soviet Academy of Sciences' publishing house *Nauka* published a book on science fiction, *Russian Soviet Science Fiction Novel*, written by Anatolij Britikov, which not only gives a thorough and very positive account of Soviet science fiction from the sixteenth century until now, but also devotes much space to sf development in the U.S.A. and Europe. The most well-known Russian sf writers, the brothers Boris and Arkady Strugatsky, the only ones comparable in quality to the best American sf authors, are subjected to considerable praise in this book; which is interesting, in view of the news early in 1970 that they had been blacklisted in Russia on account of some rather politically outspoken sf novels dealing, among other things, with a powerful country's "right" to "liberate" smaller countries. Apparently, they were not censored, at least not as much as the news had implied. In fact, the Strugatsky brothers seem now to be more popular than ever in Russia. Late in 1970, the magazine *Junost,* with a circulation exceeding

1,900,000 copies, started serializing their novel *Hotel in the Mountains*, a sf novel as outspoken as any of their earlier works.

The very popular sf book series *SF of the World*, which presents sf novels from the U.S.A. and Europe as well as from Russia, was originally to have been published in fifteen volumes, but proved so popular that it now will be published in at least twenty volumes. Recent volumes in this series have included a novel by Clifford D. Simak and an anthology of Scandinavian science fiction. Another popular book series, the *Almanach Nautshnoy Fantastiki*, a pocket series that features science fiction from all parts of the world, is even turning to the avant-garde "New Wave" style of sf. A recent novel (No. 9) features, among others, a very way-out short story by J. G. Ballard.

Russian magazines and newspapers also print a large amount of science fiction, particularly magazines like *Vokrug Sveta*, *Znanije-Sila*, *Teknika-molodezji* and *Nauka i zjisn*, all of them with very large circulations, approaching the millions. *Vokrug Sveta* (circulation: 2,700,000 copies) in particular has printed a lot of U.S. and European science fiction, mostly of the social criticism type, like Robert Bloch's *Nightmare Number Four*, a short story (or prose-poem) dealing with the advertising industry and the ultimate advertising gimmick. It might be presumptuous to talk about a Soviet science fiction boom, particularly not in the field of social criticism—the official Soviet reaction to Alexander Solzhenitsyn's recent Nobel prize in literature speaks for itself—but the interest in the genre is certainly large, and on the rise.

Poland's greatest sf writer Stanislaw Lem is also increasingly popular, not only in his native country. His recent novel *Solaris* has been published both in London and New York as the first of his many sf novels to see print in English. *Solaris* is an extremely interesting sf novel and a very sophisticated one, dealing with the concept of an imperfect God, one who is omnipotent but without omniscience, and the problems of communication between a group of human explorers and this strange entity. Stanislaw Lem has also

Illustration from a recent Soviet s-f novel.

written a book about science fiction, devoting special chapters to modern U.S. sf writers.

A veritable sf boom seems to have appeared in Romania, with a stream of book and magazine sf. The venerable magazine *Viata Romaneasca* recently devoted a complete issue to science fiction, presenting a number of native and foreign writers. Sf book series are being published, with most of the material being of native make. Romanian sf writers like Victor Kernbach, Valdimir Colin and Adrian Rogoz are immediately reviewed in the literary magazines when they publish new sf novels.

In East Germany the big name is Carlos Rasch, an author with a number of sf novels to his credit, and also the driving force behind the East German publishing of British and U.S. science fiction.

In all these East European countries there exists a more or less pronounced sf fandom, and now and then local fanzines have found their way through the Iron Curtain. It is all in the beginning stages as yet, but I am certain that the next decade will see East Europe taking new initiatives in the sf field. The U.S.A. will without doubt hold its position as the country where most sf is published, but I would not be surprised if Europe within the next ten or twenty years takes the lead in high-quality science fiction.

Science fiction is in rapid change, as everything is now. This is quite natural, and it is as natural that this development shouldn't be taken quietly by the old-time sf buffs, many of whom have been active since Hugo Gernsback started his first sf magazine, and now regard the new trends with ominous mutterings. There is still much talking about the "good old days," with which is meant the "golden" forties, and this is certainly very human and nothing to be surprised about. The revolutionary has an unhappy tendency to grow stiff with time and regard the ideals of his own youth as the apex of all development, spending the autumn of his life reminiscing about the good days of yore and complaining of the lousy times of today. The "Angry Young Men" of Britain are a typical example of revolutionaries who have become good, reactionary members of the Establishment. Bertrand Russell was one of the very few who managed to keep his intellect open to the end; but he was considered a very, very curious man.

That the science fiction readers and writers should be different in this respect would obviously be to hope for the impossible. Those who weren't fifteen years old when E. E. Smith wrote his thundering Space Operas, with the mile-long space ships and the spectacular machines, have great difficulties in finding anything interesting at all in them. A reader of today who doesn't have his mind filled to the bursting point with nostalgia can only observe that most of the pulp sf was terrible literature, that the love interest was taken directly from the sugar bowl, that the science was idiotic and the dizzying views hardly more than backdrops, sea stories on a cosmic level.

The science fiction of today is incomparably more sophisticated, and while the sf of today stands on foundations laid by the sf of the thirties and the forties, we should understand that what was good then must not necessarily be good now. In the same way, the sf of thirty years hence will probably be completely incomprehensible for those of us who grew up with the sf of today. And no doubt we will complain about the superficiality of the genre and dream back with tear-filled eyes to the "golden" sixties or seventies when there still was Sense-of-Wonder to be found.

John W. Campbell, one of the old guard who hasn't lost his Sense-of-Wonder, even though he has been working in the sf field since 1930 and has been one of the outstanding editors of sf since 1937, gives some poignant comments to this phenomenon in the preface to a tear-dripping book about Campbell's magazine *Astounding*. The book is written by Alva Rogers, who holds to the view that the pulp *Astounding* of the thirties and the early forties truly was of the "golden" age of science fiction. It is a sentimental book, a nostalgic look back at the author's youth—something that the author admits in a foreword. Campbell tears the nostalgic mood to pieces with obvious delight in his preface. The grand finale is worthy of reproducing; and it will also form the end of this study in science fiction:

THE FUTURE

So what about the Great Old Authors (please remember that 1940 was almost a quarter century ago)? Well, they're convinced that they already know how to write and aren't gonna be told what they should write by that dictatorial, authoritarian, uncooperative Campbell. They aren't going to sell their immortal birthright to Great Authorhood for any mess of dollars! And granted that the Sense of Wonder is gone, in large part, because the Old Fans are old now. But the Great Old Authors are old, too! Most of them got their scientific orientation back in the early thirties, and they've been running on it ever since. How many of them are in contact with actual research work being done today—and getting the feel for the major direction of science *now*? Who's done any extrapolation of the possibilities of super conductive systems, for instance?

They know that science fiction is about rocket ships —so they persist in using rocket ships in stories of the centuries-hence future, when it's perfectly obvious the damn things are hopelessly inefficient and impractical as *useful* transportation. And the Great Old Authors will *not* recognize that we've already *told* these stories; that we've already exercised our Sense of Wonder wondering about *those* ideas.

Will somebody tell me why the Great Old Authors will not get off their literary tails and consider something new? They hate me for shoving new concepts and new ideas at them—and damn me for *their* lack of Sense of Wonder!

The world rolls on and we either roll with it or get left behind to mumble about the Good Old Days. If you think science fiction is getting dull, it just possibly *could* be you. And I've got a pretty good idea of what's wrong but I don't know anything that can be done about it.

I don't know of *anybody* who's growing any younger. . . . (57)

Notes

1. Lord Dunsany. *The Hoard of the Gibbelins.* From *The Book of Wonder*, London, 1912.
2. "Doom Beyond Jupiter," *Harper's Magazine,* September, 1939, pp. 445-48.
3. Fredric Brown. *Angels and Spaceships.* London: Four Square, 1962, p. 8.
4. Jules Verne. *The Begum's Fortune.* N.Y.: Ace Books, 1969, pp. 103-04.
5. Ingvald Raknem. *H. G. Wells and His Critics.* Oslo: Universitetsförlaget, 1963, pp. 395-96.
6. *The Critic,* July 25, 1896.
7. *The Daily News,* January 21, 1898, p. 6.
8. H. G. Wells. *Experiments in Autobiography.*
9. Ibid.
10. Plato. *The Republic.* Book V. N.Y.: Putnam's Sons, 1930, pp. 461-63.
11. Jacques Delarue. *The History of the Gestapo.* London: Corgi, 1966, pp. 80-81.
12. Ligeia Gallagher. *More's Utopia and Its Critics.* Chicago: Scott, Foreman & Co., 1964, p. 38.
13. Ibid. p. 59.
14. Isaac Asimov. *Foundation.* London: Panther, 1960, p. 12.
15. George Orwell. *1984.* N.Y.: Signet, 1961, p. 220.
16. Frederik Pohl & Cyril M. Kornbluth. *The Space Merchants.* London: Digit Books, 1961, pp. 7-8.
17. J. G. Ballard. *The Subliminal Man.* From *The Disaster Area.* London: Panther, 1969, pp. 64-65.
18. Robert Sheckley. *The Tenth Victim.* London: Mayflower, 1966, pp. 22-23.

9. George Matthew Lewis. *The Monk*. N.Y.: Grove Press, 1959, p. 308.

0. Mary Shelley. *Frankenstein*. N.Y.: Signet, 1965, p. 214.

1. Carlos Clarens. *An Illustrated History of the Horror Film*. N.Y.: Putnam's Sons, 1967, p. 62.

2. *The World's Biggest Bloodsucker*. Luna Monthly, January, 1970, p. 8.

3. H. P. Lovecraft. *The Dream-Quest of Unknown Kadath*. N.Y.: Ballentine Books, 1970, p. viii.

4. L. Sprague de Camp (ed.). *The Spell of Seven*. N.Y.: Pyramid, 1965, p. 7.

5. L. Sprague de Camp (ed.). *The Fantastic Swordsmen*. N.Y.: Pyramid, 1967, p. 10.

6. L. Sprague de Camp (ed.) *The Spell of Seven*. NY.: Pyramid, 1965.

27. Edwin L. Arnold. *Gulliver of Mars*. N.Y.: Ace Books, 1970, p. 6.

8. Richard A. Lupoff. *Edgar Rice Burroughs, Master of Adventure*. N.Y.: Ace Books, 1968, p. 11.

29. Michael Moorcock. *Putting a Tag on It*. AMRA, No. 15, 1961, p. 16.

0. Red Boggs. *Does Conan Need Suspenders?* AMRA, No. 14, 1961, p. 16.

31. A. Merritt. *The Ship of Ishtar*. N.Y.: Avon Books, 1951.

2. William Ready. *Understanding Tolkien*. N.Y.: Paperback Library, 1969, p. 48.

3. Catherine R. Stimpson. *J. R. R. Tolkien*. (Columbia Essays on Modern Writers. 41) N.Y.: Columbia University, 1969, p. 43.

4. Robert Silverberg. *Journey's End*. From *Dimension Thirteen*. N.Y.: Ballantine, 1969, p. 183

5. Alva Rogers. *A Requiem for Astounding*. Chicago: Advent, 1967, p. vi.

6. Kingsley Amis & Robert Conquest. *Spectrum 2*. London: Pan Books, 1965, pp. 8-9.

37. Stewart Alsop. *Dr. Calhoun's Horrible Mousery*. Newsweek, August 17, 1970, p. 9.

38. Cyril M. Kornbluth in *The SF Novel*. Chicago: Advent, 1964, pp. 98-99.

39. Anne McCaffrey. *A Womanly Talent. Analog,* February, 1969, pp. 19-20.
40. *Startling Stories,* November, 1939, p. 115.
41. Robert Sheckley. *A Ticket to Tranai.* From *Citizen in Space.* N.Y.: Ballantine, 1962, p. 134.
42. John Wyndham. *Consider Her Ways.* London: Penguin, 1965, pp. 49-51.
43. Robert Sheckley. *A Ticket to Tranai.* From *Citizen in Space.* N.Y.: Ballantine, 1962, p. 136.
44. Anne McCaffrey. *A Womanly Talent. Analog,* February, 1969, p. 54.
45. Theodore Sturgeon. *Venus Plus X.* N.Y.: Pyramid, 1968, pp 151-52.
46. Michael Moorcock. *Stormbringer.* London: Mayflower, 1968, pp. 188-89.
47. Sam Moskowitz. *Seekers of Tomorrow.* N.Y.: Ballantine, 1967, p. 395.
48. Brian Aldiss. *Visiting Amoeba.* From *Galaxies Like Grains of Sand.* N.Y.: Signet, 1960, p. 144.
49. William Tenn. *Betelgeuse Bridge.* From *The Wooden Star.* N.Y.: Ballantine, 1968, p. 117.
50. *Science Fiction Times.* No. 298, 1958, p. 1.
51. "Where Are They Now?" *Newsweek,* August 4, 1969, p. 8.
52. Steve Vertlieb. *Inside a Starship Captain.* L'Incroyable Cinema, No. 3, 1970, p. 35.
53. Alva Rogers. *A Requiem For Astounding.* Chicago: Advent, 1967, p. vi.
54. L. Sprague de Camp. *Science Fiction Handbook.* N.Y.: Hermitage, 1953, p. 17.
55. Samuel Mines. *Those Four-Letter Words. Luna Monthly,* July, 1969, pp. 9, 18.
56. *Luna Monthly.* August, 1969, p. 6.
57. Alva Rogers. *A Requiem for Astounding.* Chicago: Advent, 1967. p. XXI.

Bibliography

Books dealing with science fiction.

Amis, Kingsley. *New Maps of Hell*. N.Y.: Harcourt, Brace & Co., 1960, 161 p.

Ackerman, Forrest J. *The Frankenscience Monster*. N.Y.: Ace Books, 1970, 191 p.

Atheling, William, Jr., (James Blish). *The Issue at Hand*. Chicago: Advent, 1964, 136 p.

Bleiler, Everett F. *The Checklist of Fantastic Literature*. Chicago: Shasta Publ., 1948, 455 p.

Bretnor, Reginald (ed.). *Modern Science Fiction, Its Meaning and Its Future*. N.Y.: Coward-McCann, 1953, 294 p.

Clarens, Carlos. *An Illustrated History of the Horror Film*. N.Y.: Putnam's Sons, 1967.

Carter, Lin. *Tolkien: A Look Behind the Lord of the Rings*. N.Y.: Ballantine Books, 1969, 214 p.

Davenport, Basil (ed.). *The Science Fiction Novel: Imagination and Social Criticism*. Chicago: Advent, 1964, 160 p.

De Camp, L. Sprague. *Science Fiction Handbook*. N.Y.: Hermitage, 1953, 328 p.

Gallagher, Ligeia. *More's Utopia and Its Critics*. Chicago: Scott, Foreman & Co., 1964, 182 p.

Green, Roger Lancelyn. *Into Other Worlds*. N.Y.: Abelard-Schuman, 1957, 190 p.

Knight, Damon. *In Search of Wonder*. Chicago: Advent, 1967, 306 p.

Lupoff, Richard A. *Edgar Rice Burroughs, Master of Adventure*. N.Y.: Ace Books, 1969, 315 p.

Metcalf, Norman. *The Index of Science Fiction Magazines 1951-1965*. N.Y.: Stark, 1968, 253 p.

Moskowitz, Sam. *Explorers of the Infinite: Shapers of Science Fiction.* N.Y.: World, 1963.

———. *Seekers of Tomorrow.* N.Y.: Ballantine Books, 1967, 450 p.

Rogers, Alva. *A Requiem For Astounding.* Chicago: Advent, 1964, 224 p.

Tuck, Donald H. *Science Fiction Handbook.* Tasmania: 1959, 396 p.

Warner, Harry, Jr., *All Our Yesterdays.* Chicago: Advent, 1969, 336 p.

Wollheim, Donald A. *The Universe Makers.* N.Y.: Harper & Row, 1971.

INDEX

INDEX

INDEX

INDEX

256